FERVENT FREEDOM FIGHTERS

Daniel Cosculluela

FERVENT FREEDOM FIGHTERS

Anthology of Pamphleteers from the 16th to the 20th Century

Max Milo

Max Milo, Paris, 2023
www.maxmilo.com
ISBN : 9782315012077

I dedicate this book to Guy SABATIER, who died recently,
my friend of all the enraged fights of the youth for freedom.

With my thanks to the collaborators
who have brilliantly participated in the realization of this work.

Preface
by André Bercoff

Freedom, we sometimes forget, is only used if we do not use it.

From the agoras and ancient forums to the screens of social networks, the long murmur of the mind that questions, doubts, builds, destroys and constructs, measures and disproves, constantly pushing back its own limits, has been propagating since the dawn of time. At a time when a nurse, in a cry of anger, justified or not, calls a president of the Republic "scum" and when she is searched at home and indicted, this book is more than ever timely.

Who are, indeed, these "enraged by freedom"? Daniel Cosculluela has inventoried, in the auriferous deposits of the French spirit, those who have more or less disappeared from textbooks and anthologies; those who remain in the Purgatory of rebels and the nameless, the forgotten and the proscribed, the swordsmen who, between the 16th and 20th centuries, more often knew prison than fortune, misery than glory, but whose works resound in incendiary fulgurations in the night of passivity, cowardice and abandonment.

Certainly, many of them were, at one time in their respective lives, as much celebrated as hated. But who remembers today, apart from a handful of assiduous readers, passionate researchers, specialized historians; who, today, still reads Laurent Tailhade or Gaston Couté, Zo d'Axa, Albert Libertad, Séverine or Henri Rochefort? This book is intended to be a book of discoveries and resurrections. That is why you will not find here Victor Hugo or Émile Zola, Georges Bernanos or Louis Aragon. These are not the forgotten ones of the paperbacks and other useful reissues. But would they have existed without the long cohort of pamphleteers, satirists and other spadassins of written cries that have always marked the history of the most beautiful word of all times and languages: freedom?

In a France occupied by the commissars of the *woke* and the voltigeurs of the *cancel culture,* watched over by the pawns of communitarianism and the stooges of political correctness, in a time when Orwellian nightmares are becoming basic banalities, in an inverted world where, as Guy Debord wrote, the true is only a moment of the false, it is healthy to revive the most beautiful collective immunity, provided and reinforced by those who have a chuckle at everything. Of course, here and there, some authors have fallen into racist delirium or odious hatreds, but the ramblings of a life sequence do not prevent us from finding at other times the caustic lucidity of true visionaries. Before docently condemning the totality of a work, it is still important to immerse oneself in the spirit of the time, and not to examine a writing of 1823 with the glasses of 2023.

Satire, satyre, it shoots: in all directions, on all tones, on all times. This anthology is of public health because it gives to hear voices which chose from the start to be beautiful and rebellious rather than ugly and remoches. The latter today inundate continuously some media with their gutter prose, their linguistic mediocrity and their baseness of thought. It is more important than ever to find, even if they are at the antipodes of our opinions and biases, the powerful radicalities of these dozens of musketeers of the pen and the word, who shine first of all by their talent of writing and their art to prick where it hurts. And all of them are careful not to forget their ancestor, several thousand years old, a celestial tramp in Athens, a marvelous Diogenes who, when confronted by Alexander the Great, said to him: "Get out of my sun". Let us never forget that, from the *Roman de Renart* to the *Fables* of La Fontaine, from André Chénier to Julien Gracq, all cherish the form as being the bottom brought to the surface. An essential approach at a time when words have changed their meaning and the meanings of words.

It has become obvious today, in a divided, communitarian, archipelagic, partitioned, even grand-replaced France for some, to notice the ravages of censorship, and especially of self-censorship, of sanitized language and vacuum confrontations. In this reign of generalized platitude and panic to use the real words to designate the real evils, while the street rumbles and disorder is disguised as order, it is high time to think aloud again and to find inspiration in these writers, journalists, poets, authors, priests, rentiers, workers, furious by lucidity, insurgent by intelligence, whose blazons are drawn up in this anthology, if only to reformulate the reasons for rebellion

Introduction

Pierre Dominique rightly wrote that "*polemics is a fight and the pamphlet is a weapon*".

Etymologically, a pamphlet is "*a leaflet*" which means in Anglo-Saxon a leaflet that is held in the hand. In short, there is no difference in nature between polemic, a figure of speech and pamphlet. Nor between polemic and libel, which designates a more voluminous pamphlet, or polemic and satirical volume, which characterizes a work whose number of pages makes it worthy of a literary examination. In short, and Paul-Louis Courier underlines it in his *Simple Discourse*, the pamphlet is first and foremost a matter of style and the appellation cannot suffer from being measured by the number of pages, no matter what the small and timid minds say. He even says, *horresco referens*, that it is advisable to count among them Pascal's *Provincial Letters*, "*this divine masterpiece, however, are pamphlets, letters that appeared...*" and whose grouping, historical distance and the dullness (some say the anachronism) of the subjects treated have made a textbook that is just right for teaching in high schools.

In fact, there is no intellectual life, and therefore no life at all, without polemics, that is to say, without struggle and without action.

The first manifestations of the satirical spirit can be observed in the mocking Athens where the cult of the God of derision, Dionysus, had taken deep roots. The tragedy of that time had nothing tragic about it and the name simply means goat, an animal whose skin was used to dress those who acted as satyrs during the Dionysian processions. These formed a choir, which accompanied a singer belching out songs of an insulting nature... and therefore satirical. Even as the tragic genre emancipated itself from the religious processions, it retained its original spirit, of which personal insult was the essence, as well as generalized mockery, and often its burlesque and licentious form. Nothing that society solemnly respected was spared, and from religion to social institutions, derision and public scorn were called upon received ideas and public order.

Then came Rome, a nation of jurists daubed with the spirit of seriousness, where satire was born in its singular genre: "satira tota nostra est", wrote Quintilian. With them, as with the Greeks, the theater was a popular institution, a state where the patrons assumed the expenses of the representations. The Romans also borrowed from the Greeks the use of the mask, which had itself succeeded to the most horrible daubings.

It is to Ennius, whose work has not been preserved, that the Romans attribute the paternity of the genre. But it is with Horace that Roman satire, like Greek satire with Aristophanes, reaches its highest degree of perfection. Juvenal, Persia, Petronius and Lucian of Samosate, but also Apuleius, deserve to appear in the pantheon of the genre.

Similarly in France, a country of Roman law and legists, satire became individualized while colonizing chansons de geste and mysteries, before blossoming into farces and sotties. The fabliau of the Middle Ages, composed by adventurous clerics, gallant knights or itinerant jugglers, is a tale composed in verse and often sung. The scenic art in its classical form has indeed disappeared with the fall of the Western Empire, leaving only these cultural entertainments. In the fourth century, Saint Augustine called them "*nefaria*" (harmful) and the councils of Narbonne (589) and Mainz (813) forbade them, describing them as licentious and impious.

The capitulary of Childebert the Merovingian forbids spending the nights drinking, making rude remarks... and singing. This is confirmed by that of Childeric III, directed against those who compose and sing these songs to defame others. The nobility of satire has always been its censorship by the powerful of the day and their rivals.

These fabliaux mock the ridiculousness of the time and mock the authorities and their processions of injustices and abuses. Those written in the langue d'oïl practice popular and bourgeois satire. They attack certain classes of society but do not name anyone, unlike the exuberant and independent troubadours, whose violence makes their verses weapons of war. Bertrand de Born is the one whose *Sirventes* are the most cruel, and he does not hesitate to attack Richard the Lionhearted, whom he calls *"yes and no"* to mock his indecision. So much so that Dante Alighieri scorned him in *L'Enfer,* so repugnant to the tortuous Florentine this intellectual stiffness. The summit of the satire of the Oc is reached with the denunciation of the crimes of the Rome of the North, that prostitute who, in the name of the Synagogue of Satan (i.e. the Vatican) and under the pretext of annihilating the Cathar heresy, unleashed the crusade against the independent Occitania, which they reduced to smoldering ruins at the cost of thousands of infernos, where the Perfect Ones (the most spiritually accomplished Cathars, believers, both men and women) died. In their merciless denunciation of the deceitfulness of the crusaders of the infamous Simon de Montfort, the poets of the South, such as Pierre Cardinal and Guillaume Figueras, took these heaps of rubble as their tribunes and elevated the invective to eloquence.

But in the [xi] century, the satirical spirit is cramped in the framework of the fabliau, and here appears the satirical epic. The *Romans de Renard* illustrate this widening of the field of satire. The satirists disguised as fabulists use the animal support, which they stage to establish a general satire of the vices of the society, in a kind of *"animal Iliad"* (Léon Levrault) aiming at instructing the human kind.

In various forms, since *Reynard the fox,* from the 11th to the 18th century, this epic has enjoyed an undiminished popularity. It is first and foremost about stigmatizing in the person of Isengrin, the wolf, the power and arbitrariness of the feudal baron, but also his pride and arrogance mocked by the intelligence of Reynard, the embodiment of the clergyman and, beyond that, of the bourgeoisie, which was born with an awareness of itself and its future. None of the institutions of the time is spared, neither the tournaments, courts of justice, relations of suzerain to vassal, nor the world of the convents and the clergy. Through the cat Tybert, pilgrimages and crusades are denounced; the funeral of the hen killed by Reynard is the occasion to denounce the miracles worked by this martyr. Messire chameau is the pope's legate whose only merit is to say neither yes nor no. The spirit of chivalry, that pretentious ornament of feudalism, is also treated in a burlesque way.

Then came Rutebœuf whose poems are versified pamphlets, in which this poet, who never let himself be bought, appears as a formidable polemicist, announcing the modern satire. Jean Clopinel, known as Jean de

Meung, author of the second part of the *Roman de la Rose,* is his equal and disserts about everything in a sardonic and violent way in a jumble of eighteen thousand verses. Like Rutebœuf, he condemns the greed and the avarice of the bourgeois, the venality of the judges, the cowardice of the knights and the cunning of the fair sex. They claim the respect of the rights of nature, the equality of the citizens, the body of a nobleman "*not being worth an apple more than the body of a cart driver, a clerk or a squire*" and establish the true origin of the power: "*They elected among them a big villain, the most solidly built that they found, the broadest of shoulders, the biggest, and they made him prince and lord*".

From the 14th century to the Pleiades, we must mention Eustache Deschamps, Christine de Pisan and Alain Chartier. But they are moralists more than satirists. Villon brocaded this or that prosecutor or fat canon, but it is a personal satire, a settlement of accounts, in the form of a work of art. Marot, so delicate and courtier, master in writing roundels and other praises for beautiful ladies has, in his *Enfer* and his *Epigrams,* shown a sharp and sarcastic spirit. He scratches and throws some salt on the wounds but he is not mean and remains always light. His verses always seem to make bows.

Du Bellay, the first, in the name of his friends, in the powerful manifesto that constitutes *La Défense et illustration de la langue française,* explicitly claims, by placing himself under the auspices of Horace, a satirical will.

But the friends of Ronsard are too polite, the persiflage and the cruel irony which scatter their works allow them to seize all the vices and all the ridiculousness of a society but nothing more, or rather if, in his *Discourses,* Ronsard reveals himself redoubled polemicist; he excels in the invective and the art of caricature. His target: the pastors. It is because he engages under the banner of a party, or of an idea, the catholic party, and that he translates there a personal dimension which combines ardour and passion, that he achieves this objective.

After Ronsard comes a collective work known as *Satyre Ménippée* (from the Roman name Ménippe), people of letters and people of the Church, Rapin, Gillot, Passerat, Pithou, Chrestien Durand and le Roy write, in a playful way, a charge against the leagueers of the Guise party, masters of Paris. They were Catholic but Gallic and did not want the kingdom of France to become a slave of Rome and a province of the Spanish Empire. La *Satyre Ménippée* is the burlesque report of the States General of 1593.

It is also an energetic and caustic protest in favor of national interests. This text is contemporary with the work of Agrippa d'Aubigné, one of the first true French satirists.

Vauquelin de la Fresnaye, a good Norman magistrate whose life ended at the dawn of the 18th century, tried to follow the precepts of the Pléiade, in small genres of which he composed five books of *French Satires* published in 1605. Pleasant satires which scratch or sting without hurting, as one chansonne people without ever nailing them to the pillory. Wise and quiet, this kind epicurean knows well that "it is *a misfortune that satires*", but such is his duty and his *Whip of satire* looks like a "*kind flageolet*".

Next came Mathurin Régnier, whose *Satires* are only remembered, and Motin, Sigogne and Berthelot, with whom he spent his health and his money in taverns. Together they wrote the *Cabinet satirique* and other collections where contemporary morals are censured and the failings of the V.I.P. of the time are mocked.

Saint-Amand and Dulorens, if they are not the most notorious in the genre, deserve to be cited and would be worth reading, if one were still reading and thinking. Scarron, whose models are the Spanish buffoon authors, has not fallen into oblivion thanks to the fact of having been the husband of one of the most famous mistresses of the Sun King, a fact more known than the *Mazarinades* and other Chagrined *Epistles.*

Boileau-Despréaux will be launched by Furetière whose instinct of scandal had foreseen the success of satires in the play *Sur la Misère et la Vénalité des gens de Lettres de Paris*. After him, satire, which should have flourished after a fine example, declined. Certainly Molière did moral satire on stage, La Bruyère in his museum and La Fontaine in his menagerie, but the genre lost its bite. Regnard is certainly witty in his satire against husbands, Louis Petit, friend of Corneille in his *General Satires* and François Gacon in *The Bottomless Poet*, but the latter is as if kept on a leash.

Jean-Baptiste Rousseau and Alexis Piron are more at ease in *the Epigram*, a kind of "*light*" satire very much in vogue in this polite age. In his *Odes*, Rousseau distilled venom or provoked laughter with elegance and tore his prey to pieces. Piron, Voltaire's sworn enemy, is the king of epigrams, this shortened form of satire.

Gilbert was a violent polemicist who attacked the Encyclopedists, the self-righteous of the time, whose ideas he did not share, neither in philosophy nor in literature. His masterly works, *Mon Apologie* and *Le Dix-huitième Siècle*, unjustly forgotten, testify with a terrifying realism to the decomposition of an era, of which the Great Revolution will be the culmination. And in this century of ardent struggle of which ours is the heir, it is a pity that literary history, like history itself, has been written by the victors, deliberately forgetful.

Then will come Voltaire and Rousseau, of whom no one doubts that they wrote some of the most beautiful satirical texts of the century, but also Beaumarchais, Chénier, Fréron, Rivarol, among the most known. Among the unknowns of true satire, we can count Suleau, the gavroche of the genre who persiflage the revolutionaries and falls, as a hero, at thirty years old and Champcenetz for whom the humor and the nose-thumbing magnify the courage he will show until under the knife of the Terror that he will face laughing.

Under the First Empire, writers bowed to this "*Robespierre on horseback*" that only Châteaubriant dared to challenge with his *Martyrs* full of allusions, and his pamphlet on Bonaparte and the Bourbons. Then came the Restoration and Pierre-Jean Béranger, author of songs that made the throne and the altar tremble. At his side, after the days of 1830, the political satire is assumed by Hégésippe Moreau, Auguste Marseille Barthélémy who both die poor and are today unknown.

The nineteenth century is the apogee of political satire and a great number of writers or journalists have recourse, to conduct their polemics, to satire and pamphlet. The one who is least thought of and whose power in the matter is the most accomplished, is without any doubt the great Hugo whose *Châtiments* are a splendor.

This century, of which Léon Daudet said that it was stupid, is the one of the efflorescence of all the literary styles and of the spirit of revolt carried to the incandescence. It is true that in these years there were stakes perceptible by all in a world in perpetual movement, and that multiple ideologies competed the souls and the hearts. The Great European Civil War gave the first halt to the hectic intellectual life generated by the modernization of the old societies. The agony of satire had begun.

But there is a name that we did not pronounce, not knowing what words to find to confess our admiration, that of the priest of Meudon, François Rabelais, one of the greatest satirists of all French literature. Let's just read and reread him until we are intoxicated!

This opus was thus composed according to my desires. Everything can lend itself to the most diverse and varied criticisms. Let's not talk about the style, there is none. The choice of authors? Unfair, partisan, thoughtless. The choice of texts? Arbitrary...

Moreover some authors, without valid reasons, are treated better than others. Important forts have been forgotten, very minor ones have been abundantly exposed.

The place of satire and pamphlet in literary history is awkwardly described, if not totally obviated.

So much the worse, I simply wanted to make known certain names that the Alzheimer memory of literary history has allowed to sink into oblivion. I also wished to make discover other ways of writing than those authorized by our contemporary lukewarmness. I dreamed that perhaps a certain freedom of thought and writing could be communicated to us through the discovery or rediscovery of texts and authors of the past.

I fully assume my choices and recognize that I had no vocation for literary accuracy and exhaustiveness. I said above according to which personal criteria, inevitably unfair, I made my choices. I also said that my tastes and convictions were the only reasons I could invoke.

In short, I only have my sincerity. I believe that memory is life only if it irrigates thought. It becomes culture only by inspiring our acts, from the most secret to the most spectacular. Forgetting the past is a virtual lobotomization that turns men and peoples into mutant jellyfish.

The jellyfish lives only to absorb its plankton, which it consumes by moving straight ahead, without deviating in any way, without accelerating or slowing down. It is the game, the prelude to memory, which founds humanity, gives it its diversity and complexity.

This memory stored in books and old papers, we would like it to regain its true function as the backbone of intelligence and thought.

Daniel COSCULLUELA

D'AUBIGNÉ

Agrippa d'AUBIGNÉ (1552-1630)
The *Condottiere* of Letters

"Happy who, like the face
Can show the heart to the sun!"

These two lines of a sonnet eloquently express the main and truly characteristic trait of this powerful figure of the Huguenot party and of the literature of the 16th century. This man, who personifies this heroic century and its political and religious stakes, illustrates himself in this commitment of fidelity that he demonstrated on all the battlefields: theological, poetic, warlike and human.

He was born on February 8, 1552 in the hotel Saint-Maury near Pons in Saintonge. His mother died while giving birth to him, which gave him the name Agrippa (*aegre partus*). He was the son of Jean d'Aubigné and Catherine de l'Estang, lords of Brie in Saintonge. His father, having married for the second time, married Anne de Limur who, having little regard for the orphan, had him entrusted to an uncle in the style of Brittany, Aubin d'Abbeville, judge in Archiac.

It was through this intermediary that he found himself, as a child, in contact with the man who was to become his master, the Prince of Bearn, the future Henry IV. His family opted for the Huguenot faith spread in France by Calvin in his *Institution of the Christian religion.*

He knows, and has been taught, that the Church is the synagogue of Satan, worshipping idols, corrupting true doctrine and selling indulgences, betraying evangelical simplicity for the sake of luxury and material wealth.

At the age of eight he witnessed the persecutions at Amboise, saw the mutilated bodies of the supporters of the Reformation and heard his father say to him: *"My child, your head must not be spared after mine to avenge these honorable leaders; if you spare yourself, you will have my curse."*

As a precocious child, he was taught by renowned teachers, Mathieu Beroalde and Jean Morel. At the age of seven he read Hebrew, Greek, Latin and French; at eight he translated Plato's Crito. Among his companions, Nicolas Gobelin, of the famous family, and Pierre de L'Estoile, the only papist among these Huguenots.

But events tore him away from his studious life. An edict of May 1564 drove the reformed out of Paris. Beroalde took his students to Orleans where Agrippa found his father. He obtains from his father to give up his studies to take up the military habit. While defending the city, Jean d'Aubigné receives a wound from which he will die soon after. Agrippa is completely orphaned and has no other choice than to join his uncle, who has become his guardian. He was sent by his uncle to Geneva, the capital of the Reformation, to complete his education under the great scholar Theodore de Bèze, who instructed him in the spirit of sound doctrine. But for a thirteen year old child, the austerity of Geneva was not appealing.

Moreover, he who thought he would enter the University because of his mastery of the required knowledge is relegated to the college:

"This made him hate letters and take the studies in charge" and one often applies to him the ferule according to the rough morals of the time. To compensate, the love of a charming and learned young child, daughter of his host.

But this was not enough to extinguish the nostalgia, and at the age of fifteen he ran away, on foot, and returned to Archiac. In spite of his tutor's attempts to restrain him - he takes off his clothes every night - he runs away in his shirt and is taken in by the troops of the Prince of Condé, a Protestant warlord. He participates with enthusiasm and bravery in the campaign, is shocked by the treacherous murder of Condé, participates with a group of volunteers, of which he is the captain, in the guerrilla warfare, lives intensely the fights and gains a solid reputation of boldness and cold blood.

But in winter, the campaign finished, he returned home. Shortly afterwards, the peace of Saint-Germain was signed, giving Protestantism its official place in the kingdom.

D'Aubigné is eighteen years old, he is retired. At twenty, after being bored to death for two and a half years and having recovered his mother's inheritance, the only possible solution is love.

Love, and not women, because light women, easy ones he knew during the wars. And a love that is adoration. It will be Diane de Talcy with whom he travelled through the Pays du Tendre. The final destination will be disappointment in spite of all the sonnets, in the manner of Ronsard, that he dedicates to her:

"The heavens have made me happy to love in such a high place."
"My lady and her beauty, of man make me a dog..."

Then, the beautiful one having chosen another party he vituperates:

"I implore against you the vengeance of the gods
Inconsistent perjurer and ungrateful adversary..."

He is unhappy and calls death for deliverance:

"The defeated horn surrenders and, tired of suffering,
Open to the dart of death his trembling chest..."

Salvation comes to him from events. He escaped the Saint Bartholomew's Day, the new massacre of the Innocents, having left Paris shortly before, at the head of a small troop, but events caught up with him. Henri de Navarre called him to his side with the title of squire.

For four years he lived at court. This court, more than that of Charles IX, was that of Catherine de Medici, a ruthless queen mother to those who seemed to threaten the throne. It is from this stay in this court where corruption and crime, lust and intolerance cohabit, that his most beautiful indignations are born. Of this court, d'Aubigné writes "*we wore daggers, chain mail and very often the cuirassine under the cloak"... almost always ready to cut each other's throats*. But he also plays his part, dissipates and indulges in gallantry and games of all kinds. He also writes gallant or satirical verses. Henri III succeeded his brother, who had died in strange circumstances, and the war resumed between the two parties. D'Aubigné took part first in the loyalist camp and then in 1576 in the Confederate army. The peace of Beaulieu that followed reinforced the freedom of Protestant worship everywhere except in Paris. The treaty was quickly broken and d'Aubigné resumed his independent and warlike life, enamelled with wounds and acts of bravery.

This continued until October 1577 when the peace of Bergerac was signed. Henry of Navarre, realizing that his party could not win, signed the Edict of Poitiers which restricted the freedom of worship of the Reformed to one place per bailiwick. D'Aubigné could not accept this retreat, which offended his fiery character, and he wrote a farewell to his prince:

> *"Sire, your memory will reproach you with twelve years of my service, twelve plays on my stomach, it will make you remember your prison and that this hand which writes to you has deffected the locks, and has remained pure in serving you, empty of your benefícts and of the corruptions of your enemy and of you: By this writing it recommends you to God, to whom I give my past services and pledge those of* the *future, by which I will endeavor to make you aware that by losing me you have lost your most faithful servant."*

He was twenty-seven years old. His disappointment was such that he considered entering the service of Duke Jean-Casimir, an ally of the Reformed and leader of the Bavarian bands. By accepting the peace proposed by the king and Catherine (the Gorgon), Navarre abjured Protestantism, abandoned the people of God and endorsed the triumph of the "*scarlet beast*", the Valois, stained with the blood of the Reformed. He legitimized, at worst, or seemed to ignore, at best, the depravities of this rotten court, gangrened of diviners and magicians, of whores and of sweethearts.

Unable to bear this, he returns to his land and on his way crosses the path of a young girl of the religion, chaste and reserved. Having been introduced, he comes up against the strong prejudices in vogue at all times, on the difference of conditions: his nobility is too modest.

Of these two years of retirement he says:

> *"I have neither gold nor estates, and both of them great desprise*
> *And to the esgoisé fields of the worms I hoard".*

In fact, it is during this period that he wrote *Les Tragiques*. After these two years of solitary meditation, the king of Navarre calls him back to the court of Nérac *"with caresses and expiatory promises"* and the queen Marguerite welcomes him *"in great familiarity"*.

And soon, with Catholic persecutions resuming, Navarre and his followers set out on the warpath again. On this path, d'Aubigné will be a marvelous leader of partisans, thwarting the pitfalls at the cost of often foolhardiness... and a total lack of scruples. Forced to commit himself elsewhere, in Flanders, the Catholic king is brought to deal, and the peace is signed at Fleix where Marguerite de Navarre has installed her court, and after agreement of the Protestant consistory convened a few kilometers away in the town of Sainte-Foy.

It is in these times, that having *"opportunely found in the Castle of Archiac the titles of his house"*, he obtained from the tutor of his lady the consent to the marriage.

This one is celebrated on June 6, 1583. In the meantime Diane, his unfulfilled love, had died and this disappearance inspired him to write this admirable eulogy of sublime love:

> *"Love that is only love, that lives without hope,*
> *Of myself in myself, by myself agitated,*
> *Who nacquit eternal alive to the eternity,*
> *Who surpasses in loving soul and knowledge,*
> *How close this love is to the Godhead!"*

Otherwise he is confronted with the conjugal love which, beyond the quarrels due, among other things, to the jealousy of the wife and in the absence of the dizziness of the transports, brings him the happiness in the esteem and the security. He also brings him a small Agrippa.

The return to the warlike life is done in 1585. The majority of the people remained Catholic and joined the League, instrument of the Guise and their dynastic ambitions. The Protestants felt that they were threatened.

Navarre consulted the Protestant leaders at Guîtres near Coutras. D'Aubigné was on the side of the war: "*If we arm, the King will esteem us; if he esteems us, he will call us; united with him, we will break our enemies' teste.*" This opinion won out and it was time. Henri III and the League signed the treaty of Nemours[1]. Reformed and moderate Catholics unite in a League of the Public Good.

In this war, d'Aubigné won great victories. He seized Oleron and turned it into an imposing citadel. But he also experienced defeats and prisons. And he is troubled by the attempts of negotiations between Navarre and Medici. But soon Paris is in the grip of a guisard revolution and King Henri III is forced to take refuge in Chartres and then to submit. The Pact of Union between the League and the King was signed on July 21, 1588, in spite of the tears of rage of the King, who was forced to dismiss his favorite Épernon and all the loyal royalists. But the latter, shortly after, took revenge by having Henri de Guise, who had come to Blois for the States General, assassinated by his Forty-five (favorites and sweethearts). The same people executed the Cardinal of Guise, brother of the previous king. And if the king continued the war, he was both weakened by the desertion of many leaguers and eager to stop fighting to preserve his throne and Catholicism. He offered to meet with Navarre to discuss the terms of a peace. Very quickly a truce was concluded for one year. This raised d'Aubigné's anger and he went to Maillezais in the Vendée, which he decided to fortify as an impregnable shelter. There he finds his wife and his family, increased by two boys and two girls and resumes *Les Tragiques* which he completes to compose in a climate of passionate overexcitement[2].

Meanwhile, Mayenne, Henri de Guise's youngest son, had inherited his popularity. He was the king of the insurgent Paris, organized in a revolutionary commune. Mayenne was appointed Lieutenant General of the kingdom. On the other side, Henri III and Navarre solemnly allied

1. It is said that the learner Navarre had such a strong emotion that a whole side of his moustache turned white.

2. But also of rest because since the age of seventeen, and he has thirty-seven: "*being able to say with truth that, except the times of disease and injury, he had not seen four days in a row without drudgery*".

themselves. Despite his repugnance for this unnatural alliance, d'Aubigné followed his master.

The capital is surrounded and some skirmishes take place. Henri III was mortally wounded by a Jacobin monk, Jacques Clément. Before he died, he declared Navarre to be his successor and he found himself king sooner than he had thought and desired, and half seated on a wobbly throne.

But France was predominantly Catholic and Henry, with political foresight, was preparing his conversion. This cannot be accepted by the rough and faithful d'Aubigné whose passion can be read in these words addressed to the new monarch:

"*Sire,*" he said to the king, who showed him his lip pierced with Chastel's knife, "*you have only renounced God with your lips, he has been content to pierce them, but when you renounce him with your heart, he will pierce your heart.*" We know that this dark prediction will be fulfilled. Unable to serve a cause that is no longer his, he returns home where his wife and children await him... and his work in progress. In spite of everything, he will come back to the call of his king for the last fight he will lead in the white Cornette, an elite company. But any effort to avoid the conversion of Navarre was doomed to failure. The "necessity of the State" guided him and he abjured on July 25, 1593, allowing a general truce and his legitimization. The Catholic party recognized him and the Protestant disappeared. No more rights or security for the parpaillots, this is more than our author can tolerate. In this critical situation, D'Aubigné exposes, during the assembly of Sainte-Foy, his plan of organization. The king's refusal to accede to the demands of his former co-religionists encouraged the papists to start massacring again. His wife died and in the face of this grief, to which was added the disappearance of two sons, he remained mute. But he is torn from his suffering by the assemblies that choose him to be one of the spokesmen of the Cause. He is the one that the king's men call the "Goat of the Desert"[3], and whose appearances are feared as they always express the stiffening of the Protestant party.

3. Nickname of which he will make his pseudonym when he will publish *Les Tragiques*.

The fight continued until the Edict of Nantes, which offered real guarantees to the Protestants but which D'Aubigné could not satisfy.

So he returned to Maillezais where he finished writing the epic of the *Tragiques* and decided to write his memoirs which gradually became *the Universal History.*

He rarely returned to Paris, but during his visits to the court, his satirical verve was sharpened and he was fed with everything that could reinforce his tools of destruction of the idolatrous cult that Catholicism remained for him. One will find these anecdotes in the *Confession de Sancy* and *Les Aventures du baron de Faeneste.*

Nevertheless, he accepted, for two months, to teach the rules of tournaments, jousts and barrier fights.

Back in Maillezais, he resumed his studious life, married his daughters, and wrote *La Confession de Sancy* in which he settled his account, announcing the encyclopedists, with charlatanism and Catholic paganism: the worship of saints multiplied like wedding bread by Jesus to diversify the sources of income, the adoration of stone or wooden idols, the sale of indulgences, the substitution of the gods and goddesses of paganism by the Virgin and other saints. He participated in the debate aimed at the reunification of the churches and defended the return to the doctrinal purity of the first centuries, which the papists could not accept. But little by little the Protestants submitted and these were hard years of disappointments that followed for d'Aubigné.

And one morning, still in bed, he received the news: the king had been murdered by a blow to the throat. He immediately protests "*that it was not in the throat, but in the heart, being assured that he was not lying*", remembering his terrible prediction. We are in 1610, Ravaillac has struck, his arm has been armed by the papists, but hadn't Henri betrayed the cause of God?

D'Aubigné was then 59 years old. It is in 1616, after multiple reworkings that *Les Tragiques* are finally published. This epic has seven books with significant titles: *Misères! Princes, The Golden Room, The Fires, The Irons, Vengeance! Judgment !*

Some present an apocalyptic picture of the civil war, others attack, in a passionately satirical way, all the powers responsible for this infamy, and the last ones call upon the avenging God.

There are nine thousand verses that make up this torrential and furiously current work.

This role of opposition, D'Aubigné will accentuate it more and more during the regency of Marie de Médicis and the troubles that follow. Although she confirmed the Edict of Nantes, she distributed funds that dissolved the ties of those who supported the Cause of God. Many deserted. D'Aubigné is welded, he refuses everything: *"I will have from the Queen what I desire, it is that she holds me for a good Christian and a good Frenchman"*. But corruptions and cowardice prevail.

Then d'Aubigné answers in a pamphlet: *Les Aventures du baron Faeneste,* matamore in which he caricatures the boastful and adulterated court man, chattering about his good fortunes and supposed exploits, cuistre and deserted by life. He opposes him the poet Énay, simple and determined.

But life has worn him down with its bereavements and betrayals, including the denial of his son who abjures the faith, friends who move away and bend, and poverty which undermines him and pushes him to supplications at the court of Louis XIII which he finds repugnant.

Then he sells his goods to the duke of Rohan and publishes the first two volumes of his *Universal History* which is immediately condemned. Deprived of his goods and of all freedom of action, he went to Geneva to escape the arrest warrant issued against him. He arrived there in 1620, *"to take the bedside of his old age and his death"*.

He was received with extreme deference and married Renée Burlamachi. He composed two works, *The Treaty of the civil wars* which circulated under the cloak and supports that the war is necessary when it is of legitimate defense and *the Treaty on the mutual duty of the Kings and the Subjects* where he establishes the right to the revolt against the tyranny.

The literary occupations and the tasks of fortification of Geneva, Bern and Basel which are entrusted to him nourish the last years of his life. He reached a kind of serenity that he expressed as follows:

"The sun only moves the hemisphere away from one point,
It throws less ardor but as much light.
I change without regret when I repent
Of frivolous loves and of Jeun artifice.

> *I love the winter that comes to purge my heart of vice,*
> *Like plague the air, the land of snakes.*
> *My leader bleached under the piled up snows*
> *The sun that heats them frozen,*
> *But can not dissolve them in the shortest of these months.*
> *Melt, snows, come down on my heart,*
> *That still he can't light my ashes*
> *An inferno, as he made flames once!*
> *... Here are less pleasures, but here are less pains,*
> *The nightingale is silent, the Sirens are silent..."*

He is 75 years old and a last adventure is offered to him. Richelieu enters in war against the pontifical and Spanish armies. The Constable Lesdiguières asks him about the dispositions of the Swiss cantons. Hope is born in him, he answers to this one: *"I will take back joyfully my small sword that I put in the hook, and will force all the inconveniences of the exile, the storm, and the peaceful condition that I am, with the diligence and the vigor that can be"*. His offer is accepted but the last ride will not take place.

He wrote his last works, *La Vie à ses enfants*, histoire de la dernière guerre civile de France, *La Création*, a sort of long poem of twelve songs, and the *Petites Œuvres meslées* which he completed for a second edition.

He also witnessed the debacle of the Protestant party, the Edict of Nantes emptied of its substance, the military places disappeared. The shadow of Rome spreads over the world and the light of the true faith flickers. Illnesses, companions of old age, crowded around his bedside. He struggles at first, regains his strength and persists in publishing his works, the greenness and Gallicisms of which annoy the severe Calvinist Geneva.

But his strength is waning like a candle burns and one evening he answers his wife who offers him some food:

> *"My dear, let me go in peace, I want to go eat heavenly bread".*

He dies as he lived:

"... furious with holy love".

His wish was granted on May 9, 1630 after he recited to his wife the verses of a Huguenot psalm:

"Here is the happy day
That God has made to full desire,
For us be joyful
And let's enjoy it!"

Jules BARBEY d'AUREVILLY (1808-1889)
The prophet of despair or the Believer

Barbey, Jules, Amédée, was born in Saint-Sauveur-le-Vicomte in the Manche region in 1808. Born into a small and recent Norman nobility, very austere and deeply Catholic, he spent his childhood in his birthplace and then in Valognes (Manche) where he assiduously frequented an uncle, a doctor and liberal, who had a singular influence on him. However, his educational heritage, from which he would never free himself, was stiffened by etiquette prejudices, a demand for authentic greatness and a refusal of the artifices of "*modernity*". This explains, as we shall return to, his eternal attachment to the haughty and singular dress of the previous centuries.

After leaving school, the brilliant student he was undertook his humanities in Paris where he became friends with Maurice de Guérin. After obtaining his bachelor's degree, he began his law studies in Caen in 1832. At first, the two friends created the *Revue de Caen* whose ambition was to awaken Normandy... but it did not survive its first issue.

Barbey was then in reaction against the family, republican and liberal universe, and it is in such a state of mind that his first work *Amour et Haine* (a collection of political poems) appeared.

He then returned to Paris, but, isolated and bored, he traveled for four years and then returned to the capital.

He is no longer Barbey, but d'Aurevilly, a Catholic and royalist, and yet an unbridled dandy, frequenting *the Tortoni* and other honorable meeting places, and an impetuous chaser of damsels.

He then started working for the *Globe*, then for the *Débat*, recommended by Chateaubriand, for the *Constitutionnel*, for *La Revue de Paris* and for the *Presse* d'Émile de Girardin.

He then becomes the one he will remain: the ultra-mundane dandy and the royalist absolutist who renounces... alcohol and opium excesses. Freed from these addictions, he turns to new addictions, aesthetic, ideological... and therefore identity.

His first writings that gave him access to success were occasional: *Du dandysme et de George Brummele* (1843), *Une vieille maîtresse* (1851), *Le Chevalier des Touches* (1854), *Un prêtre marié* (1865) and especially his famous collection of short stories *Les Diaboliques* (1874).

This formidable, courageous and feared polemicist, theorist of dandyism, attacks Zola, Scribe and Renan, is stigmatized for immoralism and sadism. He is against the Academy and the "*Great men of the dark day*": Cousin, Michelet, Sainte-Beuve and the fossils of the *Revue des Deux Mondes*, Flaubert, Hugo and his Misérables... He vomits the bourgeois...

The journalism assures him a relative ease and he asserts himself as the most assured and complete critic of his time.

His critical work is considerable, fruitful and varied. This literary monument, built stone by stone during a long career, was only revealed after the author's death and thanks to Mrs. Louise Read who classified and exhumed his numerous writings which thus escaped the literary vault.

Barbey d'Aurevilly had a high idea of criticism, even if it was not admitted in the heart of the muses. Novelist or critic, he is, like Balzac his alter ego, concerned with ethics more strongly than with art. In him also, the artist is always ready to yield to the moralist.

But the one who evokes and illustrates it best is Léon Daudet, who placed Barbey very high: *"My author*, he said, *is Barbey who breathes widely on a promontory, with well-punctuated sentences, ten lines long, where the incidents are solid branches that extend the trunk towards the sky. The syntax is an arborescence".*

And Paul Bourget, who knew Barbey in his old age, said: *"It is spoken Saint-Simon, an unheard-of prose of verve and color which sprang up before you, carrying in a jumble of succulent anecdotes and cruel epigrams, striking images and strong ideas, the most extraordinary verb that ever prodigious improviser put at his service."*

He died as he had lived: with his head held high and his fist on his hip, perceived as an eccentric, whose thinking, like his dress, escaped the ordinary. He kept to the end the fashionable clothes of his youth and appeared in his eighties as he did in 1889, the year of his death, dressed like a dandy of 1830.

"The striking unity of Barbey's personality," writes Daudet, *"made him enter into fame like a wedge in the log."*

A few quotes in conclusion:

> *"... passions always tend to diminish, while boredom always tends to increase."*
>
> *"It's mostly what we don't understand that we explain."*
>
> *"... in a society that is becoming more and more materialistic, the confessor is the doctor."*

Zo d'AXA (1864-1930)
The Musketeer of Anarchy

Zo d'Axa, whose real name was Alphonse Gallaud[4], was born in Paris on May 24, 1864. Young man from a good family, catholic, bourgeois and wealthy, he made mediocre studies, enters nevertheless in Saint-Cyr at seventeen years and joins the army under the colors of the hunters of Africa. The military aroma stinking up any self-respecting brain under any latitude, he quickly deserts. Generous by nature, he kidnapped his captain's wife while leaving. His libertarian wanderings lead him first to Brussels where he learns journalism in the pages of the *Nouvelles du Jour.* Then he went to Switzerland with the pretty daughter of a Brussels pharmacist and to Italy where he replaced the apothecary's daughter by a teacher's daughter who was also pretty; good libertarian taste is necessarily internationalist. Amnestied in 1889, he returned to France and founded in May 1891 *L'En Dehors* - a weekly magazine that he defined by this epigraph: "The one that nothing enrolls and that an impulsive nature guides alone, this outlaw, this out of school, this isolated seeker of the beyond, is he not drawn in this word: L'En Dehors". He signs for the first time this original pseudonym which will dress from now on all his life. This small newspaper would make any contemporary press owner blush with envy by the richness of its signatures which evokes the pantheon of letters. Georges Darien, Georges Lecourte, Henri de Régnier, Lucien Descaves, Octave Mirbeau, Camille Mauclair, Félix Fréron, Tristan Bernard, Ajalbert and Émile Verhaeren, Stuart Merill among others, the cartoonists Steinlein, Willette, Luce, Hermann-Paul, as well as the liber-

4. He would be the direct descendant of the famous navigator La Pérouse.

tarian theorists Sébastien Faure and Charles Malato and Émile Henry, who threw the bomb at the Terminus restaurant, all collaborate in this little newspaper.

This rebel by temperament, for whom "*action is the sister of dreams*", is guided by a kind of irresistible instinct towards pamphleteering. Also *L'En Dehors* rushes into a merciless criticism of institutions and morals. But this criticism does not bother with jeremiads, and the roars of revolt have for condiment this irony of which Proudhon said that it was holy. At the head of his marvelous team, every week Zo d'Axa has a field day against bourgeois society "the great culprit inciting all crimes out of respect for prejudice", the army "that ever cruel sacred beast with a thousand sharp horns made of sabers and bayonets", the family, property, morality, religion, "*a parliament that we esteem little, a justice that we suspect a lot, and a cowardly and thoughtless crowd*". However, the golden rule of the newspaper is "*silence to the whiners and the hypochondriacs*". In the land of Voltaire, those who do not rebel against all injustices and submit, out of prudence, cowardice, interest or any false good reason, to the unacceptable and the absurd, deserve no compassion.

The influence of this journal is prodigious and it leads resounding campaigns. This does not prevent fantasy. One day he wrote an article denouncing the evil stupidity of the duel, and the next day he confronted his collaborator Darien on the field to settle a philosophical quarrel. And after having given him a good blow with his sword, he asks him for a column for the next day's issue. Affirming his faith in revolt, in a free and vagabond life, out of the "*shores of the law*", he can only be labelled as an anarchist. We are mistaken, because he refuses any inféodation to any ideology, even if it is the one of the "*Holy Anarchy*". For him, there is no chapel that is worth: "*it is necessary to live from today onwards, and it is outside all the laws, all the rules, all the theories, even anarchist, that we want to let us go always to our pity, to our outbursts, to our pains, to our rages, to our instincts, with the pride of being ourselves.*"

But at that time the anarchists wanted to confront society with their fists, and the dynamite fairy was the sister of the revolution fairy. And when *L'En Dehors* comments on the exploits of Ravachol and his friends in an article entitled "Whose fault is it?", and then opens a subscription "*so as not to let starve to death kids whose fathers are relentlessly beaten by society because they are rebels*", the trials follow one another.

Arrested, Zo d'Axa is locked up, incommunicado, in Mazas. No lawyer, no visitors. He refused to answer or sign anything. After a month of this regime, he was released on provisional liberty, "*our poor liberty, always provisional*", and resumed his place at *L'En Dehors.*

Faced with new lawsuits, he went into exile in London where he had the misfortune to fall in the middle of a socialist congress where "*it was a question of parley, not action*". Spleen-stricken, he fled to Holland and hired himself on a barge that took him to Mainz by the Rhine. He then went to the Black Forest where he mingled with the lumberjacks. Then he went to Milan and attended an anarchist trial: "*It is said that Milan is a small Paris. The Milanese magistrates think so; at least on one point, they are repugnant just like their Parisian colleagues. Isn't the magistracy the same everywhere? And can it be otherwise? It is even undoubtedly the reason which makes that through all the countries the memory of the fatherland remains to you: it goes up like a nausea when one sees the vileness of a judge*".

As a result, he was arrested in the middle of the night and they wanted to take him to the police station on foot. "*In this case,* he explains, *you will carry me, and, of force*". He will say later: "*but also could I show myself in such company? All these people smelled of the prefecture from afar. And if, on the way, one had crossed some night owl I would rather have shouted to avoid the worst confusion, to at least rehabilitate me in the eyes of the passer-by, I am not a policeman, I am a criminal!*"

As a result, Zo d'Axa was expelled from Italy. In Trieste, which he had reached on foot, he embarked for Piraeus with Italian deserters and organized a riot with them on board the ship. He was in Greece where he slept in the ruins of the Parthenon; the East attracted him and he wanted to go to Constantinople. He passed the Dardanelles and it was Kavala and Mytilene, "*formerly Lesbos, which became virtuous in old age, and it is much less picturesque*", then Smyrna and finally Jaffa on January 1st, 1893. He was arrested when he disembarked, kept in custody, in a cell, at the French consulate. He escaped and took refuge in the British Consulate, which was considered inviolable... except for him. Thrown in irons on the ship La Gironde, he was the object of unhealthy curiosity from the passengers who asked him: "*Scoundrel, what did you do*?" He replied: "*I cut an old woman into thirteen pieces and it gave me a headache*!"

In Paris, Zo d'Axa was sentenced to eighteen months in Sainte-Pélagie. Having refused to sign a petition for pardon, he was released on July 1st, 1894, for the national funeral of President Sadi Carnot, who had been liquidated by the anarchist Caserio. Waited for by plainclothes cops at the exit, he refused to leave the prison. He is expelled. Picked up, he is put on the violin at the police station of the street Cuvier. He escaped and, as in the Brassens song, the good people tried to arrest him and succeeded. He spent twenty-four hours in the police station and was released. He published *De Mazas à Jérusalem (From Mazas to Jerusalem), which* he had written in prison and in which he recounted his odyssey. Adolphe Retté wrote the following about this diary: *"A diary," he wrote, "appeared (a long time ago), a whip in which bells tinkled with sobbing laughter, slammed, toupilla magistracy and legislature, High Brass of the States-Majors and Lowers of the Banks, leaders and leaders, marked the obscene backside of the bourgeoisie with red.* The Outside *was, which made the spinning tops waltz under starlight. Zo d'AXA, this strange man, happy to be himself, without party label, without political connections, this anarchist could not tolerate himself for long..."*.

He is riddled with debts and in spite of the success of the work before which all the critics bowed[5], somewhat disillusioned by the denial of certain collaborators and deprived of the means necessary to the resumption of the newspaper, he decided to remain silent and to start again to travel. In this he is faithful to the conclusion of his book: *"For quite a long time men have been made to travel by showing them the conquest of the sky. We no longer want to wait until we have conquered the whole earth. Let us each walk for our joy. And if there are still people on the road, if there are beings that nothing awakens, if there are born slaves, undecayed peoples, too bad for them! To understand is to be in the vanguard. And the joy is to act. We do not have time to mark the step: life is short. Individually we run to the assaults that call us. One spoke about dilettantism. It is not free, this one, not platonic: we pay... and we start again".*

This trimardeur who never believed in the promises of the fairy anarchy but never flinched when he was assimilated to the compa-

5. Clémenceau wrote: "*From Mazas to Jerusalem* is a beautiful lesson in disrespect."

nions, is reproached by them, supreme insult, to be an intellectual and an aristocrat.

The latter do not accept that he shares equally his contempt between the masters and the slaves and proclaims, quoting Carlyle, *"I vomit the ruling classes and the ruled classes disgust me. This trifler, this haughty rebel for whom morality is a chapter of aesthetics, renounces a battle judged sterile and will wander for a few years in the universe where he walks "his tawny goatee and his ironic and clear gaze" (Léo Campion).* And then in 1898 comes the Dreyfus Affair, the Affair that opens two years of ferocious struggle. France was in turmoil. People are for or against, no middle ground. Zo d'Axa emerges from his tower of silence, caught up like the others in the great drama. The difference is that he does not take sides: *"If this man was not a traitor, he was a captain. Let's move on."*

And he launches his *Feuille* to all the winds of revolt. Written by him alone, it is illustrated by Steinlein, Luce, Auquetin, Willette, Hermann-Paul, Léandre or Couturier. And each one hits the nail on the head, like a paving stone in the frog pond. He scourges the sheep of Boisdeffre, the forgers of the General Staff in *En Joue... Faux*. He attacks the children's prisons in *Enfants Martyrs, a* biribibi of children devoted to penal colonies. He scathes the vulgar public and the tabloid press in *Dix Assassinats pour un Sou*. He denounces the profit-hungry landlords in *On Détrousse au coin des Lois.* And the honest worker, the proletarian with the calloused hands of all the socialist and anarchist schools is not spared, not more than the *"rhetoricians of the Social, promising future well-being". "We would fail in our pleasure if, after having properly saluted the judiciary and the army, we did not hasten to bow to the people, with all available respect. That the landlords are chauvinistic, in the name of their tenement houses; that the financiers praise the army that stands guard in front of the Caisse; that the bourgeois acclaim the flag that covers their merchandise, is effortlessly explained. Even that some, half-philosophers, people of calm and tradition, numismatists or archaeologists, old poets or prostitutes, prostrate themselves before the force, it is still understandable, but that the ilots, the mistreated, the Proletariat, are patriots, why then? It is the unbreakable slouching of the mass of the exploited that creates the growing and logical ambition of the explorers. Whether he is from the mine or the factory, the Honest Worker, this sheep, has given the scabies to the flock. To educate the people! What will it take? His misery has taught him nothing. The victim becomes an accomplice. The unhappy one speaks about the flag, beats his chest, takes off his cap and spits in the air: I am an honest worker! It always falls on his nose".*

THE HONEST WORKER ONLY GETS WHAT HE DESERVES

But his masterpiece? It is the election of the candidate of *The Leaf*: "*I always believed that abstention was the silent language which it was advisable to use to indicate its contempt of the laws and their makers. To vote, I said to myself, is to become an accomplice. You take your share of the decisions. One ratifies them in advance. You are part of the gang and the herd.*

How can one refuse to bow to the legislated Thing if one accepts the principle of the brutal law of numbers? By not voting, on the contrary, it seems perfectly logical to never submit, to resist, to live in revolt. One has not signed the contract. By not voting you remain yourself. One lives as a man that no Tartempion should boast of representing. We disdain Tartalacreme. Only then one is sovereign, since one has not crossed out one's right, since one has not delegated anyone. One is master of one's thoughts, aware of a direct action. One can disregard talk. One avoids this idiocy of asserting oneself against parliamentarism and electing, at the same time, the members of the parliament".

And he adds that he was wrong, because the foreigner is watching and that the duty of good Frenchmen is to elect a parliament worthy of the greatness of the country. And to present the most qualified of the candidates: the null donkey, since he will count all the blank and null ballots.

Here is his program poster:

Citizens,
You are being deceived. You are told that the Chamber composed of *fools and crooks* did not represent the majority of voters.
This is not true!
A chamber of jocular deputies and rigging deputies represents, on the contrary, wonderfully, *the voters that you are.*
Don't protest: a nation gets the delegates it deserves.

Why did you name them?
The room represents the whole.
It takes fools and cunning, it takes a parliament of ganaches
and Robert Macaire to personify at the same time all the professional
voters and the depressed proletarians.
And that's you!
Vote, voters! Vote, the parliament comes from you. One thing is,
because it must be, because it cannot be otherwise.
Make the room in your image. The dog returns to his vomit.
Go back to your MPs.

DEAR VOTERS
Vote for them! Vote for me!
I am the Beast that the Beautiful Democracy needs.
Vote for me!

On the day of the election, Zo d'AXA travels around Paris walking the White Donkey. We sing:

"It's a donkey, a donkey, a donkey,
we need a donkey".

The aliboron candidate was arrested by the police under the jeers of the crowd and taken to the pound. Zo d'Axa then abandoned him, saying "*it doesn't matter anymore, he is now an official candidate*". And in *The Leaf* entitled "*He is elected*", he writes:

"In connection with the elections in France, the gazettes of the whole world have, without malice, brought together the two notorious facts of the day. In the morning, at about nine o'clock, Mr. Félix Faure went to vote. In the afternoon, at three o'clock, the White Donkey was arrested.

I read about it in three hundred newspapers. The Argus and the press mail cluttered me with their clippings. There were some in English, in Wallachian, in Spanish; still I understood. Every time I read Felix, I was sure they were talking about the donkey.

And the last issue of *The Leaf* is a kind of testament. It is entitled *La Dernière aux Anarchistes*. About the explosion of a powder magazine in Toulon, Zo d'Axa remarks that the efforts of the dynamiters look pitiful next to this firecracker and he shouts to those who do not disarm: *"no more chapels, systems and theories, the individual above all!"*

And he concludes: "It is immediately that they want to live; it is the hour that they free themselves from the guardianships, and from the words of order. Each one its road. During all the events, apart from all the parties, they launch the cry of revolt".

For Zo d'Axa is tired of *"the inert and spineless masses cooking in the pot of servitude"* (Victor Méric). Too bad for the individual if he gets stuck in the quicksand of stupidity and ignorance. This philosophy has its requirements which put off those who revere the cloud makers of the singing tomorrows. This approach is not made for the *"palates* of *cream-licking children"* (Jean Richepin). D'Axa has said all he has to say and he is on the move again. He travels the world again, from the Americas to China, from Japan to India and Africa. He lives in a barge on the rivers and canals. Disdainful of artificial cities, he avoided people but ended up stranding in Marseille where he spent his last years. He was often seen riding his bicycle and, for twenty years, convinced that men everywhere were equally duped and despicable, he kept silent. Carrying a rolled-up blanket on his shoulder, he throws it down at each stop and lies on it, disdainful of hotel rooms. A true vagabond.

When the great planetary massacre broke out, when the teachers of the old workers' movement, who took him as a dilettante, shamefully betrayed the revolutionary cause, he did not change, faithful to defeatism. The Russian revolution and the Bolshevist dictatorship, a sham of bourgeois oppression, did not fool him. While in Paris in 1921, he replied in *Le Journal du Peuple* to a journalist who accused him of denial (suspected him of having denied himself): *"Keeping silent would perhaps not be enough to preserve me from the honor of appearing as a repentant. The silence, broken for a moment, will be light to me just now to be modestly naked. The last friends of L'En-Dehors and La Feuille know the meaning of a past that the present does not intend to deny. For a long time, against the ugliness of time, we reacted together. We were called anarchists, the label did not matter. In short, there are only two parties: wolves and dogs forever hostile. And not only two parties: two instincts, two ways of feeling. Yes, I was writing for pleasure, the pleasure of saying what I thought, in fact what I still feel.*

What is it then to live, if not to spend according to its nature, a moment? I like the morning on the roads near or far, and without pen, without other ambition or goal than to understand the clear day outside the floating mirages, outside as well as always, the sheets of writings near.

Pallor of the words. I hardly indicate, fast... at least not a false nose, it's embarrassing. In the small happiness of birth, absurd and convenient privilege, the capitalist society, before the final bankruptcies, exempts me some pecuni. I use the last assignats to the walks which still please me. And to displease does not displease me.

Too bad, and damn for those who suspect that a glimmer of freedom modifies the substance of my thought. It accentuates the nuances...

... The only certainty is to Live and without waiting. So let's live: action, word or silence. A matter of time, an individual case. And as little foolishness as possible."

It is suggested to him to take again his pen, he answers that he does not care about the future and about "*the tomorrows which will be in centuries*", "*the promised Land will be the one where we will rot*".

Until his last day, at the end of August 1930, he will live, "*caring very little about the suffrages of fame, strong of the only esteem of some friends*". He who wrote that "*the escapee from the social galleys, who would no longer climb into the flagged ships of religion and the fatherland, would not embark either on the rafts, without cookie, of the humanitarian Medusa*", kept his word all his life of rebel.

He left us a precious message that only those who survive under the rubble of contemporary stupidity understand: "*to circulate a little by the world, to glimpse the thickness of the masses, to find everywhere flourishing the same transposed duperies, the beliefs and the fetishisms rooted to the bone, it is true, did not lead me to edifying illusions. To breathe, to breathe elsewhere. To be nothing in the vain business. Lamp of pure air, wind from the sea. And undoubtedly nomadic.*

What is it to live, if not to spend, according to its nature, a moment?"

Henry BAÜER (1851-1915)
The Musketeer of the Pen, natural son of Alexandre Dumas

His motto was "*Live Free*" and he lived by it. He proved more than once in his life that he intended to put his actions in conformity with such a principle, even if it cost him honors and situations.

He was, in short, a man and a journalist of the kind we hardly know anymore in our time when omerta is the common law of rats.

From the end of the Second Empire to the beginning of the First World War, Henry Baüer knew all sorts of states and fortunes, communard then prisoner of the Versaillais, convict in Caledonia and companion of Louise Michel who held him in high esteem, a hard-working journalist, then an admired and feared writer, engaged in multiple fights, glorious and uncertain, to end in a disgrace that prolongs our amnesic time.

He was indeed the son of the great Alexandre Dumas with his legendary literary and amorous prodigality. All his life he respected his father's rule expressed in these terms: "*My son, when you are the son of Alexandre Dumas, you live the high life, you dine at the Café de Paris, and you don't deny yourself any pleasure...*"

As a worthy son of his father, he collected everything: loves, work, fights.

A bohemian student in the Latin Quarter, he recounts his life in his *Memoirs of a Young Man*. Smitten with Proudhonism, trained in contact with Longuet and Rigault, he joined the Commune without hesitation and made his first forays into journalism in its newspapers, in *La Résistance*, in Blanqui's *La Patrie en Danger*, and in Jules Vallès's *Cri du Peuple*. He was a major in all the battles until the last day.

Arrested after the end of the insurrection, he was brought before the Council of War and sentenced to deportation to New Caledonia. He remained there for seven years and his indomitable character earned him persecution from the chiourme. Thus, for four years, three times a night, a supervisor knocked on his door and shouted: *"Are you there?"* And he only moves away when the convict answers.

Delivered from the Caledonian hell, at the age of thirty, he got married and resumed his activities as a journalist. It was at the *Réveil*, a newspaper founded by Valentin Simond, that Baüer did his real apprenticeship. This daily newspaper, almost entirely literary, was an innovation in the press. Among its editors, a poet, Paul Verlaine. Among the unpublished works published: *Sapho* by Alphonse Daudet and *Les Sœurs Rondoli* by Maupassant.

It was Alphonse Daudet who noticed him and appointed him as his successor as drama critic when the newspaper sank, but he was taken over at *L'Écho de Paris*. He deployed his full measure there.

In the Dreyfus affair, Baüer gives his full support to Émile Zola, who is his friend and whom he considers his master in naturalism.

Baüer fights, day after day, for a current realist theater that will eventually find its place in the *Théâtre libre* created by Antoine. When he is in conflict with Antoine, he supports a new avant-garde theater: *L'Œuvre* de Lugné-Poë. He contributed to the discovery or the imposition of Otway, an English author of the 17th century, August Strindberg and Oscar Wilde, but also Mirbeau, Maeterlinck, Dostoyevsky, Ibsen, etc. He is at the height of fame and power, but he faces and overcomes prejudices, suffers affronts and receives insults, especially those, vehement and funny, of the prodigious Léon Daudet.

Then his interest will be focused on Louis Lumet's *Civic Theatre* whose vocation is to capture the interest of the popular public by creating epic and national frescoes such as *Danton* by Romain Rolland. It was already a question of applying art to popular education.

If Baüer is a great journalist, he is also a true writer. If one cannot dwell on his first play, *La Revanche de Gaëtan,* written in Nouméa in 1879, which is conventional and formalist, one can retain *Une Comédienne* (1889), a novel that brings together scenes from the life of the theater, in a naturalist style to excess, but interesting as a study of the life of actors of the last century.

In 1900 he wrote his first real play, *Sa maîtresse*, a comedy in four acts which was given at the Théâtre du Vaudeville. It is an apology for free love and female emancipation. *Chez les bourgeois,* published in 1900, is also a thesis play opposing a paternalistic boss and his revolutionary nephew. *De la vie au rêve,* published in 1896, is a collection of short stories in the spirit of Maupassant.

But where his true talent shines through is in his autobiography *Mémoires d'un jeune homme* (1895) and in the collection of five years of columns in *L'Écho de Paris, Idée et Réalité* (1899).

Dramatic critic, Baüer is also a committed writer who gives his opinion on a political event, a book... It is a spectrograph of an era by a witness who does not hesitate to compromise himself.

But his commitments earned him enmity, and the affair of *Ubu-Roi* by Alfred Jarry, which caused a huge scandal, sealed the end of his moral authority. His opponents, among them André Gide and Léon Daudet, were furious and the latter described Baüer as "*Dumas père for cottages of necessity*".

In a few weeks his situation collapses and he leaves *the Echo of Paris* for *the Petite République* of Gerault-Richard. His chronicles are less successful and his resources diminish. But he remains the disinterested supporter of all the victims of official conformism, such as *Louise,* the comic opera by Charpentier.

If we pay tribute to him in some agapes where Alphonse Allais, Tristan Bernard, Henry Bataille, René Boylesve, etc. are faithful to the appointment, he is more and more unused and forgotten.

In his retirement, he ended his life by making an inventory of the precious objects in the churches, inventories provided for by the 1905 law on the separation of the Churches and the State.

The declaration of war in August 1914 violently clashed with his absolute pacifism. He did not give in to the bellicose delirium that swept away so many fine socialist and anarchist minds and did not accept that so many young human lives were sacrificed to the interests of the magnates of industry and international finance.

Seriously ill, he entered a nursing home and died, lucid and fearless. His son Gérard would later say: "*He remained faithful to the choices and decisions that had kept him away from honors and profits. I owe it to him to have known how to esteem, as they should be, the free spirits who maintain the purity of their convictions above cleverness and opportunism.*"

That's all we have to say.

Pierre-Antoine BERRYER (1790-1868)

The Cicero of Legitimism

He was born in Paris in 1790 into a bourgeois family. His father was a renowned lawyer, a counselor at the Parliament. After studying at the Collège de Juilly, he was admitted to the bar at the age of twenty-one and married, the same year, the daughter of a director of the navy and war. He soon asserted his royalist opinions, despite the ruin of his father during the Restoration. This did not prevent him from defending, alongside his father and Dupin Aîné, the generals Debelle and Cambronne in 1816, as well as Marshal Ney. The latter was executed but he saved the lives of the other two.

In the following years, he defended the cause of the freedom of journalists, during trials opposing them to the authorities, but also to the generals Canuel and Donnadieu who engaged in a ruthless repression during the insurrections of Grenoble (1818) and Lyon (1820).

A supporter of freedom of education, he joined the campaign of the royalist legitimist newspaper *Le Drapeau blanc* against the Royal University and published a pamphlet on the subject in 1827. He defended Félicité de Lamennais who was attacked for his ultramontane theses, which earned him prosecution and the hostility of Gallican Catholics.

In 1830, he entered politics and, solicited by the ultras, he accepted to be a candidate for the deputation in Haute-Loire. Elected with a very strong majority, he refused to be part of the cabinet of the prince of Polignac and left Paris. After the revolution of 1830 which transferred the crown on the head of the descendant of the regicide Orléans, he remained almost alone in the Chamber to represent the royalist and legitimist France and protested, at the sides of Chateaubriand, by declaring, on August 7, 1830, that this one does not have quality to deliberate on the vacancy of the throne or elect a monarch. In vain, and in this new regime, the July Monarchy, which succeeded the Restoration, he was an opponent. Although a convinced legitimist, he was in favor of the abolition of the censal suffrage and advocated universal suffrage. He opposed the indictment of the former ministers of Charles X who were sentenced to life imprisonment in the prison of Ham. Triumphantly re-elected in Haute-Loire in 1831, he tried to dissuade Auguste de la Rochejacquelein from organizing an uprising in the Vendée bocage in favor of the Duchess of Berry and *the "miracle child",* the Count of Chambord. Arrested, he was judged and acquitted by the court of assizes of Blois. Re-elected in 1834 in four constituencies, he chose the Bouches-du-Rhône and received an enthusiastic welcome in Marseille where he went. After the death of Charles X in exile, he remained faithful to the eldest branch of the Bourbons and joined the Count of Chambord, swearing an oath of loyalty to him. Continuing his activity as a lawyer, he defended in 1844-1845 the right of association of workers and, at the same time and in the same spirit, the freedom of religious congregations. Re-elected in 1848 to the Chamber of Deputies, he tried, sitting on the right, to unite the royalists in order to allow the restoration of the monarchy.

He was among the protesters of the coup d'état of Louis Napoleon Bonaparte in 1851, and voted with some representatives gathered at the town hall of the 10th district, the dejection of Louis Napoleon. Arrested, then released, he did not run for re-election to the legislature but did not give up his ideas nor the right to propagate them.

Elected in 1855 to the French Academy, which had become a public place of opposition to Napoleon III, he asked to be exempted from the official visit to the Emperor, under the pretext that it might be unpleasant for the Emperor to find himself in front of his former lawyer[6]. He made a return to political life in 1863, taking advantage of a release from it and was elected deputy of Marseille.

Continuing his career as a lawyer, he defends his young colleague Jules Ferry, who is prosecuted for having violently denounced in

6. He had been part of his defense council during the Boulogne case.

Le Temps the disemboweling and devastation of old Paris by the prefect Haussmann. During these years he never ceases to argue the benefits of the freedoms that the monarchy allows and the balance of the natural institutions that found it.

In 1868, suffering, he left Paris for his property in Angerville in the Loiret.

Feeling his end coming, he addressed a last missive to the Count of Chambord:

> *"O my lord,*
> *O my King, I am told that I am approaching my last hour. I die with the pain of not having seen the triumph of your hereditary rights, consecrating the development of the liberties which France needs.*
> *I take these wishes to Heaven for your Majesty, for her Majesty the Queen, for our dear France.*
> *In order to be less unworthy of being heard by God, I leave life, armed with all the help of our Holy Religion.*
> *Farewell Sire, may God protect you and save France.*
> *Your faithful and devoted subject"*
>
> Berryer.

He died a few days later, on November 29, 1868.

Auguste BLANQUI (1805-1881)
The Revolution Man

This man is above all a myth and, as such, stripped of all his attributes as a living being. His theoretical production is known only to a few initiates. The ideas attributed to him come from what his epigones, and especially his adversaries, have said about him. What remains of him is an image of perseverance, even obstinacy and heroism: a professional revolutionary, organizer of many plots, expert in secret societies, who spent almost half his life in prison.

Yet this man lived, and this life allows us, certainly, to understand him better and to situate this existence and its importance in the century. Above all, it opens the door to an understanding of the revolutionary and proletarian phenomenon before its irremediable integration into the spectacular market society and illustrates the birth of the two currents of socialism in France: that of national socialism, which rapidly evolved into fascism, and that of a more internationalist nature, which espoused the cause of capitalist modernization.

Auguste Blanqui was born nowhere, that is to say in a place that only emerged from the anonymity of the communes because of the fame of its enfant terrible. This place, Puget-Théniers, saw the arrival one day of a civil servant, a sub-prefect of the Empire, Jean-Dominique Blanqui. He was a professor of philosophy and astronomy in Nice, which was then in the possession of the King of Sardinia, and he was rather sensitive to new ideas. Thus, when the Republic invaded Nice, he was at the head of those who demanded the attachment of the County to France. So he was appointed as a representative of the Committee at the Convention... which transformed it, on January 31,

1793, into the department of the Alpes Maritimes. Dominique Blanqui was elected deputy.

He was arrested for moderatism; he protested against the Montagnard coup of June 2, 1793, and was thrown into prison. He was freed by a new coup d'état on 9 thermidor.

During these ten months of incarceration, in fear of the fateful call for the guillotine, he receives beneficial visits: those of the daughter of his landlady. She was fourteen years old, he thirty-six. He will wait for his majority, in 1797, to marry her and end his life as a deputy; after the Convention that he had reinstated, he had been propelled to the Council of Five Hundred.

Life in the provinces is difficult for a young and pretty Parisian woman. She gets bored, allows herself to be courted, flirts willingly, argues with her jealous husband and soon gives birth to seven children. The fall of the Empire was the fall of her civil servant husband. Fortunately, she made a nice inheritance and this allowed her to escape from poverty, because her husband was shunned by the restored monarchy, which was suspicious of former Republican officials.

Louis-Auguste was born on February 1st, 1805 in Puget-Théniers. He witnessed the entry of Austrian and Sardinian troops into the city. He saw the three colors trampled underfoot and the excesses inherent in any occupation: ransacking and arbitrary liquidations. He was deeply impressed by these events, which he would later say marked the course of his life. At the age of fourteen, he joined his older brother in Paris in order to lighten his parents' load. He went to school at Charlemagne, among the children of the wealthy or the aristocracy (or both), and surpassed them all in intelligence and memory.

At the age of seventeen, he was revolted by the death of the four sergeants of La Rochelle involved in a carbonarist plot. He promised to avenge them and joined the secret society in 1824. He was still a Bonapartist, mainly because of his hostility to the monarchy and his uncompromising nationalism. After having dabbled in journalism at the *Courrier français* and the *Journal du Commerce*, and worked at the École du Commerce, he accepted a position as a tutor in the South-West with the son of an Empire general. It is a period of meditation and probably of ideological formation but also of character development. The Blanqui who "*went back*" to Paris in 1826, enrolled in the Faculty of Law, was arrested in his characteristics: he was severe and austere, an absolute abstainer from alcohol and tobacco, a rigorous vegan. Does he know it or does he think about it, he already embodies a certain vision of the Revolution, the one that is dressed in absolutism.

He took courses at the Sorbonne and met Amélie-Suzanne Serre, a student at the boarding school where he gave some lessons. This lasted eight years and they got married in 1834. In the meantime, Blanqui collaborates with the newspaper *Le Globe* founded by Pierre Leroux in 1824. This newspaper is a tribune of opposition which welcomes, from Sainte-Beuve to Chateaubriand, from Ampère to Victor Hugo, all those who do not submit to the absolutism of Charles X. One is republican or bonapartist, liberal or socialist.

The Three Glorious Years of 1830 will shatter this facade union. On one side, the frock coats, gravely discussing a future to be shared, on the other side, the coats that beat the pavement and set up barricades. Blanqui proposes to his colleagues, frightened by so much audacity and unconsciousness, to form an insurrectional committee. They refuse. He exclaims: "*the weapons will decide, as for me I will take a rifle and the tricolor cockade*".

The great bourgeois who had taken the lead in the movement silenced the guns and imposed a Duke of Orleans, known as Louis-Philippe, at the head of a necessarily unchanged state.

Blanqui, a political apprentice, learns quickly, and his discourse hardens, as shown in his 1831 *Address to the Committee of Schools,* a true call to insurrection for a real revolution. This earned him - he had already done a probationary stay in the dungeon for having strayed on a border road - a few weeks in the prison of La Force where he rubbed shoulders with former barricaders of all persuasions. He struggles to define himself and his thinking amalgamates elements of Saint-Simonism, Fourierism, Owenism and Babouvism. This confusion will be long to dissipate.

This did not prevent him from being active at the head of the *Society of Friends of the People* whose program was a social republic.

Accused with fourteen of his comrades of treason and violation of the press laws, he was incarcerated in Sainte-Pélagie. He was acquitted at the trial of January 1832 where his plea, said Henri Heine, "*sounded the revolutionary tocsin*" but the court of appeal reversed the decision and sent him to prison for one year. He was ready to lose his life, especially since cholera was killing indiscriminately (his father died at the age of 75). He owes his survival and his newfound freedom to his mother, whose role will not be denied throughout his prison career. He can finally get married, we are in 1834.

His political system was then in a period of crystallization and the monthly magazine *Le Libérateur,* which he founded at the time, allowed us to follow the process of its development. His vision of history was classic for the time. Two classes confront each other, oppressed and oppressors, one of which embodies progress, which will triumph, and with it reason (rational law). The only romantic note and original touch in this common vision of a humanity ardently and boldly advancing towards a better life is that it is in France that this rational law must first triumph. France will then brandish the torch that will light the firebrand of freedom for other peoples. This rational law requires the pooling of the means of production, leading to equality in the redistribution of the resources produced. To achieve this, a revolutionary elite, conscious and organized, leading a people overwhelmed with work and intoxicated with misery, to the insurrectionary takeover.

At the same time that the glitter of his theory crystallized, plots and insurrectionary movements multiplied. From 1834 to 1839, conspiracies followed one another under the aegis of the Society of Families and the Society of Seasons. Blanqui, but also Barbès, were the inspirers. Arrested with his lieutenants, he was tried in August 1836, sentenced to two years in prison and imprisoned in Saumur.

There he intensely felt the emptiness of the absence of Amélie and their son Estève. Fortunately, the marriage of the Dauphin gave the prisoner an amnesty in 1837.

He immediately resumed his conspiratorial activity within the Society of Seasons and its ally the Federation of the Righteous. The latter, made up of German immigrant workers, was led by the tailor Weitling, whom we know from his correspondence with Marat.

Europe of the time is in the grip of all the demons of revolutions. From the infamous merchant England, the one of the slums of Manchester and Liverpool, to the severe Germany, not yet unified but already quite Prussianized, revolts against all the institutions, shaken by the crises resulting from the accelerated development of the capital which shakes the conservatisms, are rumbling. Everywhere secret societies and conspirators are stirring. And, as we know, France has a duty to enlighten the world and to pave the way for the reign of Reason. So in 1839 the insurrection is triggered by the Society of Seasons and the Hôtel de Ville is invaded. A revolutionary government was proclaimed on the balcony. But only a few hundred people joined the insurgents and Victor Hugo, walking in Paris that day, did not notice anything unusual.

After the failure of this revolutionary masquerade, the captured insurgents were tried for *"incitement to civil war"* before the Court of Peers. The sentences were heavy. Barbès was sentenced to death, others to very heavy prison sentences. Blanqui, who was captured only after a long flight, refused to defend himself and denied his lawyer the right to plead. He is in turn sentenced to death.

The king commuted the sentences of Barbès and his own to life imprisonment. The tomb of their freedom was given to Mont-Saint-Michel, one of the harshest prisons in the kingdom. It is during this incarceration that Amélie dies, whose parents take the child, whom they will raise in contempt of the father. This event struck Blanqui, who remained faithful to the memory of his wife all his life. It also adds to the physical and psychological torture of incarceration, this atrocious feeling of powerlessness that seizes any prisoner with regard to the *"outside"*. He tried to escape with the help of his mother, and was caught at the same time as Barbès.

The conditions of incarceration are so harsh that tuberculosis and depression strike the prisoners, who are not treated. Thanks to the intercession of various friends, it is decided to transfer Barbès, whose hemoptysis is becoming worrying, and Blanqui, whose condition is cachectic. The first one will go to Nîmes, the second to Tours. But Blanqui's condition worsens and a college of doctors declares him incurable. Fearing the consequences of his death in prison, the king pardons him, but Blanqui refuses the pardon and is kept in prison. He then spontaneously recovered and was able to benefit from the lighter regime that was granted to him. A press campaign in 1847 allowed his release.

The reports of the prefects say it, *"the catastrophe is imminent".*

The economic crisis bordered on bankruptcy, unemployment, which had not been helped at the time, was considerable (200,000 people in

Paris alone) and food shortages were spreading among the working classes. The Orleanist regime is discredited in all circles. Balzac writes:

> "*Above the charter,*" says Balzac, "in the Cousin Bette, there is *the holy, the venerable, the solid, the amiable, the gracious, the beautiful, the noble, the young, the all-powerful penny*!"

The republican banquets mobilize more and more participants, thus testifying to the defection of a part of the possessing classes with regard to the monarchy, the fall of the economy depriving the regime of any legitimacy. These banquets became real popular demonstrations in Paris as well as in the provinces. It is on the occasion of one of them, on February 20, 1848, that hostilities are triggered. Forbidden by the authorities, it was postponed to February 22 and moved from the more popular 12th arrondissement to the more aristocratic Champs-Élysées, in order to bend the authorities. In front of the resistance of these, the republican deputies protest and go to bed. But the Parisian people did not give in, they invaded the streets shouting "*Guizot to the gallows*" and "*Long live the reform*". They were joined by students who protested against the banning of three professors, including Michelet. Barricades were erected and the National Guard joined the insurgents. Shortly after, the Chamber was invaded and dispersed. A provisional government is established in the Hôtel de Ville. Blanqui was not part of it. He left Blois when the fall of Louis-Philippe was announced and joined Paris the same evening. Naturally he soaked up the atmosphere of the capital and was pleased to see that the air was red. He does not support the provisional government and engages against Lamartine in the quarrel of the red flag.

Let's stop for a moment on this episode that is too little known. Bakounine in his *Confessions* evokes with emotion the barricades "*drawn up like mountains and rising up to the roofs*"; he will see the workers, in the intoxication of the triumph, singing patriotic airs while "*brandishing red flags*". But this flag rubs shoulders with the tricolor still haloed by the struggles of the Great Revolution whose tradition without panties maintains a falsified memory.

When on February 25 the red flag is in the process of becoming the national flag, this soft paste of Lamartine, ci-devant member of the provisional government, cries of orrage. He makes of the red flag a "*sign of terror and distress*" and affirms that "*the floating and undecided mass of these poor and ignorant men collected in the suburbs raised the red flag only because this color excites the men like brutes*". That day therefore, the crowd, irresistible, invaded the Town Hall with the cries of "*The red flag! The red flag*". Taine and Lamartine tried to calm the tumult and partially succeeded. Then they met to deliberate with Carnier-Pagès. Armed men then entered the session room and camped themselves in front of the rulers. The worker Marche, 25 years old, who was at the head of them, became the spokesman of the crowd. In his left hand he holds a red cloth and in his right the barrel of his gun. "*The electricity of the people*, writes Lamartine, *seems concentrated in his look*". And he develops, for the last time perhaps, the program of the proletarian revolution. This program that Lamartine declares at once "*the program of the impossible*". And to propose to go to consult the people who are trampling outside. In front of his eloquence as sonorous and empty as brilliant, the crowd, this eternal dupe, is dazzled. But during several days the most obstinate groups resist and try to force the decision. There takes place the riposte of Blanqui who, arrived the day before in the capital, writes a manifesto:

> *"To the Provisional Government,*
>
> *The republican fighters read with deep sorrow the proclamation of the provisional government which re-established the Gallic rooster and the tricolor flag.*
> *The tricolor flag inaugurated by Louis XVI was illustrated by the First Republic and by the Empire; it was dishonored by Louis-Philippe.*
> *We are no longer, moreover, of the Empire or the First Republic.*
> *The people wore the color red on the barricades of 1848. Let us not try to wither it.*
> *It is only red with the generous blood shed by the people and the National Guard.*
> *It floats, sparkling, over Paris; it must be maintained.*
> *THE VICTORIOUS PEOPLE WILL NOT BRING THEIR FLAG."*

The truth is that Blanqui does not conceive of the republic as anything other than socialist, nor of socialism outside the republic.

He then founds the Central Republican Society in order to make a new, and true, i.e. social, revolution. Because it is necessary "to *abandon the men of the City hall to their impotence..."* and *"... to remake August 10".* Because the city is in full ebullition. All the currents compete for the opinion and the newspapers flourish. Among the 122 that counts G. Delmas[7] there are notorious organs like Proudhon's *Le Représentant du Peuple,* Cabet's *Le Populaire,* Raspail's *L'Ami du Peuple,* Considérant's *La Démocratie pacifique,* and ephemeral leaves with ronflants titles: *Le Sanguinaire, Le Volcan, Spartacus, Robespierre, Le Tribunal Révolutionnaire,* etc. Then there are the clubs that spring up in most cities and offer a platform for all dreams but also for all delusions. Lyon had nearly fifty of them and Paris nearly two hundred. To extinguish the social fire, according to a tactic that was to be successful, the government organized elections. Blanqui warned the people against this maneuver and tried to regroup the radical clubs. Only twenty or so responded to his call and published a proclamation in which they read that socialism and democracy are the two lasting and inseparable foundations of the Republic, that the words Liberty, Equality, Fraternity are hollow if they only cover scarcity, *"that it is not enough to change words, it is necessary to change things radically"* and to move towards the complete emancipation of the workers.

But they then sought to smear him and this is the story of the Taschereau document. This lawyer, who had turned to journalism and was a supporter of successive regimes until he became Secretary General of the Seine Prefecture under Louis-Philippe, then a deputy under the Second Republic, published an article on March 31 in which he made Blanqui a police informer. This false police officer intended to listen to the tribune of the political scene has a certain impact despite Blanqui's refutation and the unfailing support of Proudhon, Cabet, Raspail and Considérant. A trial between Taschereau and Blanqui saw the conviction of the latter despite the total absence of evidence. The dissension between the animators of the clubs, Lamartine's objective, is however realized because of the attitude of Barbès and various other leaders. Thus the great demonstration of April 16, which was to bring together all the revolutionary currents, was parasitized by these quarrels and suspi-

7. Revolutionary curiosities, the red newspapers. Some will even count 283 of them.

cions and by the important work of the snitches. It was to cries of "*Death to the communists*" that the demonstrators were welcomed by a docile bourgeois crowd and an armed force composed of national guards and mobile guards. It is the last jolt of the proletarian giant. The elections that followed shortly after confirmed his death, Lilliput triumphed, Blanqui and his friends were beaten to a pulp.

But the social question persisted and attempts were made to divert attention from it by inviting the people to support a Polish insurrection for the independence of this territory occupied by Russia. A demonstration took place on May 15, after the bloody riots in Limoges and Rouen, where hundreds of workers were killed or injured. The crowd, once again, entered the Chamber of Deputies and called Blanqui to the podium. He salutes the cause of Poland but also evokes the situation of the proletariat in France. He is the only one to give his speech a social content. A derisory attempt to create a revolutionary government is swallowed up in confusion, after the intervention of the National Guard. The leaders of the clubs are arrested and, among them, Blanqui, after eleven days on the run. In June, the last act is played out with the dissolution of the Ateliers nationaux, a social charity enterprise that was supposed to respond to the workers' demand for the right to work. The decree of June 21 enjoined men between the ages of 17 and 25 to enlist in the army, while the others had to work as diggers in the provinces. The government, on the other hand, had planned everything to deal with the discontent; its minister of war, General Cavaignac, had all the fighting units put on a war footing. The confrontation, during what will be called the four bloody days, pits 50,000 insurgents on one side, poorly armed and poorly equipped and directed, against more than 80,000 perfectly equipped and supervised men, not counting reservists and mobile guards. While the prefecture published the figure of 1,460 killed on both sides, the English newspapers put forward the figure of 50,000 dead, 14,000 imprisoned and 4,000 deported to camps. June washed the bourgeois humiliation of February in blood, and with the corpses of workers, faith and dreams in a (communist) earthly paradise were buried. Soberly, the Assembly, resuming its work, will pronounce the funeral oration of the proletariat saying that "*anarchy had been defeated*" and thanking general Cavaignac. From these events Blanqui draws a drastic revision of his conceptions on progress, republic, socialism and the nature of social classes, but he also measures the fundamental role of the permanent armies as a decisive instrument of the repressive apparatus of the State.

The revolutionary period ended with a major political trial in March 1849 in Bourges. Thirteen defendants appeared before the High Court on charges of incitement to civil war. Among them, Blanqui, but also Barbès, Raspail and the worker Albert. All of them challenged the jurisdiction of the court and, with the exception of Blanqui, the main accused, "*the great accursed one, stigmatized by all*" (*Le Peuple*, March 15, 1849), refused to present their defense. What are they reproached with if not being socialists? He refuses to consider it as a utopia.

> *"When the people are fasting, no one should eat. Here is my utopia, dreamed the day after February. How many implacable enemies it has aroused in me! It was not however about resurrecting a republic of Spartans, but about founding a republic without ilots. Perhaps my utopia will seem the most insane and the most impossible of all. Then God saves France.*

The verdict was rendered on April 2, six of the accused were acquitted, four to five were sentenced to five to seven years in prison. Blanqui, Barbès and Albert received ten years. With Raspail and Flotte he was sent to the citadel of Doullens in the Somme. It was there and on Belle-Île, where he finished serving his sentence, that Blanqui completed his political doctrine.

In Doullens, where they arrived on April 13, 1849, Blanqui and Flotte occupied the same cell. It was cold and damp, like the others, in this citadel built by Vauban two centuries ago. Then there was no drinking water, some was sent from the neighboring town, and the view was limited. But the inmates can garden and receive food. They could also write and do all sorts of intellectual work. Blanqui studied economics and history, religion and astronomy. He kept up an assiduous correspondence with friends outside the prison and, as a good vegetarian, spent precious time washing his vegetables and preparing his meals. In October 1850 he was transferred to Belle-Île-en-Mer. This was a measure of isolation. His detention lasted seven years. In November 1857, he was transferred to Corsica. He then spent twenty-three years in prison. He was freed thanks to the energetic intervention of his sister, Madame Antoine, in August 1859, despite the desire of the government to deport him to Guyana. His family had become smaller over the years; Adolphe and Sophie, his brother and sister, had died, another sister had emigrated to Latin America. His son Estève had become so distant from him that he offered him asylum in exchange for renouncing politics. Blanqui does not even answer. The France he rediscovers, after eleven years of confinement, has changed. Industry tends to concentrate and with it the owners of capital. Mass retailing appeared with Le Bon Marché, La Belle Jardinière and Le Louvre. Then came Le Printemps and La Samaritaine. As for the people, they became apathetic again because it was a period of full employment, but the material conditions of life did not improve. Wages have fallen, and so we see the generalization of women's and children's work, with the fourteen or sixteen hour day, for twelve legal ones. What to do! Blanqui remains an activist more than a theoretician. Engels describes him best: "*a political revolutionary in essence and a sentimental socialist only, sympathetic to the sufferings of the people, but devoid of socialist theory.*" Blanqui himself writes: "*thought is exhausted: ... The word is*". So he prepares the publication of a newspaper by meeting, everywhere in Europe, the enemies of the system and of the emperor Napoleon III. Everything was ready, funds, editorial staff, presses, when the police put an end to the adventure. Blanqui was arrested with five other people and tried in June 1861. The prosecution had nothing in its files but a press offence and twenty-five years in prison. Then the president says: "*You have kept the same ideas*", "*perfectly*" answers Blanqui, the magistrate continues: "*Not only the same ideas but also the desire to see them triumph*".

"*And I will keep it until death*", the accused thundered. These convictions will cost him four years of prison that he will be sent to the Conciergerie and then to Sainte-Pélagie.

The protest against the unfairness of this judgment will be very strong and led in part by Marx himself.

At Sainte-Pélagie, the twenty-seven months he spent there were months of intense and thorough study. History, economics, demography, philology, philosophy, literature are devoured by the imprisoned gargantua. He learns everything, and reads, in French as well as in English and Latin. Then he wrote, engaging as always in an active correspondence.

And he received journalists like Eugène Pelletan, Alfred Sirven, politicians like Scheurer-Kestner and Georges Clemenceau[8], writers like Juliette Adam. Finally, he met those who shared his detention, such as Jules Miot and Vermorel or Gustave Tridon, who was to become his very faithful lieutenant.

This one, freed, will become the official director, Blanqui being the occult, of the newspaper *Candide* launched thanks to the financial support of Doctor Lacambre. This bi-weekly with a large circulation for the time, 10,000 copies, will have eight issues before being banned by the police. In the meantime, Blanqui had been hospitalized due to his very poor health. After a year's stay in the Necker hospital, he escaped with the help of his friends on the eve of his release, fearing a new arrest followed by deportation. We are in 1865. He will reside in Belgium, then land of welcome with England of many exiles, at his friend Doctor Watteau. He was sixty years old.

Blanqui then worked on the organization of his party and the diffusion of his doctrine. Among the works that contributed to this, we must mention one that was quite successful, *Les Hébertistes* by G. Tridon, whose preface was written by Blanqui. At the time, each republican or socialist current discovered a spiritual filiation with the great ancestors. For Blanqui's party, these were the Hebertists, the only ones to embody the conscience and the heart of the revolution, true apostles of reason and science, protectors of the plebs and vigorous defenders of liberty, equality and atheism (fraternity being somewhat undermined by the cult of the Guillotin machine). The Blanquists were also close to them in their patriotism, which explained their distrust of the International. This explanation is also valid for the social composition of the party, where one finds mainly students and intellectuals.

As for the party, it resembles the Société des Saisons of yesteryear with its 800 to 2,500 members organized in units of ten, grouped in Paris and its suburbs. But these members also know how to play the cuckoo in all sorts of societies and organizations such as the Freemason lodges. There are also attempts to penetrate the nascent workers' organizations. Blanqui, who, like Marx, did not consider the unions as a means of emancipating the proletariat, nevertheless instructed his lieutenants to "*pay*

8. Then intern at La Pitié opposite the prison.

more attention to the workers". The difficulty of this propaganda lies in the Blanquist conception that the reforms are counter-revolutionary and the struggles for the immediate objectives, a waste of time and energy.

When the International Working Men's Association was created in 1866, Blanqui was reserved and only decided to participate in its first congress in Geneva because of pressure from Paul Lafargue, Marx's son-in-law, who knew Blanqui and his main disciples well. But the Blanquist delegates were so provocative that they were expelled.

Blanqui then wrote his famous text *Instruction pour une prise d'armes,* which can be considered as a theoretical statement responding to the Internationale. This text testifies to the gulf separating the two men, Marx and Blanqui, and their two theories. The latter is not a Marx before the letter, a beardless Marx. His theory of the coup de force, even if it appeals to the action of the proletariat, but not exclusively, is foreign to Marxism (and to Proudhonism). Marx will say of these conspirators that they "*improvise the revolution, they do not take into account the circumstances. They are the alchemists of the revolution and they share the confusion and narrowness of vision of the first alchemists.* But he has a great respect for him and would be very happy to meet him. This respect was reciprocal, but it did not lead to any rapprochement, despite Marx's attempts at the second Congress of the International. Blanqui did not believe in the future of the International and did not understand its approach to the masses.

During the demonstration that followed the assassination of the young Victor Noir in January 1870 by Prince Pierre Bonaparte, the Blanquists were present, marching around their old leader hidden in the crowd. On the occasion of the unrest that, for several days, shook the capital and rebounded on the workers' struggles, dozens of opponents were arrested. Blanqui took refuge in Brussels. He returned on August 10, 1870 convinced that the military disasters he had suffered created a climate favorable to insurrection. He therefore ordered the removal of the Villette barracks. Vallès nicely recounts in *L'Insurgé* this fiasco, which saw passers-by indifferent to the cries of "*To arms!*" and "*Long live the Republic!*" shouted by some insurgents. "*Before appealing to the people, it is necessary to feel their pulse to make sure that they have a fever.*"

A few months passed which saw the rout of the imperial expedition in ridicule and shame. After the capitulation of the emperor in Sedan on September 2, 1870, and under the pressure of the Parisian people, in the first ranks of which were the Blanquists, the deputies proclaimed the republic. But the popular uprising of September 3 and 4 brought to power only puppets whose only objective was to block the road to social revolution. Blanqui was naturally pushed aside but he considered that the defense of the territorial unity, of the national unity, therefore of the fatherland, was the priority. All the more so since the illusion remained in him that, as we have seen, the republic could only be social. So on September 7, he launched the daily *La Patrie en danger*, whose unbridled patriotism sank into chauvinism and hatred of the Germans, "a *people of brutes*". The club of the same name that he creates at the same time with Eudes, Granges, Regnard, Tridon, etc. ignores social demands in favor of the war to the death. But Blanqui's influence remained weak and he was only elected commander of the 169th National Guard Battalion after Clemenceau intervened.

Blanqui quickly understands that the government is preparing a capitulation and he violently attacks "*the lackeys in all livery who have never risked a hair of their head nor an hour of their liberty for the democratic cause*."

When on October 28 Bazaine negotiated the surrender of Metz, when the Prussians seized Le Bourget on October 30 and when it was said that Thiers negotiated a peace treaty with more humiliating conditions than the one that followed Waterloo, the capital was in turmoil. The government was deposed and its members arrested. Fourteen new ministers were elected by acclamation, Blanqui among them. If not all of them accept the power, he seizes it and exercises it. But the armed support is missing. The elections consume the defeat of the insurrection and Blanqui has to hide. His newspaper ceases to appear. But the accumulating defeats and the food shortage that overwhelms Paris maintain a climate of riot. A popular uprising is prepared by the International but the government takes the lead, closes the clubs and arrests the opponents. Blanqui was imprisoned in Figeac. He was still there when the Paris Commune began on March 18. He was then transferred to the sinister fortress of the Château du Taureau near Morlaix. Attempts to exchange Blanqui for hostages were rejected by Thiers. To endure his detention, Blanqui took refuge in cosmography and even wrote a pamphlet: *L'Éternité par les astres (Eternity through the stars)* which was published in 1872. He appeared before the court martial in 1872 in front of a full house attracted by the spectacle of an old man of sixty-seven having spent more than thirty years of his life in prison. He was sentenced to life imprisonment and deprivation of civil rights. Unable to bear the journey to New Caledonia, he was imprisoned in Clairvaux. He remained there for seven years and was released following a campaign for amnesty on June 12, 1879. That same year he was elected deputy for Bordeaux and then invalidated. He will run again and will finally be defeated by a handful of votes. He also engaged in an intense correspondence and multiplied his pamphlets: *Ni Dieu Ni Maître, l'armée esclave et opprimée...* and multiplied his public meetings. He took part in the newspaper of his party which had this unambiguous title: *Ni Dieu Ni Maître.*

But on his return from a meeting on December 27 he was struck by apoplexy and died at the age of seventy-six after an agony of five days.

He was buried at Père-Lachaise on January 5, escorted by a large crowd that paid unreserved tribute to the only true professional French revolutionary.

Léon BLOY (1846-1917)
The purifier of souls

If the name is known to all, the work, both today and yesterday, has retained only a few chosen. He is, however, one of the greatest pamphleteers of his century and one of the most original writers in literature.

Léon Bloy was born in Périgueux on July 11, 1846. His family was of old Périgourdine stock on his father's side, well-to-do craftsmen, but not rich. His mother's side was more affluent, but not wealthy. His father, who had done some studies, was an office manager at the Ponts et Chaussées, and his mother devoutly took care of her seven children, whom she entrusted to the Virgin Mary with a special devotion.

From his childhood it is worth remembering that he had, according to his own words, *the gift of tears*, which he considers to be a sign of predestination. For the rest, he evokes a kind of melancholy, a disposition to daydreaming, he even speaks of the despotism of dreams, all of which translate into a torpor, an almost autistic withdrawal that makes the child a designated victim for all his peers. But this sleep of the vital impulse has its volcanic fury, thus in the high school: "*One day however I revolted, the malice of my fellow students having exceeded I do not know which limits. I stole a refectory knife, fortunately harmless, and after an emphatic bravado, I rushed at a group of forty young fools, injuring two or three of them. I was relieved, foaming, crushed by blows, superb. My knife had done little harm, only a few scratches, but my father had to take me out of the stultifying stay and keep me at home.*"

Here he is, unschooled and continuing his studies at home. Bloy's diary of adolescence and youth tell us nothing about this period. Except that he had a well-ordered life, the winter in Périgueux, the summer in the country residence of Fenestreau. The work was done in the offices of the father who was in charge of the supervision and the initiation to the copying of illustrated documents in view of a future engagement at the Orleans Railway Company for which he worked.

The education also includes readings, introduction to music and cultural evenings with the parents.

There are no rough edges in this life which imitates, more or less, that of all the petty bourgeois of the time. In this daily boredom, little Léon dreams of becoming a poet. He writes verses that he reads to his father one evening, who coldly rejects his vocation.

And nothing else? Yes, all the same; brought up as a Christian, as we have said, he loses his faith at the age of fifteen because of "*the extreme fury of the nascent passions... Several years will pass thus during which Pride, Sensuality, Sloth, Ignorance, Envy, Contempt, the most ferocious Hate accumulated in me and grew until the paroxysm.*" This state of diabolical possession explains the maniacal hatred that he then deploys against Catholicism.

> *"Before," he says* (so before his conversion), *"I was not indifferent to the Church, no, certainly that is not what one should say, but I hated it and this hatred, I beg you to believe, was nothing vulgar, a deep hatred, and I cannot help smiling rather sadly... I could not hear the Holy Church without blushing with fury and* (here is the little known project that his hatred had inspired to this demoniac) *I remember well to have gathered, me, poor imbecile runt, the elements of a great work against the Christian doctrine, which, certainly, would have been terrible, because I would have written it with my blood and I would have made pass my whole soul in the inflamed expression of my blasphemy."*

This mental deviation leads Leon Bloy during the Paris Commune to develop apocalyptic visions:

> *"In my eyes as an apostate,"* he wrote to Abbé Anger-Billard, a friend of Barbey d'Aurevilly, *"the burning of a few public monuments and a small number of private properties, the fall of Cologne, the slitting of the throats of several hundred enemies of the people,*

and a few other pranks known to the whole world, were extremely pitiful results, and quite unworthy of the expeditious justice of the self-respecting revolutions. ME, I had dreamed better. The three hundred thousand heads of the citizen Marat would not have been enough for me and the oil would have vainly solicited my suffrage. The democratic equality taken from the lowest possible level had to, according to my views, realize a social level such as it did not remain any more under the sun that the Bourbeux and the Croupissants. My line, an ideal delegation, started like a topographic arrow from the presumed aristocracy of virtues, that is to say, from the Priesthood, and went rapidly, after having passed through the aristocracy of money which disappeared into the Red Sea, to the aristocracy of triumphant goujatism and to the high barons of hereditary scum. All superiority, all human relief had to fall, to sink and perish in the cesspool of a definitive promiscuity."

Fortunately, he will defeat the beast... after many avatars.

In the meantime, the young man arrived in Paris in June 1864 with a small viaticum of 160 francs collected by his father. He first worked at the Orleans Company with a remarkable ardor and all the more noticed that it did not last more than a week. For the climate of the company was more conducive to idleness than to work that no one required. This lasted for a year, before the demon drove him to enroll in a drawing course. There he met new friends with whom he created a reading circle. They met at the home of the parents of one of them, the young Victor Lalotte, read verses and commented on literature in grandiloquent terms.

But the instability that would characterize Bloy's personality and life was already at work and he left Pils' drawing studio. At this time he begins to break with the anonymous, but peaceful, career traced by his father and works only part-time at the office of the Orleans Railroad, and a kind of moral distress invades him. He wandered around the city, meeting new people, going to cafés, billiards and girls. Indecision nags him, which leads him to consider a career in journalism, without giving up painting, while cherishing other dreams. Very quickly he left his job for good (his dismissal was welcomed with relief), and navigated from small jobs to miserable jobs.

It is the beginning of a new career, that of a tapper, which he will pursue with assiduity throughout his life. For he became acquainted with the debts that quickly formed a string, ginning up his daily misery.

From this period date his first known articles addressed to *La Rue* de Jules Vallès, who refused them, but also a copy of Rogeard's pamphlet *Les Propos* de Labienus. He is, he tells us, then this "*republican and perfect socialist.*"

But Providence was watching, and it came to disturb the young man's despair. One day, while he was selling Voltaire's *Complete Works* to a bookseller to lighten his library and weigh down his stomach, a man with a large scarlet-lined cape, a lace ruffle and a wide-brimmed hat passed by: Barbey d'Aurevilly. Bloy follows him, asks to admire him, moves Barbey who invites him to enter his house. They talk, Barbey is seduced and a strange and decisive friendship is born between them. It is at the origin of Bloy's spiritual and political conversion. Barbey's book, *Prophètes du passé,* composed of portraits of counter-revolutionary figures (Bonald, De Maistre, Doneso Cortes) is a ferment of the long alchemical process that leads to the conversion. The passion for the Absolute that he recognizes in Barbey, the frenetic taste for violence that inhabits him and the insatiable need for justice lead him to feel called, to provoke a kind of illumination, to generate a mysticism of the imagination. He creates in himself the conditions of the trance that he then welcomes as a blessing. He himself dates his conversion to June 29, 1869, but he does not give the time.

He then went to war in 1870 in the Cathelineau corps with the mobile troops of the Dordogne. For him this war was a crusade: "*passions invaded France, it is the Protestant leprosy over our ulcer of Cartesianism*". It is thus necessary to rid Europe of the followers of Luther and Calvin. Also the defeat is easily explained. It is "*the great catastrophe*" which manifests the anger of God. Sergeant Léon Bloy, demobilized, joins a corps of volunteers sent to fight against the Commune. The "soldier of Christ" justifies this commitment by his condemnation of the democratic principle.

> *"I am a former republican, and with what ardor I was one, God knows. Well, for years I have meditated night and day on these things and I have arrived quietly, without any tremors, without any*

inner violence, at the irrevocable and absolute condemnation of the democratic principle. I have condemned it in the name of human nature, in the name of reason, in the name of God, as a nameless falsehood and a flag of eternal doom."

Not having been engaged in the slaughter which washed with the blood of thousands of workers the fear of revolution that had arisen in a scorched bourgeoisie, he returned to Périgueux, having been refused the certificate of good conduct issued to all other volunteers. It is true that his state of mind had changed somewhat. In a letter to a friend, he writes:

"Oh, my friend and confidant, my soul bleeds and I weep as I write to you... M. de Cathelineau simply believes in the disinterested enthusiasm of people, most of whom are, I believe, worthy of the prison. And it is with such men that the three times small Mr. Thiers wants to save France! In truth, one wonders how God himself could manage to do something with this people."

He stayed two years in this city and it is during this stay that he discovered Blanc de Saint-Bonnet, author of two works: *La Restauration Française* and *De la Douleur*, with whom he engaged in an assiduous correspondence in which he paid tribute to the theorist for his contribution to the formation of his thought.

In 1873, he returned to Paris and thanks to the introduction of Saint-Bonnet found employment with a Mr. Pages, organizer of the Catholic Committees of France. But in a short time his lack of assiduity and his negligence earned him his dismissal. The invocation of Our Lady earns him an immediate, if modest, position with a notary. During this period Bloy is alone; he visits parish priests, meditates and ignores everything about the world that is agitating around him. But he is not fooled and describes the state of his camp at the time thus:

"The backsides were still cooking from the German boot. There was only talk of returning to God. One piled into Catholic circles to hear the good word of Mgr Mermillod, telling what he had suffered for Jesus Christ or the ecumenical babblings of M. de Mun. One clung madly to the Count of Chambord, supposedly the great Monarch,

announced by the prophecies, and whose illegitimate belly was to save everything. People rushed to pilgrimages singing liberating verses. One voted the erection of a sanctuary to the Sacred Heart, on the walls of which would be read these helpful words: Gallia poenitens et devota, *and each one brought his stone, because it was the national Vow, strangely forgotten since. What else? The Augustinian Fathers of the Assumption founded the Prosperous* Pilgrim *and the Profitable* Cross, *for the irredeemable debasement of Christian thought or feeling."*

Barbey and Saint-Bonnet worked together to get him out of his inactivity and introduced him to Louis Veuillot, director of *L'Univers,* who welcomed him immediately. He collaborates irregularly, too much for his taste, and is so formalized by it that he writes of Veuillot that he is *"a formidable cad".*

For all that, the five articles he writes are brilliant, eloquent and vigorous. But they have nothing exceptional. Also the hope to be assured of a journalistic income is only an illusion and testifies to the fact that Bloy is beside the point. But he persists and publishes in *La Restauration, a* legitimist organ created by Georges de Cadoudal. This confirms his journalistic position with a specialized public of journalists and writers but does not feed him, *"I almost died of hunger...".* Because his function of secretary of Barbey d'Aurevilly is only honorary. Disappointed, he gave up journalism and proposed to enter the literary career. He then participates in the group of the Republic of Letters to which belong Catrille Mendès, Richepin, Paul Bourget, who call themselves the *"Vivants"* and present themselves as the school of *"modernism".* Within this group, which soon met in the salon of Nina de Villard, there were, in addition to the first three mentioned, François Coppée, Léon Cladel, Armand Sylvestre and Émile Goudeau. Within this society Bloy appears as *"a starving failure".* He did not see himself as such and tried to convert. Richepin and Bourget are targets of his fiery proselytism. In vain.

It is at this time, and in this state of mind, that he meets the writer Ernest Hello. This one, twenty years older, is little known and little read. But he was enlightened, convinced that God's victory could only be achieved through his own triumph. God was patient, Hello was less so, and the waiting made him desperate. This suffering wrung from him these words that one would think belonged to Bloy twenty years later.

> *"I have been treated by men," he said, "as the Virgin Mary was treated by them... I am reminded of this word of the Scriptures, the stone rejected by the architects has become the cornerstone of the building... If I had an action, free and effective, I would open the door to you and to many others... I feel in my destruction the greatest misfortune that has befallen God and men... I feel the absolute insignificance of everything else. I feel, as I have never felt before, the infinite vanity of everything that is not my deliverance. It alone is the salvation of all. Whoever thinks of anything else wastes his time... Alone among all men, I would be able to give justice and glory. And still, moreover, every day that passes for me in inaction takes away from God his glory, from mankind his bread, from myself my life. Each day that passes for me in inaction represents such a sum of misfortunes and crimes that it is impossible to count them..."*

Providence, eager for a twist, chooses this moment to introduce into Bloy's life a young prostitute of thirty years, Anne-Marie Roulé. For him, there is no doubt that Providence is confronting him with the demon co-tenant of Miss Roulé. In *Le Désespéré, a* literary transposition stripped of mystery, Bloy describes himself as possessed by his "inner goat". This possession, both painful and passionate, is shaken by the death of his father, to whom he arrived only after the funeral having lost, by love or by desire, a night· This night of pleasure was also the night of his father's agony and this fed the neurotic feeling of guilt that animated him. Hence the decision of abstinence, so quickly abandoned, in front of the impetuous call of the sensuality.

So he decided to settle down and take a job at the Chemins de fer du Nord in order to live a Christian and middle-class life. However, he soon resigned and took refuge in the Grande Trappe de Saligny. The return to the world took place after two months and was accompanied by two miracles: a creditor paid his debts and Anne-Marie was converted. But the real miracle was the offer to collaborate with the Catholic newspaper *Le Foyer illustré* and then with *La Revue du monde catholique*. There he met a priest, the Abbé de Moidrey, who was revolted by the reticence of the ecclesiastical hierarchy with regard to the miracle of La Salette (the apparition of the Blessed Virgin on September 19, 1846 to two shepherds and the delivery of a message on the punishments likely to befall people unfaithful to the word of Christ). Here he is on pilgrimage with the abbot, who dies during the trip.

From then on, Bloy felt invested with a sacred duty: to write a book on La Salette to the glory of Our Lady of the Seven Sorrows. He wrote this book under the dictation of the Virgin and nine thousand angels, with the help of Anne-Marie, a pythoness engulfed in this supernatural which so well suited his hysterical nature. This delirium between the two of them led to a work entitled *Le Symbolisme de l'Apparition,* which was not published by his daughter until 1925. This work accomplished the evolution of Bloy's Christianity into a private, esoteric, hermetic and almost heretical faith.

Anne-Marie's condition, between delirium and deprivation, deteriorated and she had to be interned at Sainte-Anne on June 20, 1882.

A very long crisis begins; it will end only with the meeting of Jeanne Molbech, where *"the spirit of prayer left me... I was given over to the unbridled lust of my carnal sense... I set myself against God..."*

This period, according to us of a great richness, is that of the *Black Cat* and the *Pal.* But also the one during which he probably wrote *Le révélateur du Globe, an* apology of Christopher Columbus where he asks for his beatification.

Under the direction of Rodolphe Salis, the club, created by Émile Goudeau of the Hydropathes group, had gone from being a light cabaret to a highly respected literary café. And it is then, in this place to which was associated a review of the same name, that Bloy becomes a character. He imposes his ferocity and has cards engraved where he declares himself *"entrepreneur of demolitions".* And he rubs shoulders with Willette and Caran d'Ache, Ponson du Terrail and Charles Crès, Paul Mounet and Coquelin Cadet in the columns of the journal and on the stage.

And so he attracts the attention of Francis Magnard, the basileus of *Figaro,* who offers the young and promising barker. He keeps quiet for three months, writing what is expected of him. Then he thinks it's time to distract himself by settling accounts with Richepin, whom he curbs in a nice way but without manners.

Magnard being more complacent than courageous and *Le Figaro* what it remained, it is Bloy who is asked to leave.

The return to Le *Chat noir* and the publication of Le *Révélateur du Globe*, which was hardly a success, did not bring him any prosperity. He had no more luck with the collection of articles from the *Chat noir*, which he published as a collection under the title *Propos d'un entrepreneur de démolitions*.

He pinpoints in a bloody hunting table some glories of contemporary literature and hopes today disappointed.

He would later regret these youthful excesses. But the time had not yet come, and he wished first to create his own store of ferocity. It was *Le Pal*, inspired by Alphonse Carr's *Wasps* and *La Lanterne* de Rochefort, whose first issue appeared in February 1885. It is a question of "To say the truths to everyone on all the things and that they can be the consequences of it". He adds at once "I declare my irrevocable will to *miss essentially of moderation*". Such is the program of this journalism of combat and convictions which is opposed, of spirit and form, to the journalism of submission and complacency.

But *Le Pal* is a bitter failure and ceases its publication after the fourth issue. The public was not seduced by this outpouring of rage, this tidal wave of gall which proposes to dissolve, in opprobrium and contempt, the literary notabilities that are Zola, Jules Ferry, Vallès, About, Richepin, Ohnet, Sarcey, and even, Victor Hugo: "*this imbecile llama of which* no *one is unaware of the pitiful intellectual senility*".

Moreover, literary men are not enough for him, he still has to vatiate politicians, ministers of religion, officials of all kinds and, unforgivable crime, journalists, incense-boxes specialized in the waxing of vanities. Let us read it:

> *"It is fifteen years old, our Republic, pubescent, without virginity, fallen from the bloody vagina of Treason, Jezebel of the brothel, adorned with filth, monstrously fattened with fornications, (similar) to some very ancient Lust that would have been painted on the wall of a hypogeum... Republic of the wine merchants and pimps."*

This republic is that of the owners:

> *"People of cowardly imbeciles or repulsive tartufes, whose moral wealth is now a kind of bourgeois honesty to raise the hearts of sows".*

The clergy itself is not spared:

> *"Those above all who should have resisted and fought against the retaining wall of the clergy, a surprisingly crumbly mass of mediocrity, baseness, cowardice and infamy, made even less consistent by the mixture of a few rare flints of the word."*

What indignant Léon Bloy and gives such a breath to his imprecations, it is what characterizes, according to him, his time, the mediocrity. Faced with this defilement of the soul, no compromise is possible, hence the requirement of intolerance.

But he is forty years old, has had fifty jobs, lost three wives, failed at everything, and is engulfed in a sticky misery. What use is it then to be full of genius?

To write a novel, promised to Paul-Victor Stock, which tells *"the crushing of a superior man by a mediocre society"*. It is *Le Désespéré* published in 1886.

In the night where this great shadow staggers there are however two fireflies which accompany it, Villiers de l'Isle-Adam and Huysmans.

Their trio formed *"a union of anger"* (Bardèche). Each of them praised the merits of the others, provided moral and financial support and tried to promote the work of the companions.

This was not enough to ensure the success of Le *Désespéré,* which Stock had to give up, frightened by a "madness" of Bloy, and which was taken over by a bookshop commissioner. Nobody or almost nobody talked about it and few bought it.

In 1888 luck smiled again and offered Bloy a collaboration with the famous weekly *Le Gil Blas.* Once again it did not last. Eleven articles and a year later, he was fired.

Thus the misfortune returns and the misery. Then there is also the death of Villiers and the quarrel with Huysmans. There is also the meeting with Jeanne Molbech who will become his wife. She is young, Danish and poor. This meeting and this love will be the pretext of a transfiguration. They get married in 1890 and Bloy, with all his strength restored, takes up his somewhat neglected pen again. He also went to Denmark for a lecture tour which was not without success. On his return, *Le Gil Blas* called him back and finally, in 1892, he published *Le Salut pour les Juifs,* a response to Édouard Drumont's pamphlet *La France juive.*

In this small volume of barely 150 pages, he postulates that the Bible is not the history of the Jewish people but that of the people of God and, consequently, of God, as told by himself. It is therefore a question of deciphering it, and it is a work of exegesis in which he engages. It emerges that Jesus is the perfect Poor Man whom the Jews crucified out of hatred for them and adoration of money. Only the conversion of the Jews can therefore save humanity because it would mean their renunciation of money, and therefore the end of their rejection of the Redemption which would then be promoted. In short, the crime (the deicide) was necessary for the fight between good and evil to take place and for the latter to triumph. This theology, which combines good and evil, reintroduces the latter into the history of Creation in a gnostic world. It leads to a valorization of the role of the Holy Spirit that will be the inspirer of the ultimate fight.

Theology demanding and hermetic of which Bloy is a lonely and imaginative prophet.

The years 1893 to 1895 were years of hardship. He published *Belluaires et Porchers, a* collection of articles published in *Le Gil Blas,* and a book of stories inspired by his memories of the 1871 campaign, *Sueur de Sang.* Without success. *Histoires désobligeantes,* another collection of stories, was no more successful. Moreover, Bloy is bored at *Gil Blas* where his pen is held back. He cannot pour out his heaps of slaps on the face of his enemies and must use the weapons of irony and sarcasm. He tries to reason himself by saying that he *"cannot be a pamphleteer forever"* and by basking in the material security that this regular collaboration offers him, but it is not enough.

However, Providence is watching, taking on the tragic mask of anarchy. When Laurent Tailhade is wounded by the bomb dropped at the Foyot restaurant, Lepelletier of *the Echo de Paris* titles his article *"Une bombe intelligente" (A clever bomb).* It is a reminder that Tailhade had loudly approved a previous attack by Vaillant in the Parliament. Bloy immediately published a paper in defense entitled *L'Hallali du poète,* in which Lepelletier was called *"a sponger who had been desalinated for twenty years by all the spittle".*

The offended sends his witnesses to Bloy who challenges them. In those days of journalism, which was not yet fuddy-duddy, there was no question of honor. Jules Guérin, editor in chief of *Gil Blas, took the* place of his journalist. The duel takes place, he is wounded and Bloy is fired. It is the return to misery.

Before being absorbed by it, he has time to publish *Léon Bloy devant les cochons, an* answer to all his detractors, which was published on the day of the assassination of Sadi Carnot. Another failure.

Then torments began to assail him on all sides. His newborn child, André, died, probably of croup. He manages only with difficulty, and by beating whoever will let him, to pay his rent. Then he starts drinking absinthe. His wife suddenly falls ill, risks dying but recovers. Then another of his children, little Pierre, dies. And this is what he writes, and which can be found in this very beautiful book that is *The Poor Woman*:

> *"In the presence of the death of a little child, Art and Poetry really look like very great miseries. The moans of the mothers, and even more, the silent swell of the fathers' chest have a much different power than words or colors, so much the pain of the man belongs to the invisible world".*
>
> *"It is not exactly the touch of death that causes so much pain, since this punishment has been sanctified by the One who is called Life. It is all the past joy that rises up and roars like a tiger, that breaks out like a hurricane. It is, in a more precise way, the magnificent and desolate memory of the sight of God, for all the peoples are idolaters you have said so much, O Lord! Your sad images only know how to adore what they think they see, for so long they no longer see you, and their children are for them the Paradise of Voluptuousness".*

He is desperate, downcast and finds the strength only to survive. For this he lives on the side as a mercenary of letters. However, he completes *La Femme Pauvre*, the counterpart to Le *Désespéré*, an autobiographical novel recounting his unhappy love (necessarily) for Berthe Dumont.

It is such a failure that it will take the publisher twenty years to sell the two thousand copies printed. And this, in spite of the vibrant, but lonely, praise of Séverine and Octave Mirbeau. *The Journal* published simultaneously in Belgium is not more successful.

Then Bloy decides to start a new life, and since the French public refused to recognize the greatest of French writers, he went to look elsewhere for the right tribute to his genius. He left for Kolding in Denmark, and from the very first days he declared *"I am at war with three quarters of the population"*. During this stay in Barbary, he saw only *"cockroach and ligamentous brutes"*. He stayed there for eighteen months before returning to France. We are in 1900.

Insensibly the misery will be lightened by the presence of obstinately generous friends *"I recognize a friend when he sends me money"*, and the renewal of the literary network which is insensibly created around the master, whose works, and especially *the Diary*, have more unconditional fans than readers, let's name Rachilde, Jehan Rictus, René Martineau, Séverine. And then there are great joys. The death of Émile Zola for example:

"The newspapers confirm the good news, the cretin of the Pyrenees would have died in his literature, he would have been picked up in the excrement." But he did not give up his pamphleteer work and collaborated with *L'Assiette au beurre* where he gave three articles (including one against colonization and another on journalists, entitled *L'aristocratie des maquereaux*). He also publishes the last of *L'Église* where he offers himself to the slaughter of *"sad priests and some other servants of the devil"*. The success is of esteem but is accompanied by a small harvest of enthusiastic articles.

And so, in 1905, at the Autumn Salon, the painter Léon Bonhomme exhibited a portrait of Léon Bloy. It was a sign that was added to the others like a promise. From then on, in the pavilion on the rue du Chevalier de la Barre, friends met every Sunday.

Everyone brings something and we have dinner. There was always some left over for Monday and Tuesday because friendship knew how to be generous.

Then comes 1908 and this major work, where Bloy reconnects with his youth, brings together all the moments of his life in a generous, powerful and masterful text: *Le Sang du pauvre (The Blood of the Poor).*

It is a merciless denunciation of the exploitation of man by man, but also and especially of money. For *the Blood of the poor* is money, says Bloy, *"It expressly sums up all suffering. It is Glory, it is Power. It is Justice and Injustice, it is Torture and Voluptuousness"*. And to add *"the joy of the coward has for substance the pain of the poor... The rich man is an inexorable brute who is forced to be arrested with a scythe or a pack of machine guns in his belly"*. Then to denounce the vampirism by the indifference and the hardness of heart which characterizes the modern Catholics, deserters and apostates of the true faith. Money, which has become the blood and soul of civilization, has replaced faith. The idolatry of which it is the object is a blasphemy against. "*On the last day all accounts will be settled in a terrifying finale*" (Bardèche). In short, God will be the instigator of the great evening.

This last great book of Bloy is of a prodigious modernity[9].

He denounces the standardization of the (anti) human condition accomplished by the economy, underlines that it is not even the goods and their possession that are the justification of the enslavement to Leviathan but the desire for them. This intuition, at a time when the economy was being born, attests to Léon Bloy's own dimension. This major work, by the author's own admission, one of his most important, was a failure: 91 francs in royalties.

The fourth volume of the *Journal* met its thousand readers and widened the circle of the chosen ones. We even see the revolutionary Victor Meric, in *Les Hommes du Jour,* writing that his work is colossal and defies the ravages of time.

Bloy is then a refugee out of time, leading a life of a good family man, refusing all forms of modernism and of the stupid and arrogant progress (the car, the plane, the cinema...). Little by little his fame grows and flattering articles bloom here and there.

In 1912, he published *L'Âme de Napoléon* because the story of Napoleon "*is the face of God in the darkness*", translating "*Napoleon prefigures the One who is to come*". This book, like the others, is partly inexplicable if one refuses the Bloyan postulates and others in another dimension, supernatural, of the world where the symbolism of history can be decoded, "*as long as one has the keys, one accepts those proposed by the author: historical facts are the Style of the Word of God.*"

This work, however hermetic, is the first to be the subject of a collective study in the review *Les Marchés de Provence.* The conspiracy of silence is definitively broken and the one who is called "*an Ezekiel of the sewer and*

9. Thirty years later... perhaps this assessment of lucidity should also be tempered.

a mucky Jeremiah" finally gets the place he deserves among recognized writers. The reprints begin.

When the war broke out, "*it is my personal unworthiness that has determined the divine anger and I am, in reality, the only guilty one*", he published *Jeanne d'Arc et l'Allemagne* and then *Au Seuil de l'Apocalypse* in 1916 (the seventh part of his *Journal*).

But his strength is declining, "*I can no longer count on my body...*" he writes. However, he continued to write and in 1917 he published *Les Méditations d'un Solitaire.* He believed that his strength had returned, but on November 3, 1917 he had an appointment with death. It is punctual.

The man of refusal, the Herald of God joins the story.

Aristide BRUANT (1851-1925)
Modern Villon and general of guys

"Near Sens, in Courtenay, in the land of wine, I was born...
sings Bruant in verses entitled *En Bourgogne.*

Courtenay, it is the sweet France but also a city, sorry a village, full of history. I should even say history. Three Byzantine emperors and a king of Jerusalem, in short, the whole era of chivalry is summed up in the loops of two rivers, the Loiret and the Yonne, which adorn like necklaces, castles and marshes. And then, very close by, the village of Chantecoq, Gallic of a Gaul not yet colonized by the Roman merchants, where Louis-Armand-Aristide Bruand was born on May 6, 1851. He will become Bruant by becoming a chansonnier. But he is first of all an only child, handsome, intelligent, docile, that a prosperous middle-class environment having known how to take advantage of the Revolution (it was made for that) destines to high studies. Then it was the imperial high school of Sens where the child-poet *"plays with the wind, talks with the clouds",* made his first, and brilliant, weapons. But the wheel of fortune turned and, in 1868, his family was ruined by the risky investments and negligence of a father who ran estaminets. The whole family moved to Paris, their childhood was over. Aristide will be successively a jumper at a lawyer's office and then a jeweler's worker. At the age of nineteen he has a job, but the war comes to throw the trouble in his existence.

A patriot in need of heroism, he remained so until the worst, when he joined a group of "francs-tireurs", the Gars de Courtenay. The debacle of the imperial army, then of the Versailles troops, deprived him of triumph. For a few years, he lived a laborious and self-effacing life, busy feeding his family of broken arms. Not really, because during his free time, he wanders around Paris and discovers, it is banal to write it but essential to understand the genesis of this street poet, a city behind the Haussmannian mirror with its workers fresh from a martyred revolution, its ruffians and its ribalds, its proletarian women that the versaillais called the knitters... And he, the intellectual, discovers that he understands Latin better than the language of the streets. His curiosity is sharpened, reinforced perhaps by the seduction he discovers with his daughters, so much less stuffy than the trivial little bourgeois women. From day to day he goes out to discover, listen, see, feel, pushes doors and crosses thresholds. He is shy, but he is less and less afraid of the gouapes and marlous. He even feels won over by a familiarity that distracts him from his daily gloom. His parents, for whom he is the only stable source of income, pay him a substitute, so he will not do his military service. Tired of the jewelry business, with no future when one does not have substantial capital, he turns to the civil service. Here he is an employee of the Chemins de fer du Nord. From 1875 to 1879, he maintained himself in this state of physical prostration that engenders this sweet security of a guaranteed future. More precisely, he fights against this contagion of subjugation, this shrinking induced by obedience and servility, by a greater attention to those who are outside, the scoundrels, the outlaws, the dregs of policed societies. He now knows their language and their morals, and is passionate about the green language, its life and evolution, from Villon to Vade and to that of the fortifs. From his linguistic discoveries he nourishes poems and songs that he sings at night in a caboulot. He will know his first successes there. And then one day, a guy accosts him and sends him to Robinson's, Place de la Nation, where the fee is 2F50 per night, plus wine. The man who gave him this tip was called Sellier, he was a cooper and would become one of the greatest French tenors. And it works so well that the compliments decide Bruant to launch a challenge. He is going to sing for the least complaisant audience, the one of the *Amandiers*, composed of stonewomen and marlous. It is a triumph. He was soon spotted by an impresario of the time and appreciated by the famous Paulus. He also resigned from the railroads, to the great displeasure of his saprophytic parents. He even begged his mother, to whom he gave all the money he earned, to give him five francs to join the Society of Authors and Composers. Then it is the period of the army. Because the replacement only allows to delay the deadline of a gloss. So he is incorporated in the 113th regiment of line of which he will write, he is always so cocardier, the song of march. This song will be taken over, with some modifications, by many other regiments. He even wrote, encouraged by his colonel, other martial hymns, such as *La Noire :*

"For her, in the shadow of the flag
We'll get our skin punctured".

Let's move on quickly...

After the trestles of *L'Époque*, those of *La Scala* and then of *L'Horloge*. In a few years, the young Bruant became an artist with a refined outfit: a jacket, "rosewood" pants, a fancy vest and a magnificent eight-reflector on top. This dandy who collects successes is adopted by the chic public and frequents the right people. He also had literary connections and even established active collaborations with some of them, Jules Jouy for example. But from one day to the next, he is transformed: corduroy jacket and breeches, sombrero and scarf in crimson. The hair is thrown back and flattened, and the final touch to the picture: a hidalgo cape: "*In the carnival of everyday life, I arrogate to myself the right to disguise myself*" Is that all? No. He also says:

"Whatever you assume, the show is over. No more funny verses and catchy little choruses. If I write any more, to earn the spoonfuls of my own, my friends will sing them. I promised the inimitable Paulus, he will have them, and he will make applaud a Bruant which does not exist any more. But, beware! a new Bruant is born, and I have the presentiment that he will say two words to the crowd of partygoers, daddy's boys, idlers, incompetents, that he will shout to them the human suffering, and all the threatening hatred of the wretches that their outrageous luxury, their immeasurable stupidity does not cease to irritate". And of those, of which he will be from now on openly the singer, he says addressing to the seated ones: "*they frighten you, thank them for not understanding that they could terrorize you more*". Because his contempt perceives for

the pranksters of the night neurotic of the two sexes, fond of slumming without risk. The first place where the disciples of the muses meet is *Le Chat noir,* in memory of Edgar Poe, created by Rodolphe Salis, a painter-decorator. This first cenacle is composed of Jean Lorrain, Villiers de l'Isle-Adam, Albert Samain, Georges d'Esparbes, Toulouse-Lautrec, Willette, Alphonse Allais, Moréas, Caran d'Ache, Xanrof, etc. All of them, emptying their drinks, attracted the literary onlookers who came to listen to the fine minds declaiming and discussing. As the club's popularity spread, it even had an eponymous newspaper. To celebrate his arrival Bruant composes a ritornello which quickly becomes famous:

> *I seek my fortune / Around the Black Cat / In the moonlight, / In Montmartre at night.*

Complaint of the bambocheur, nose to the wind, in search of good fortunes in the absence of the one measured in cash and stumbling. For *Le Chat noir, Le Lapin blanc, Le Clou* and other caboulots, including that of Maxime Lisbonne, future colonel of the Commune, *Le Bagne* where one was served by mock revolutionary fries while waiting to found a bistroquet supplied with water from Lourdes for aperitifs, only sparingly fed their artists.

So when Salis moves his *Chat Noir* Bruant takes over the patents and gives birth to the *Mirliton.* In this mythical place of an era, a style was created that would be parodied but never imitated.

There, the customer is greeted by invectives and jeers: "*Ah! Ah/Ah! That's your face, that's your hoe!*" And the gentleman is called a pimp, the lady a broad. And as the snobs bleat with pleasure at the idea of getting sloppy, they ask for more. Then comes the success which is not only of esteem.

Courteline, who named *La Crécelle, Le Mirliton* in his novel *Messieurs les Ronds-de-cuir* describes the atmosphere as follows:

> *"Everything, from the owner's scarlet shirt to the gigantic kazoo that was held to the ceiling by an imperceptible wire, seemed to be a resounding challenge to common sense. They thought this place was funny, and, in short, there was a lot of it. Along the*

walls, whose ragged tapestries masked the plaster between the holes, basins and beard dishes ran, mixed with guitars without strings, with frames without paintings, with paintings without frames. Next to a fanciful sun, made of a night pot in its center and an unequal radiation of boarding axes and Tunisian chibouks, a large portrait of Derouet (the name he gave to Bruant) showed him as a soldier of the 113th line, laughing, tasting a quarter of wine on a clear landscape background... And all this seen among the crowd of heads, distinguished through a packet of smoke like an artificial sea bed through the cloudy glass of an underground aquarium, giving rise in their minds to the idea of a junk shop, where everything was sold, even human flesh."

And he repeats Bruant's words:

"Shut your mouths! Silence to the people of the Faubourg! There are some here, who came in a carriage, just to be treated like carrions. Look at the ambassador of what's-his-name over there, with her loaf of bread and her pencil. Go on, you old cow!"

Bruant is the man of the moment. All the newspapers speak about him, day after day. And all the polygraphers pilgrim to this place, behind the academics, and the ancestors of the swampy bobos. With his success, Bruant rents a small estate at the top of the hill where he lives with François, his handyman. In the neighborhood he is the darling of the gorselines who recognize his fatal beauty. Because the popular chansonnier, he insists on this appellation, is truly popular. In him are recognized the old men of the Bat' d'Af, the pimps of the Glacière, the soldiers' girl of Grenelle, the waitress of the Bastoche, the butcher boys of the Villette. All the little people and the outsiders, the desperate, the stoners, all of them recognize themselves in his songs: *À Montparnasse, La Noire, À Biribi, À La Goutte d'Or* and in his nostalgic music with refrains cut by sobs. And when he writes and sings :

"And on the rocker to Charlot
He paid, without saying a word,
In La Roquette, one beautiful morning,

He made those of Pantin see
How to know how to die a kid
From the Beast!"

It is emotion, real emotion, which makes the eyes flow and the throats become hoarse. Nothing to do, says Bruant himself, with Richepin's *"gueux d'opéra-comique qui s'expriment en alexandrins..."*. But his stories of dying of hunger, also listen to those who cannot understand, who came to the world with the silver spoon in the mouth. So *"I revenge myself by insulting them, by treating them worse than dogs. It makes them laugh to tears; they think I'm joking, while very often it's a whiff of the past, of the miseries suffered, of the filth seen, that comes back to my lips and makes me speak as I speak."*

In 1888 one can see an old lady, of quite suitable aspect holding by the hand a small boy going every afternoon towards the square Saint-Pierre. This lady is Mrs. Bruant mother and this little boy, her grandson, also named Aristide. This one was the son of the popular chansonnier and the Marioni, also a singer. One day the mother, who was not in good health, left this world and entrusted the child to her sister. And this one comes without way to give him to his father who also simply entrusts him to his own mother. As he takes his fatherhood in hand, he gives birth to his first book: *Dans la rue*. An immediate success, the book is snatched up.

Here is what Jules Lemaître and Laurent Tailhade have to say about it:

> *"But here comes the hairless and terrible face of Mr. Aristide Bruant. A singular character. Imagine Coppée's head stripped of its grace, turned sinister and macabre, his lip bitter and scornful, the head of a handsome convict in a melodrama who would be the lover of a duchess; a suit of black velvet with ribs, which is a combination of the worker's coarse velvet burgundy and the romantic pourpoint, and on which a scarlet shirt collar is folded down, all of which is very arranged, very concerted, very theatrical. Add the most biting, cutting, metallic voice I have ever heard, a voice of riot and barricade, to dominate the roar of the streets on a day of revolution, a superb and brutal voice, which enters into your*

soul like a blow from a surin in the straw of a pante." And, taking hold of the book: "the picturesque in the ignoble, a cynicism of an imperturbable serenity. You will discover there amazing deformations and transpositions of morality."

Laurent Tailhade who arrogates to himself the right to lack indulgence, will declare: "Aristide violent and contained, he possesses a field of vision limited on purpose, but, by that very fact, of an unequalled clarity, a microcosm where are inscribed harshly - like the black silhouettes on the rubric of the Etruscan potteries - the characters that he has seen. He knows their emotions as well as their appetites, he knows the unforgettable word that fixes them forever." And, speaking about the songs: "The voluptuousness is absent, the sexual emotion appears there hardly, without refinement nor depth. One never feels, in its rhythms, the wild smell of the lust. Love is imposed on the woman as a chore, on the man as a source of legitimate and welcome profits. Aristide Bruant, copious in words of mouth, is, for sure, one of the least erotic poets of the French language".

Henry Baüer called him the "Dante Alighieri of the Parisian underworld". As for the clowns of the Palais Bourbon, they called each other by interjections à la Bruant. The success is such that Bruant launches his own newspaper: *Le Mirliton*, irregular monthly, says the headline. Some of the best writers, Steinlen, Toulouse-Lautrec, Courteline, Jehan Rictus, Alphonse Allais... There are even advertisements! Montmartre became more and more important. At nightfall, alone, in couples and sometimes in processions, the night owls head towards this forest of luminous signs where all kinds of pleasure dispensers cohabit: taverns, theaters, balls, hotels for priced trips to the seventh heaven, various bars and cabarets with songwriters. With the girls in the streets and the pimps not far away. In short a gigantic cesspool of which Bruant mocks in acerbic terms, the sordid consumers who contribute to the perpetuation of this garbage. He tramples their carrion and keeps his love for the others who put off their misery to distract this fauna. We see then, we hear especially, Yvette Guilbert, as who would say Madonna, the voice, the beauty and the intelligence in more, and Félicia Mallet, tragedienne of a modesty and an independence of spirit inconceivable at the time of the dripping media complacency, add to their repertory the songs of Bruant. The Bruant genre is so launched that copies are paraded on the Parisian and provincial stages and that he becomes the darling of the people of the world who aspire to decorate their receptions with his presence.

But he has not changed, he has not mellowed, and the popular ardor that welcomes his stripes sounds like a protest against the financial rot of the time: Panama and M. Suez, Grévy's son-in-law and his little business of decorations, Cornelius Herz and his group purchases of deputies. One is also frightened by the anarchist bombs that pulverize a few half-soldiers of capital here and there and this fear, with which one associates, a little, Bruant, gives such pleasant shivers, my dear...

In addition to his fame, Bruant's fortune is consolidated. Profits from the Mirliton and royalties form a substantial pactole. For example, *Mad'moiselle, écoutez-moi donc* and *La Chaussée de Clignancourt* brought the co-authors, Jouy and Bruant, 20,000 francs. Also with a repertory which grows richer from day to day, the capital of the popular chansonnier swells and allows him the realization of an old dream, to become owner and even lord in his native country, Courtenay. Every summer, he will come back to find the Cléry, which slaloms with the willows, the peasants who are true friends and his dogs to which he is bound by an inordinate love. In the winter, there are concerts and tours. Because he is called, implored, everywhere in province and abroad.

In Lyon, the silk industry protested against the incitement of the canuts to revolt that his repertoire would convey. In Marseille, he was called "*the Danton of the Parisian song*". In Bordeaux, Paul Berthelot of *La Petite Gironde* wrote: "He intones the red mass, the Gloria of the girls, of the pimps... He evokes all the anathemas and the rales of the refractory, in a powerful shortcut, with brutalities of etching *biting the copper...*". In Algiers, he sings *Biribi in* front of parterres of spahis and hunters who cheer the meeting of a Work with the reality that inspired it.

After a few years of this regime, he is forced to go and rest his voice in Mont-Dore where he meets friends and especially friends. Among them were Sarah Bernhardt, the diva Jane Pierny, Andrée Mégard and a very pretty young woman. She is introduced to him. It is the singer Tarquini d'Or. We are in 1895 and they will not leave each other until the death of the poet thirty years later.

Notwithstanding the passion that unites them, Mrs. Tarquini d'Or, before committing herself, had declared to him: *"I have responsibilities that I like to assume alone. You will let me earn my living as I am used to. I want to do it".*

She had a child, Brutus, and it is for him that she sometimes accepts extraordinary performances in France and abroad. But during these separations they write to each other every day. And what Bruant reveals about himself in his correspondence is moving.

Here is the letter he wrote to her after the death of his dog Pili:

> *"Pili is no more, my dear sweetheart, it is a great sorrow for me. I have to force myself not to cry like a child. You know that I was attached to this good little animal who loved me for fifteen years. You remember her joys and sorrows when we were away. She won't come to wait for us at the station, when we return, our old Pili!*
>
> *She died this morning at eight o'clock. I took her last breath and kissed her goodbye for both of us, as I wrote to you. I saw her pass away hour by hour. She didn't suffer much, but her stomach couldn't take anything more, and all night long I heard a small painful gasp that hurt. It's terrible to see someone you love and who loved you return to nothingness!*
>
> *I buried it myself, in a box with the piece of blanket you gave it and one of my old red shirts. There she lies next to my desk. Tomorrow I will say a final goodbye to her and bury her in our vineyard. Poor Pili!*
>
> *All night long I thought about the two of us, about our separations that take away our best days, and what the hell is that? To this! Because finally, we will die too, my dear, and what a pain for the one who will stay! It is to never think of it.*
>
> *I'm in pain, sweetie."*

Because Mrs. Tarquini d'Or had to resolve to adopt her husband's dogs, which she did with no difficulty, there are a dozen of them living at home, richly fed, warmly loved, vagabonds and pedigree dogs, "*dogs of manants or dogs of princes*". He loves them all, welcomes them, shelters them, takes them in... and chases away with sticks those who mistreat or do not support the "*quat'pattes*".

Bruant having moved to the Marlin de Lifart which requires some work and maintenance, he needs to increase his earnings. So he agrees to write daily serials, very popular in the newspapers of the time, in collaboration with Michel Morphy and Arthur Bernède. They are the *Bat' d'Af, Fleur de Pavé, Captive, etc.*

Then, with the same people, he started to work in the theater and for months he made the beautiful evenings of *the Ambigu.*

Finally, he took up the challenge presented to him by some friends to run in the 1898 legislative elections in the working-class district of Saint-Fargeau. Two documents illustrate this campaign.

An election poster and a program in verse.

LEGISLATIVE ELECTIONS OF MAY 8, 1898

BELLEVILLE-SAINT-FARGEAU

ARISTIDE BRUANT

People's candidate

Citizens, Voters,

The many friends and admirers of the great
popular chansonnier Aristide Bruant have decided
to put forward his candidacy for
protest, clearly republican, socialist,
patriot.
All the enemies of the capitalist feudal system and
of the cosmopolitan Jewry, a true Syndicate of the
Treason organized against France, will vote for
the humanitarian poet, for the glorious singer of
Belleville.
It is in Belleville-Saint-Fargeau that Bruant
began. It is in Belleville that he knew his
first successes.
It is to his old Belleville that he returns
logically by recognition.

BELLEVILLOIS !
You always cheered for him when he came
Lend a hand at your charity events
and solidarity.
Vote en masse next Sunday for the people's candidate:

ARISTIDE BRUANT

The Initiative Committee.

If I were your MP,
Ahoy! Ahoy! Let's hear it!
I would add Humanity
To the three words of our motto...
Instead of talking every day
For the republic or the empire
And to make long speeches
To say nothing,

I would talk about the little gods,
Granny girls, poor old men
Which, in winter, freeze in the city...
They would be hot like in summer,
If I were to be appointed as an MP,
In Belleville.

I would speak about the sad beggars,
Purotines beating the crap out of each other,
Flat bellies, hollow bellies,
And I would talk about a crib
For the poor girls without a bed,
That we push away and send back
In the street! ... with their little one!
Mothers of joy!

I would talk about their cuties,
Of these pitiful cherubs

Whose poor little buns
Do not know the water of the baths,
Cherubim whose soul and blood
Rotting in the air of the slums
And that we see pass, the white complexion
And the red eyes

I would talk about old people with a limp
Who would like to work again...
But which the workshop does not want any more...
And that drags until dawn
On the hard pavement of Paris,
- Their refuge, their invalids -
Strayed... hunted... ashamed... bruised,
The empty guts.

I would talk about the little gods,
Granny girls, poor old men
Which, in winter, freeze by the city...
They would be hot like in summer,
If I were appointed as a Member of Parliament
In Belleville!

The public meetings are original and often turn into recitals. But his popularity did not reach the ballot boxes, where only 525 ballots were cast in his name... The national socialism does not make recipe!

If he escaped the shame of becoming a deputy or even worse a minister, it was to become a bellowing boss. He bought *L'Époque* and associated his wife with its management, whose artistic escapades he could not stand. She has ideas to develop the business and organizes classical matinees and more diversified evenings. The public wants Bruant and creates a commotion when he is not there.

But the popular chansonnier is not amused and has only one desire, to find Courtenay. He sold his store and returned to Paris only to escape the rigors of winter in the country. He then devoted his time to writing a dictionary of slang which, with the help of Léon de Bercy, established its history.

Until 1913 he was dormant and no longer walked the stage. To those who reproached him for not working anymore, he answered: "*Nature is beyond me*". In fact, he creates a true communion between man and his land, which he surveys in order to watch it live and live from this contemplation.

Only once did he give in to a request. At the request of the fashion designer Paul Poiret, he sang at *L'Oasis* for the farewell of Yvette Guilbert. After the evening, he fled and returned to his land, relieved.

The worst is yet to come. In 1914, the Great European Civil War broke out, sounding the death knell of Western civilization and bringing about the assumption of the commodity. His son, his double, Aristide, takes part in it. An officer who graduated from Saint-Cyr, he embodied the highest French patriotic and military tradition. At Longuyon a bullet pierced his arm. At Noyers, two shrapnel bullets caused more serious injuries. He won[10] the war cross and the Legion of Honor. He went back into action with the rank of captain and had his shoulder ripped out at Boureuilles. However, he returned to the front in Verdun as a volunteer. He was wounded in the head.

He returned to his regiment and took part in the attack on Craonne on April 16, 1917. He lost his life.

Bruant joins thousands of fathers and mothers in the blue nights of distress. In spite of the appearances, preserved of strength and vigor, the oak is uprooted. The Faculty discovers him besides an angina pectoris, the sap becomes rarefied.

And yet he accepted a few years later a contract for a singing tour at the *Empire*. We are in 1924, he is 73 years old. These concerts will be a triumph, all is rented to go to see and hear the poet of the rabble and the gueuses, his voice of riot and barricade. The public is subjugated, those who knew him and those who discover him.

"Standing? as moved as we were," wrote Henri Béraud *in Comœdia, "with his fists shoved into the pockets of his roulier jacket, he formed, in the middle of the stage, only a brown velvet stain. And, without taking a step, he led us from Belleville to Batignolles, from Batignolles to the Bastille; a few verses of psalms in an almost dead slang, short and lively lines, the whole monstrous city came to life, from the sewers to the*

10. There are those who receive it for services rendered to the society of the spectacle and those who earn it with blood money...

chimneys; and we understood then, young and old, that this song is the song of the poor, and that Bruant's harshness hides (as always!) a heart of good man, a heart that beats, in truth according to the inimitable rhythm of the popular heart."

The day after, the novelist whose place is so great in contemporary literature, the author of the admirable *Vitriol de lune*, will complete in *Excelsior*:

" ... *I was at* the Empire *only a passer-by, only a curious person... Perhaps like many others, I was looking for the ghost of my youth and childhood at the side of the resurrected Trouvère... But then Bruant made the miracle. And the fidelity of Paris, which greeted him as soon as he appeared with an endless applause, was perhaps only recognition*".

And Francis Carco, who owes him so much, adds: "*Stunned by the spotlight, pale, stiff, almost clumsy, because one felt that this too large stage hardly suited him, he threw out his first song like a challenge. This booted man, pulling his leg and not a ham, was he, Bruant, whose refrains were hummed in the past and whose glory had run around the world? Perfectly, it was him, in person. He was still going strong after more than thirty years. His repertoire had the same accent. It carried. He kept all his verve, his sinister and pathetic gouaille, his poetry, his enthusiasm. He produced a great effect and finally acted so directly on the public that, from the galleries, men and women, remembering the tunes that were played to them, took up with the 'grandfather'*".

We're the Happy Ones

We're the pimps who don't get cold feet.

This singing tour increases his popularity. Biographers abound and new performers, such as Mistinguett, sing his repertoire.

But it is no longer time and a few weeks later a cerebral hemorrhage overwhelms him.

It's over. He will be buried in Burgundy, alongside his lineage, wearing his legendary costume.

Those who want to pay tribute to him can go to meet him in Subligny.

André CHÉNIER (1762-1794)
Or the martyred poet

The one of whom Brasillach said "*I don't think that among the French poets André Chénier is one of the greatest, but he is certainly the one whose destiny is the most moving*", was born in Constantinople in 1762 where his father was Consul General of France. His mother, whom he himself believed to be of Greek origin, was a Lomaca from Catalonia. Three years later, Madame and her five children returned to Paris, as the Consul was appointed to Morocco. She opens a brilliant salon where Chénier and his brothers get the taste and the intelligence of the ancient culture and beauty. He pursued solid studies at the Navarre College where he rubbed shoulders with many young heirs and made solid friendships. Among them the young and already brilliant Camille Desmoulins and a certain Joseph-François Baudelaire (Charles' future father).

In 1782 he joined the Angoumois regiment garrisoned in Strasbourg as a cadet-gentilhomme (i.e. officer), but, not obtaining the sub-lieutenancy he coveted, he put an end to his military experience and moved with his books and papers to the family house. That same year, 1783, the illness of gravel (those nephritic colics that he evokes in his poems, by the expression "*the burning sands*") appears.

Nevertheless, he decided to travel with some friends, the Trudaine brothers, and planned a trip to Italy and Greece. Illness stopped him in Switzerland. He will never know this Greece of which he will become the bard.

Frequenting the salons, and adding to the easy loves some tumultuous liaisons, he wrote his first poems and sketched several texts: *Essay on the Decadence of Letters, Liberty, Hymn to Justice,* which testify that he is then no longer "*politically-correct*". In 1787 he accepted a modest job as an embassy secretary in London to support himself. He will stay there until 1790.

Having returned to France, he participated in the revolutionary movement by founding the Society of '89 and by engaging in journalistic activities. He is then a moderate and a poet a little precious. On Greece, as in all things, he had the ideas of the men of his century. It was for him the tolerance and the joy of living and graceful fables which one called mythology. It was a delicate myth, "*this miniaturist Greece*" (Brasillach) above which, however, he managed to rise, and an almost exclusive source of inspiration (even if he was curious about all poetry but closed to that which he called "*the uncultured and brave Muse*" of the English). While in London, he undertook two scientific epics that would remain in draft form and an essay, *L'Amérique,* which praised this New World and the Insurgents.

In short, without the Revolution, he would perhaps have remained an unknown poet or one of those authors of the second ray that we (re) discover on the occasion of the launching of a new literary fashion.

But, if he sees this revolution being born with sympathy, he is quickly frightened by its developments. Writing for *Le Moniteur* and *Le Journal de Paris* (where he succeeded Condorcet), he propagated the moderate ideas of the Club des Feuillants, and very early on, and the supplements of the *Journal de Paris,* which he financed with his own money, testify to this, he protested against the Terror, which he showed to be much earlier than the dictatorship of Robespierre. It is through the glorification of rebel soldiers, the establishment of all kinds of counter-powers, the constitution of building committees that denounce suspects, the looting and assassinations committed by bands of self-proclaimed patriots... phenomena and political maneuvers that arouse his indignation, that he denounces the process leading to the dictatorship of the Jacobins and the misuse of the Revolution.

He writes, to denounce patriotic hysteria and hypocrisy:

> *"If this party has invented on purpose for its opponents a jurisprudence other than that of the constitution and of justice... If troops of assassins have set fire to, looted, and devastated their houses; if, in many places, they have been beaten, massacred, torn apart, and sometimes eaten, and their wives and daughters insulted, whipped, raped, and sometimes had their throats slit ; and if this party, when it did not dare to approve entirely of all these actions, at least tried to inspire indulgence for the villains who had committed them, calling them the people, saying that the people were misguided; and*

if afterwards, when the first impression was somewhat weakened, it denied them with the most derisory impudence..."

and denounces "... *the jokers and jesters of tréteaux, the knights of industry, the deserters, the men withered by the decrees of taking of body, prisoners of justice, condemned as refractory thieves, etc."*

Thus, in his essay *The Altars of Fear*, he denounces this creeping terror: "*Ancient peoples had erected temples and altars to fear*".

His last article in the *Journal de Paris*, on July 26, 1792, is directed against the warmonger Brissot and those who, under the eternal pretext of "*the Fatherland in danger*", justify all the evil deeds and all the scoundrels. He left Paris for a short stay in Normandy, exhausted and demoralized, and returned to Paris in early August. In his last days of freedom, he saw the royal power he held dear disappear and devoted all his energy to writing note after note and memorandum after memorandum in view of the trial of Louis XVI and the refutation of all the calumnies poured on the monarch in the name of the principle, stated by Saint-Just, "*that one cannot reign innocently*". His commitment is so strong that one could believe that he participated in the team of advisers who organized around the lawyers de Sèze and Malesherbes the defense of the king.

The year 1793 saw the assassination of Louis XVI on January 21 and the establishment of the Revolutionary Court on March 10. The Committee of Public Safety, after having eliminated the Girondins, decreed, that is to say formalized in September, the Terror.

André Chénier went into hiding in Versailles, where he lived for a year until his arrest on March 7, 1794. His interrogation by an illiterate policeman is "*a model of silliness without spelling*" (Brasillach). Talking to this policeman from the "*house next door*" he was asked about his relationship with the suspect Coté.

He was incarcerated the next day in the Saint-Lazare prison before being transferred in July to the Conciergerie where he wrote his *Iambes*. On July 25 (7 Thermidor), he was tried before the Revolutionary Court for, classically, plotting against the security of the State. It was an ordinary trial, the minutes of which were written in advance.

He was guillotined late in the afternoon of the same day at the age of thirty-two.

Two days later, Robespierre fell and the Terror was over.

Paul-Louis COURIER (1772-1825)
Winegrower, pamphleteer and former horseman

Who remembers Paul-Louis Courier today if not a few Hellenists? For he was a great among them and a specialist in the history of journalism. Some people in Périgord wonder what it means for the street where the Departmental Council and the Prefecture are located to bear this name, imagining that it is an "*illustrious unknown*" among their ancestors. Paul-Louis Courier was however very Parisian. He was born as an illegitimate child in 1772 in the capital, to a rich bourgeois father and a man of much spirit. Lover of a certain Duchess d'O, he was threatened with assassination by his husband and took refuge in Touraine. This allows him to devote himself to the education of his son and to transmit to him this aversion for a certain category of nobles and this taste so perfect for the antiques. Jean Paul Courier de Méré is indeed one of those strong spirits, voltairian, who gives his all to the ideas of the time and supports them with a solid culture. Moreover, this convinced republican transmits his passion for demolition to his son. This son was destined for a military career, and more precisely for the engineering corps. At the age of fifteen, he entrusted him to mathematicians who attested to his ability to understand everything and his lack of curiosity for the supposedly exact sciences. What his father considered as an entertainment, literature, was for him an unceasing source of seduction of all kinds, and Greek literature in particular. Nevertheless, the young Courier sacrifices to his father's views and enters the military artillery school of Chalons. He was there during the Prussian invasion of 1792 and the skillful and energetic resistance of Dumouriez, the future traitor, gave him the time to complete his studies. In 1793 he was commissioned as an artillery officer and sent to the border. The era was full of heroes and many families were proud to have at least one. Paul-Louis was not one of them and his contempt for war was rooted in his first contact with it. The noise of the camps, the learned marches, the plunder renamed of the name of conquest, and the massacre of the name of liberation, do not exert on his spirit any seduction. For all that, 1793 was the height of the revolution and the period when, with a little education and character, one could claim a rapid advancement and a glorious future. Hoche, general of the army, was twenty-three years old and his chief of staff only eighteen. Courier is not one of those passionate supporters of the Republican cause, eager for stripes and heroism. He spends most of his time scouring libraries and writes to his mother *"I like to reread books that I have already read many times, and by this I acquire a less extensive but more solid erudition. I will never have a great knowledge of history, which requires much more reading, but I will gain something else, which is better, in my opinion."*

In 1795 the young junior officer that he was still left the army in front of Mainz without authorization. He took refuge in Albi where he began to translate some Latin works. He was then wanted as a deserter and owed it to some friends to escape the prosecution and condemnation he was facing. His military career was limited by this fault and was sanctioned by a position as a quartermaster in the Toulouse region. He learns then, we are at the end of the Terror, to dance with application, to run the balls and the parties. This was a reaction against the morbid austerity of the conventional period, a reaction that characterized the early days of the Directory, where feasts and pleasures of all kinds saw the survivors of the dark years of dictatorship of the incorruptible and his followers rush to the party. He liked it so much that one day, he had to leave Toulouse to escape, like his father before him, the wrath of an outraged family.

Here he is in Italy, we are in 1798, then under the Bonapartist boot and he is distressed by the spectacle of degradation and oppression that the peninsula offers, subjected to the regime of greed and arrogance of the new French owners. He was also repulsed by the veiled submission of the local elites who courted the parvenus of the occupying forces. Finally, he witnessed the shameless and shameless plundering of the republican predators who left a field of ruins when they withdrew. "*Say,*" he wrote to his friend Chlewaski, *"tell those who want to see Rome, that they should hurry, because every day the iron of the soldier and the claw of the French agents wither its natural beauties and strip it of its finery. Permit me, Sir, who is accustomed to the natural and noble language of antiquity, to find these expressions too flowery, or even too ornate; but I do not know of any that are sad enough to paint for you the state of decay, misery and opprobrium to which this poor Rome, which you have seen so pompous, has fallen, and of which, at present, even the ruins are being destroyed. In the past, as you know, people came here from all over the world. How many foreigners who came there not only for one winter, spent their whole life there! Now there are only those who could not flee, or who, with their daggers in their hands, are still searching in the rags of a people dying of hunger for some coin that has escaped so many extortions and robberies... The monuments of Rome are hardly better treated than the people... I still mourn a pretty Hermes child, whom I had seen in his entirety, dressed and hooded with a lion's skin, and carrying on his shoulder a small club. It was, as you can see, a Cupid stealing the weapons of Hercules; a piece of exquisite work, and Greek, if I am not mistaken. There remains only the base, on which I wrote with a pencil: Lugetes, Veneres, Cupidinesque, and the scattered pieces, which would make Mengs and Winckelmann die of pain, if they had had the misfortune to live long enough to see this spectacle. Everything that was in the Carthusian monastery, in the Villa Albani, in the Farnese's, in the Honesti's, in the Clémenti museum, in the Capitol, is taken away, plundered, lost or sold. Soldiers, who entered the Vatican library, destroyed, among other rarities, the famous Terence of the Bembo, one of the most esteemed manuscripts, in order to get some of the gilding with which it was decorated. Venus of the Villa Borghese was wounded in the hand by some descendant of Diomedes, and the Hermaphrodite,* immane nefas! has a broken foot..."

Let us judge after that the civilizing and liberating mission of France in Europe and the croaking of the right-thinking historians on the emancipating role of the Great Revolution. The verve of the future pamphleteer is exercised in these first writings with all the integrity that he will never cease to show. He multiplies himself in perilous excursions of curious and antiquarian, on the lookout for any novelty that his insatiable cultural bulimia made him desire. He is known for the courage of his artistic wanderings, his indifference to the danger revealed by a little-known anecdote. When the French were forced to leave Rome, Courier wanted to say a final goodbye to the Vatican library. He forgot the time of departure of his division and when he came out he was the only Frenchman in Rome. It is evening and he is recognized by the light of a lamp in front of a Madonna. People shouted "*giaccobino*" and a shot fired at him killed a woman. In the tumult created by this accident, he reaches the palace of a Roman nobleman who loves him and helps him to escape. After having crossed, in adventurous conditions, a Provence that is not very welcoming for republican soldiers, and having lost his papers and money, he arrives in Paris in a pitiful state and suffering from tuberculosis.

During the Consulate Courier remained the obscure soldier that he was, but he began to write various opuscules, *L'Éloge d'Hélène* and *Le Voyage de Ménélas à Troie to reclaim Hélène,* whose lack of pamphleteering character should not hide the elegance of the style.

At the end of the Consulate, he was entrusted with the command of a squadron of the occupation forces in Italy. He was still there when the First Consul proclaimed himself Emperor. During the referendum organized by the future Caesar, to the question "*Do you still want the republic or do you prefer an Emperor*? His opinion however is quite different: "*A man like Bonaparte, soldier, chief of army, the first captain of the world want that one calls him Majesty! To be Bonaparte and to be Sire! He aspires to go down...*" This energetic statement reveals an independent character, and his discretion, a not very vigorous character. In fact, the period strikes Courier especially by its ridiculous side. He is not at all sensitive to the antics that are for him the antics of the new aristocracy. In his letters written from Italy his rebellious spirit takes on the features of the most biting satire. The Empire reveals itself in all its mediocrity with this new etiquette, spoken by barons crippling the language, these decorations and titles grotesquely amphigouric and these inordinate ambitions that the distributions of titles and kingdoms try in vain to satisfy. Courrier is not an admirer of the Revolution; the Convention appeared to him as brutal and inhuman and the Directory, as venal and insipid. His contempt extends to this imperial regime which is only the caricature of this new class domination. In 1808 he withdrew, not having obtained the leave of absence he had requested.

But the 1809 campaign gave birth to a new and ephemeral ambition: to achieve glory at the Emperor's side in Germany, which seemed to open its arms to the victor over Spain. He became acquainted with the true nature of the Napoleonic wars: men and officers killed by the thousands, rivers of blood and mud mixed together, massive destruction of houses and crops... These are the victories of Essling and Wagram!

Courier will be forever estranged from the war and will devote his life to literature. He went to Italy where the famous episode of the manuscript of *Longus* was set. This one, sheltered by the library Laurentinc in Florence, included an unpublished passage which filled the missing part in all the editions of this novel. Inadvertently, and carried away by the joy of his discovery, Courier spilled ink on a few Greek words that formed the pates that made him hysterically denounced to the world by librarians scandalized by such vandalism. Attacked by some booksellers who pursue him with their vindictiveness, he answers them in a *Letter to Mr. Renouard,* named after one of them, bookseller in Paris where the gall flows thickly in the style of Voltaire, scourging Fréron or the Pascal of the *Provinciales,* agonizing the cagot party. This text draws attention to him and the Minister of the Interior wants to prosecute him for destruction of documents, when the Minister of the Army wants to prosecute him for desertion... Because he left the army again without authorization. He got off scot-free, but in return he renounced all use of his pen. He only studied and traveled until 1815, the fall of the Empire and the restoration of the Bourbons.

The spectacle of this time which sees the bankrupts of Coblentz, that Rivarol despised so much, and a family heir to the throne of Henri IV return without shame in the vans of the foreigner and impose the usual persecutions to the defeated, does not fail to shock the sensitive and proud soul of Courier. He then stops disavowing himself as a soldier of the Empire.

The man who became, a few years ago, a Touraine winegrower now assumes his history as a soldier of the Revolution, if not a revolutionary. He is therefore a winegrower by choice, a soldier by duty, a writer by taste. If he remained a soldier and never claimed any promotion, it is because he wanted to be a citizen-soldier and because he hated corrupting power. Released from the writing ban, he is available for his destiny. His first pamphleteer writing is only six pages long, but what pages! It is a petition addressed in December 1816 to the Chambers and bearing the title *Je suis Tourangeau.* It is the picture of the royalist reaction, the white terror, in a small village, Luynes. The whole of France can recognize itself in this account of the tyrannical activities of a prefect who arbitrarily arrests 500 people, several of whom die in prison. This satirical genre in which Paul-Louis Courier will excel is the *Libelle.* This one is not stopped by any censorship and spreads at the speed of anger and indignation. Decazes himself, then prime minister, will use it against the extremists of his party that he does not control anymore. He even tries to attach himself to the polemicist who refuses with height any subjection. However, in the face of the rapacity of people well in court who want to take away his goods, he agrees to frequent the Parisian salons for a while. This is enough, and is still enough today, to inspire the greatest respect to the local representatives of the State, notably the prefect.

Here he is in the small papers of this servant and that satisfies him: *"he thanked, greeted, and did not return"* (Alexis Carrel).

In 1820, Courier presented himself to the Académie des Inscriptions, towards which his passion for Hellenism inclined him, where he intended to succeed his father-in-law Clavier. Rejected by this one he addresses to the academicians a letter *To Sirs of the Academy of Inscriptions and Belles-Lettres.* He accuses it of having been founded *"only to compose mottos for the King's tapestries and, in a need, for the Queen's sweets".* His letter never had any success because of the reproach that it was inspired only by the malice and the resentment of the rejected candidate. He nevertheless deploys a mockery "at the same time buffoonish and serious which excites the laughter at the same time as it raises the indignation and the contempt, such as one admires them in the immortal Provinciales". This is what we read in a preface to the writings of the pamphleteer, which may well be his own work, but is no less true. The same year, the *Letter to the editor of the Censor* appears.

> *"The small collection of letters to the censor,"* says Courier, *"began to popularize the author's name. Until then, the eloquent and courageous denunciations with which he had pursued the iniquitous magistrates who were imposing their despotism on the timid and mute population of the countryside, had hardly resounded beyond the department of Indre et Loire.*

He was the patriotic writer of his commune, of his Canton; he was not yet the popular man of all France. The letters of the censor, quite widespread, revealed to the public this talent and this new courage of a sincere friend of the country, whose spirit raised above all prejudices sees everywhere the truth, says it without any fear, and says it in a way to make it accessible to all, vulgar, and, if one wants, even trivial and village.
Add to this that, by a prodigy quite unheard of, this writer, who seems to seek only common sense, expresses himself with a purity and an elegance of language entirely lost nowadays, and which imbues his writings with an inimitable character."

In this writing, the winegrower of La Chavonnière, whom one wants to exclude from the elections, struggles, alone, and approaches only the strict local question. But he does it in such a way that his argument by its quality and its precision takes a national value that it preserves today.

In 1821, *Le Simple Discours* appeared. A subscription having been opened to offer to the Duke of Bordeaux, then in foster care, the domain of Chambord, the town council of Véretz, his village, deliberates on this subject. And Courier intervenes in this debate by denouncing the courtiers who make a national offering of a tribute imposed on most people. By simply changing some words, one could find in it a matter for castigating contemporary speeches on obliged solidarity. But no one today would dispute that. At the time, Courier was brought before a court of assizes and sentenced to two months in prison and a 300 franc fine. This writing, which is based on the true, natural morality, is reproached for its social amorality.

He answers therefore by publishing the relation of the lawsuit, it is the libel *To the devout souls of the parish of Véretz,* then he goes in prison to Sainte-Pélagie.

He left to publish a *Petition for villagers who were prevented from dancing,* the court in front of which he appeared once again limited himself to reprimanding him.

But the conclusion that Courier draws from this new repressive episode is that from now on one can only resort to the clandestine press.

For two years, without making himself known while allowing himself to be recognized, he publishes *the First and the Second Answer to the*

Anonymous, a lively painting of the struggles of a young priest struggling with earthly (and carnal) love. Then came *Le Livre de Paul Louis* and *La Gazette du village*, satirical essays by an "*enemy of the government*".

Finally comes the unjustly ignored masterpiece that is the *Pamphlet of Pamphlets.*

> *"This work,"* said Courier in the anonymous notice, *"is, strictly speaking, the justification of all the others.*
> *The author, who has always known how to squeeze into a few pages the truths he wanted to tell, sets out to demonstrate that the pamphlet is, by its very nature, the most excellent kind of book, the only one that is truly popular because of its very brevity.*
> *The big works can be good for the idle ones of the living rooms; the pamphlet is addressed to the laborious people whose hands do not have the leisure to leaf through a hundred pages. This happy and ingenious thesis is supported in a way that one would gladly call dramatic.*
> *The opinion of a Parisian bookseller is put in front of that of an English baronet; the one pretends to scourge, the other to glorify the author of the title of pamphleteer; and from the debates come out a crowd of these good truths which go to their address".*

And with him a celebrity that disconcerted the author himself. He becomes the curiosity of the salons and the public sheets that are the newspapers (as one says the public girls) suddenly see in him the Rabelais of the politics, the Montaigne of the century, etc. Very quickly however he gets used to his reputation.

In this work, there is a sentence that is both cryptic and prophetic: "*Paul Louis, the cagots will kill you*". He still has that appalling character that he was already known for in the army and which earned him, as it always did, enmities with the neighborhood, for we know that he always had *a* sort of "*trial by fire*", and with his wife. When the latter was pregnant, having "*conceived suspicions about his fidelity*", he left Véretz, leaving her fifty francs to make her deliveries..."

Delescluze, the art critic, who tells the anecdote, also concludes in the ladrerie of the polemicist, because, a posteriori there is reason to see there a lucidity that the future confirms.

He was indeed murdered on April 10, 1825 in his own woods by a certain Frémont, an alcoholic gamekeeper, whose hand had been armed by two brothers, lovers of his wife. But a doubt remains, because during the trial the gamekeeper is acquitted. A second trial, provoked by the arrival of a new witness, sees his widow and the surviving sponsor absolved. Should we conclude that this was a political assassination disguised as a crime of passion? Doubt will never cease to play its little music.

Gaston COUTÉ (1880-1911) : Peasant Poet

The father of all Brassens and the people's blackbird

"What do you want to remain of a bird that can't sing?"

This question of Victor Méric concerning the Blackbird of the people, the guy who went wrong, is not innocent. Time passes, and the famous, the acclaimed, the celebrated and the self-confessed immortal, are now only cold ashes in the extinct and deserted hearth of memory. From time to time a performer, Lavilliers for example, puts one of Couté's poems in his repertoire. But what about his story, his life, his sufferings and his struggles?

Gaston Couté was born in Beaugency in the Loiret in September 1880. But it was in Meung-sur-Loire, the *"nasty town of three thousand souls"* that he spent his childhood. His childhood was nourished by the landscapes of the nearby Sologne, the sounds of the Beauceron dialect and the spectacle of peasant life before the Great Civil War of 14-18.

His observation post: the mill of his father, the miller, a place of obligatory passage at that time, a place of conversations, gossips and confidences. And then, as a good student, but not very hard-working, he runs through the woods and fields, steals and contemplates, discovers and feels. Michel Ragon said of him that he *"would gladly give even today.... All the Parnassians and half of the Romantics".*

Then he entered the Pothier high school in Orléans, where he discovered a passion for medieval poets, starting with poor Villon, his ancestor, who was interned in Meung by the ferocious bishop Thibault. He also met a certain Pierre Dumarchey, the future Mac Orlan, who would remain his friend. And he begins to write his first poems, in patois, in which are already all the themes that he will love.

From the outset, he was interested in the *"tramps"*, the miserable tramps and other beggars, denouncing hypocrisies and other social tricks. These texts, which circulated among the students, were not to the liking of the pawns, the teachers and the management. A year later, in 1896, he sends his first texts to the magazine *La Meunerie française.* Then he quickly abandoned his studies, which did not interest him, and became a collection clerk while publishing his first works in *Le Progrès du Loiret, Le Bulletin de la meunerie française* and the *Revue littéraire et sténographique du Centre.*

There he met young poets, such as Da Costa, director of the *Revue littéraire et sténographique du Centre,* with whom he founded the *Cabaret du Lézard d'Or,* which gave shows at the Café de l'Europe. In front of the success of this one they must emigrate towards a larger room.

It is in the Hardarineau room, tells Edmond Heuzé, "*that Gaston Couté, brought to the program, opened the fire with 'Le vieux moulin.' His bony face, his long bushy hair, his anarchist look, his sparrow-like figure, annoyed the audience. Very calm, he advances and towers over the public which is decidedly resentful under the provocation. Hands in his pockets, he waits for the silence to be re-established, then begins...*"

In the course of this year 1897, he was transferred to the Perception of Ingré, five kilometers from Orléans, and could continue to frequent the Cigaliers and Da Costa.

But very quickly he went up to Paris. And it is the Butte Montmartre which welcomes him and where he will know his first successes, in *the Âne rouge,* in the *Noctambule,* where he meets Jehan Rictus, in the *Funambules...* At the time, the Butte, with its slopes that slope down towards Place Pigalle, Place Blanche and Place Clichy, was the picturesque refuge of a whole swarm of artists, writers, rapscallists and losers, Montmartre and its bistros, Montmartre and its clubs where this exotic fauna reigned, an object of curiosity for provincials and foreigners on the go. This bohemia, so charming to the foreign eye, was not necessarily laughable for those who tried to live for nothing and often from nothing. For one did not always eat and if one knew how to do without, the food and sometimes also the lodging, it was necessary to help oneself with alcohol. A bock was not expensive, and one could always find fifteen sous or a complaisant bistro that accepted to be paid in cloth or in declamation of poems. But bohemia is okay for a while, and only if you come out of it almost unscathed, otherwise it drains all strength, absorbs all energy and sterilizes all thought.

We are in 1899-1900.

Couté's first successes are called *La chanson d'un gâs qu'a mal tourné, Les Conscrits, Le Christ en bas, l'École.* And this fame led him beyond the Butte, to the Left Bank. At the time, he was not yet twenty years old. He often took the pseudonyms of Pierre Printemps or Gaston Koutay. Then he took his stick and went on the road with Maurice Lucas. This journey led them to Orleans, Blois, Courcheverny, Romorantin... until Gargilesse. At each stage Couté declaimed his texts in the evening and Lucas executed pastels which were sold at a tombola. The success was modest and the two companions soon returned to Paris.

As soon as he came to Paris, Gaston Couté was in contact with the anarchist and socialist revolutionary press. It is in *Le Libertaire* and the *Journal du Peuple* of Sébastien Faure, weekly and then daily, that he publishes certain texts that he lets acclaim sometimes, listen to distractedly often by a public of snobs eager to indulge themselves, or of gogos.

It was then that Victor Méric went to see him one evening to ask him to participate in a singing evening organized at the Maison du Peuple. As soon as Couté knew what it was about, he accepted with enthusiasm. This allowed him to leave the adulterated circles frequented by the bo-bo of the time and to give the best of himself to this popular public which made him the "*Mistral of Beauce*" according to the word of Xavier Privas. For his colorful, direct poems, with bold, brutal images, stripped of artifice, went straight to the heart of the public, stirring their imaginations. Would you like to read a sample? Here is one entitled "*La Complainte des Ramasseux d'Morts*":

Cheu us, the lend'hand of the battle,
We came from the farmers...
I sowed a few bales of straw
In the ass of the manure grave;
And, our mare, one shot and gone
I soumm's gone, shaving the edges
White fords, frozen vineyards,
To go and raise the dead.

In my acreage of "Guérouettes",
I've picked up holes:
With Penette...
I've picked up holes;
Two moblots, one Bavaroués!

Holes in the front of the clods, poor bastards,
Strokes lying flat
As if asleep in the condom
By this early morning of ice.
They're already stiff as a board:
I found his arm again
- A red wool braid on the sleeve -
In the field in Tienne, in the hollow of a ra...

As for the s'cond, it was all in one piece,
But a ball had twisted the forehead,
And the bright blood of his youth
Sinking through a nasty round hole;
He was a funny guy
With one of those nice muses
That make the girls laugh.
I'll load it in my tombezieau!

... The 'trouesième, with his helmet with ch'nille,
Had stayed in our house:
He had a whole family shit
That he explained in his jargon.
He knows how to tease the funny guy,
Li made subeziots,
Or was it on his shoulders...
He will not have seen his little ones again!...

Young people who have not seen the war,
Let's have a drink! Let's not talk about it!
And may the coming year be prosperous
For the grooves and for the "airlocks"!

Bring in charr'té's of ruddy bunches,
Of fat alfalfa and free spikes,
But you never make a crop like this
To our harvest ed of souésant'-dix.

In my acreage of "Guérouettes",
I've picked up holes,
With Penette...
I've picked up holes:
Two moblots, one Bavaroués!

Well, isn't this a masterpiece? And this one:

Ahoy! Over there! The fat vicar,
Who lead a deceased to the ground,
The dead do not need you anymore,
Because they have to leave their money,
To buy your holy water,
That's not what brings them back to life...

And all this to say until the thirst of the hatred of the rich and the upstarts, of their prejudices and their morals, the horror of the war and the social injustices, his tenderness for the poor, the deprived, in a word the proletariat of the cities and the fields.

Then one day, the recognized and admired poet, although marginalized by the opinion makers, decided to enter politics.

It was not a question of making a career for himself, for he had a great contempt for political politics, but of collaborating with the journal *La Guerre sociale.* She was four years old in 1910 when Couté joined its ranks. It was born in Clairvaux, a former Cistercian abbey converted into a prison, from the meeting of a certain number of prisoners who had signed the anti-militarist poster known as *the Red Poster.*

In a first issue of Le *Pioupiou de l'Yonne,* Gustave Hervé, its editor-in-chief and that of *La Guerre sociale, a* history professor who was dismissed for anti-militarism, wrote: "*I would like all the garbage and all the manure from the barracks to be gathered in the main courtyard of the district and for the colonel, in his large feathered hat, to solemnly plant the regiment's flag there*. This article entitled "*The flag in the dung*" announced the tone of *La Guerre sociale* which had a circulation of 60,000 in 1910. This made it a major political "*Journal*" ahead of the *Annales politiques et littéraires* (170,000), *Les Temps nouveaux,* by Jean Grave (8,500), *Le Libertaire,* by Sébastien Faure (8,000), *l'Action française,* by Daudet and Maurras (4,000)... In addition to Victor Méric, Eugène Merle, the cartoonists Grandjouan and Delannoy and Miguel Almereyda collaborated on this newspaper. The latter had founded the Young Guard, which specialized in confrontations with the police, the "Cossacks". It was Almereyda, the father of the future Jean Vigo, who invited Couté to give a weekly news song. The political song of current events had then a great importance in that it popularized widely, in a direct and accessible way, the themes of the newspaper. These songs are a model of French song: cheeky, malicious, sparkling but also revolted and virulent. They were repeated in the workshop, in the street, on the evenings of meetings.

Here are two of them, chosen almost at random:

A song?

SONG OF REVOLT OF THIS JULY 14

Air: La Marseillaise

The rough shoulder of the people
Threw down the Ancien Régime
On a day of righteous anger:
The people did not benefit from it! (*bis*)
And, in our tricolor era,
The odious reign of the bourgeois
Replaced that of the kings:
Our serfdom still lasts!

Refrain

Courage workers! In a black battalion
Let's walk, let's walk...
It will come our Revolution!

These people are coming, comrades,
Under our noses, execute
Their hypocritical masquerades
In honor of freedom (*bis*)
But, while the lanterns shine
Hervé falls asleep in Health
To stifle the Truth
They have remade other Bastilles!
They only have these words in their mouths:
Progress and Humanity!
But if from his fierce grave
Aernoult[11] could resurrect... (*bis*)
Because to remake nature
Of our Boys with too proud a forehead
In Biribi, gloomy hell,
They reinstated torture.

They also talk about Justice
By evoking eighty-nine,
But they let their police
Cutting off Liabeuf's head (*bis*)
And Briand, valet of our masters,
Has for us insulting airs:

11. Aernoult, assassinated on July 2, 1909 in Djenan-ed-dar (Algeria) by the military chaouchs. Aernoult was a roofing worker. In 1905, towards the end of the year, the strike of the subway workers broke out. There were incidents at the château, near Romainville, during the strike: fox hunting, disturbances at a construction site. Aernoult had joined his comrades from the "Terrace". He was from Romainville. He was recognized and denounced to the police. He quickly went to the mines of Courrières. In absentia, he was sentenced to two months in prison for strike action. A few days before the Courrières disaster, Aernoult returned to Romainville. Death had not yet claimed him. But the prison claimed him. He was arrested and tried, and this time he was sentenced to ten months in prison. Barely nineteen years old, he was locked up at the Petite-Roquette. One day he received a visit from a barracks "flatterer": "When at your age you have a conviction," said this character, "the best thing is to enlist in order to rehabilitate yourself! Weakened, distraught, Aernoult gave in; on his release he left for Africa, enlisted in the African Hunters. He was then a handsome guy, robust, solid, a guy as blond as a young girl, not mean for a bit, not nervous, quiet and good humored. Soon exhausted by chores beyond his strength, beaten by Lieutenant Sabatie, Sergeants Casanova and Beignier, victim of a thousand abuses in his cell, panting, bleeding, gagged and then put to the toadstool in the throes of agony, he died at the age of twenty-three, his body dead of blows. "Will we recognize that he was hit on the head? asked a worried captain. - No," said the major, "it will be believed that he knocked himself out against the walls of his cell" (*La Guerre sociale*).

He knows that we are no longer in the time
Where traitors were guillotined!

But that will change, comrades...
O valiant people of the Faubourg,
Who once made barricades,
You will rise one fine day (*bis*)
And this day our hearts will be at ease
Seeing you with us,
Little soldiers, little pioupious :
Worthy sons of the French Guards.

(From July 13 to 19, 1910)

At the same time Couté collaborates with *La Barricade*, created by Méric, where he signs *Le Suberiot* (the whistler). He met Maurice Allard, later deputy of the Var, and André Morizet, future Senator of the Seine. This collaboration will not end until his death.

And during this time Couté continued to frequent cabarets and especially the *Lapin agile*, which Francis Carco remembers so well, where he was seen in the company of Roland Dorgelès, Max Jacob, Pierre Mac Orlan, H.P. Gassier, Jules Depaquit. The evenings continued in the Latin Quarter at *La Chope de la Haye* and ended in the sticky early morning at Les Halles.

From time to time he escapes and returns to his hometown, he plunges back into his youth, finds his father but also his fields and woods and this tongue so tasty to the palate. He gets his cherry back and then comes back and starts drinking again.

Because he drinks like all those who frequent the brewery, this poor people's salon. He drinks and he is sick, already affected by the tuberculosis that was to take him away.

Then one day, we are in June 1911, after a night similar to the others, around six o'clock, he declares: "*I am exhausted*". His friends put him in a cab that took him back to his hotel, Place du Tertre; he was so pitiful that his concierge called a doctor who sent him urgently to the Lariboisière hospital. He died there soon after, alone.

He will be buried on June 30 in Meung-sur-Loire.

Who remembers today the one to whom Victor Méric paid tribute in this way:

> *"Poor Couté, dear companion, old friend! We had chatted all night. You had confided to me your rancour of revolt, of unrepentant 'refractory.' You pushed back the collar towards which so many domesticated animals aspire. You lived on the fringe, fiercely free, sparing your friendships, only giving yourself knowingly, closed to anyone who did not vibrate with you. It paid off. You drank. We all drank. We drink foolishly, because we have nothing else to do and it warms our spirits. And because one forgets, with many. But bohemia is terrible. We taunt her. It takes its revenge.*
>
> *This small, skinny man, with eyes of flame, with pursed lips, was a great poet. He went singing, the beggars of the cities and the fields, in his tasty jargon, with his inimitable accent of the soil. He flogged tartuferies, magnified miseries, wept over the reprobates and sounded the tocsin of revolts. A great poet, you are told. How is it that nothing remains of his work, only scattered songs, couplets that we hum? Ah, it's quite simple. The poor little poet gave away his productions, as he went along, for a few cents.*
>
> *And he never heard from them again."*

Georges DARIEN (1862-1921)
The irregularity of letters

His real name was Georges Hippolyte Adrien, the son of a merchant of novelties and ready-made lingerie. He was born in Paris on April 6, 1862.

His father, a Calvinist, had married a Catholic woman whom Georges Hippolyte did not like. As a result, as soon as he finished his studies at the Lycée Charlemagne, he went ahead of the call of his class and enlisted at nineteen as a volunteer in the Train squadron. A rebellious and negligent soldier, he was transferred, following venial breaches of the rules, to the first company of disciplinary pioneers at Gafsa in Tunisia. He was released in 1866 after thirty months in prison and returned to Paris where he settled in a garret in order not to replace military servitude with that of his family.

In order not to depend on anyone, he did not apply for any job, which implied that he had at least a small income, and began to frequent the literary world, especially young symbolist writers. For three years, he did seemingly nothing. In fact, he observed, explored the field, read a lot, spoke little but listened attentively. During this period of maturation, he conceived several literary projects, novels and plays. The most urgent for him was *Biribi,* completed in 1888, whose violence frightened the publishers and which wanted to inaugurate the game of massacre. For such is his project, to indulge in a ruthless game of massacre whose targets and victims would be the icons of society in putrefaction. Such a project is admirably developed in an article of Émile Bergerat published on July 14, 1888 in *Le Gil Blas.*

"The great men of this world are those who provoke and hasten the solutions of problems by personal solutions and who venture to give an opinion, good or bad, but ready-made, to their contemporaries, wrote the son-in-law of Theophile Gautier. *They have been called tyrants! Why? Perhaps they are only less fatalistic than the others in a civilization of fakirs, thumb-twisters.*

"In the bullring of the Federation Street, the other day, one of these men was born to us, I greet him. He is from Spain. He is a simple bullfighter.

"Realizing that this eternal question of the bull's death threatened to turn into sawing and nonsense, he grabbed the bull by the horns and killed it.

"His success was immense. It had to be. Glory to him! Glory to Señor Lagartija, who enriches France with an opinion on something! This is the most difficult thing to do in our country, and one risks one's life, you should know that. From now on, our judgement is the following in bullfighting. "You have to kill the bull, because someone dared to kill it, in Paris, the first one.

"In all things, you see, what constitutes the great man is to dare to kill the bulls that nobody kills. There is no other secret in art, in science, in politics, in anything. One only enters the Book of Memory on this condition, so much humanity is amazed to see a man who is a man. The philosophy that determines this bullfighter to take it upon himself to kill the bull, when all the spectators tremble at the same time and desire to see him kill it, is the same as that of a Napoleon or a Columbus, and does not require a soul less than theirs. It requires the same genius and the same luck. The more I advance in life, the more it appears obvious to me that nothing is useful in it, neither gift, nor work, nor virtue, and that only those have lived who... killed the bull.

"And what bulls to kill in France! Think of it! French society, as we owe it to the rush of new interests and old traditions, cannot be better compared than to a Spanish bullring, full of banderilleros, picadores, espadas, and brilliant bullfighters, gaudy and mounted on rosses. The people overwhelm the amphitheater's stands, and they pay to see some old institutions disemboweled, some secular routines gutted, having only skin and bones, bleeding ancient abuses

good for the knackers. Of course, he hates them and mocks them, but he feels sorry for their comical antiquity, and he remembers that they were pallbearers or couriers before they were rossinantes. But, finally, they must be sacrificed since they are no longer useful, not even to drag the omnibus of democracy.

"The beautiful bulls run from the torils, young, strong and fast. But they have balls on their horns!...

"Here are the picadores, the banderilleros, the bullfighters and the colorful troop of the brave. But they are unarmed and reduced to the simulacrum of their exercises. They will not kill the bull, which will not kill the rosses, and everyone will be safe and unharmed after this ridiculous comedy. Isn't it the exact image of this uncertain age with skeptical tendencies? The progress has balls to the horns, and it simulates the disembowelment of the sacrosanct and pitiful carcasses that the sensibility did not dare to sacrifice. Our bullfighters are bullfighters for fun and have only the costume, the red scarf and the wooden sword. Who do we kill here? Neither the future nor the past. The bulls are stunned like oxen in a slaughterhouse, in the wings, and the people wonder where the game is, what it consists of and why it is so famous, since it is all in the form of a joke.

"To act! This is what the new peoples alone dare to do, and this is what the old ones, spoiled by the dream, can no longer resign themselves to... This horror of acting is so great among peoples of Latin blood, and among all of us, that we have come to effeminate the beautiful word "act" and have turned it into "action"! All our vexation is in this awful barbarism and more deliquescent than all the neologisms of the symbolic!

"Ah, when will those brave men come to us, whose race we have been, and who, without fear and risking everything, will kill the innumerable bulls of the social arena! How one awaits them! How we would love them! Come, divine Messiahs of the Initiative! Let us kill bulls! Let's kill the bull, and long live Señor Lagartija!"

It is this role of apocalyptic messiah that Darien wants to play and *Biribi* was to be the first drum roll. But he hesitated to entrust his manuscript to Charpentier, a publisher ready to ride the wave of the military novel that Zola and his coterie of the *Soirées de Medan* had encouraged and then abandoned. The second wave of naturalist writers was committed to the impassive description of a world that was open to all raging (ravaging) brushes. Abel Hermant published *Le Cavalier Miserey* and Henry Fèvre *Au Port d'Armes,* mœurs militaires. Then comes *Sous-Offs* by Lucien Descaves who will win the prize of literary martyrdom.

For four months, the newspapers went wild, for and against, and a trial even made headlines.

Savine, preferred to Charpentier as a potential publisher, has procrastinated, multiplied the frigid haggling and *Biribi* appears only in 1890, shortly before the acquittal of Descaves. The previous title of Darien *Bas les cœurs,* a *picture of the war of 1870 seen by a child,* did not leave any trace on the surface of the literary swamp. He wrote a few novels and even provoked a debate in Parliament that led to the virtual abolition of the military prison. In *Le Gil Blas,* Séverine, who signs Jacqueline, wrote *"I would not be surprised if legal proceedings were taken against this book; I would almost wish it if the truth were to come out of the scandal, and entirely, with its hideousness, its atrocities before the shivering magistrates".* Damien, in fact, like Lord Lagartija, is ready to finish off the bull by appearing in a court of law to mortally weld his wounds. But the army and its sponsors had interest in silence and oblivion. They are going to obtain them. Let's stop for a few moments on this book, almost mythical and so little read. No one has equaled it in violence, except L.F. Céline, the great cursed. In this volume, half novel, half autobiography, Darien recounts the joyful torments to which men guilty of minor breaches of discipline, that imperious military dogma, were subjected. He describes the liturgy of redemptive sanctions: the sites where the condemned were exposed, the toadstools, the tombs and the gags, all the instruments of the agony of the poor guys that the military belly could not assimilate and to whom a fate of excrement was reserved. He also tells of the glorious corps of chaouchs, most of them Corsican, and their exploits, how, eager to celebrate at the chief town, they feed the war council with disciplinarians. For they sit there as witnesses and accusers. Then the gallooned monsters play cards for the life and liberty of a poor fellow, and the one who wins will hold the leash and go wading in some slum. These pages quiver with hatred and anger but also with compassion and pity; the style is sober, of a rigorous classicism. These images charged with all emotions will influence thousands of young people who will rise up, the Dreyfus Affair is to come, against militarism.

The publisher Savine, noticing the Donquichottesque vocation of his foal, then designates another target for him. He was to lend his pen to the ferocious Drumont to execute one of his Jewish targets. At first Darien accepted, but then, sensing the tortuous and unhealthy scheme, he recused himself. He then produced *The Pharisees,* a violent pamphleteering charge against the two acolytes. The book is mediocre and somewhat lacks its effect.

At the same time he collaborates with *L'En dehors* de Zo d'Axa, a political and social pamphlet, in which he engages in an all-out offensive against prejudice. Angry and unsociable, he confronts his director in a duel, guilty of having vilified this practice in a vigorous article. Wounded, he continues to collaborate with the newspaper. After the disappearance of the latter, he founded *L'Escarmouche* which he ran alone. This did not prevent him from leading his literary life in parallel and working with Descaves, the author of the famous novel *Sous-Offs* condemned for contempt of the army, on the theatrical adaptation of his book. He added a hoax book, *Les Vrai Sous-Offs,* in which he parodied a militaristic charge against Descaves' book.

But political passion has its risks. For the anarchists of the pen must assume the acts of the anarchists of the field. And the time is for direct action, illegalism and individual recovery. So in 1894, when new repressive laws threaten the libertarian milieu, every anarchist is suspected, by anticipation, of criminal designs. Fleeing persecution, Zo d'Axa, Pouget, Malato, Zevaco, Darien and many others crossed the Channel and took refuge in an England that welcomed outcasts. Darien, who spoke and wrote English wonderfully, acclimated easily. Although his life was not well known[12], it seems that he got married and worked as a bookmaker. But above all, he explored London and its surroundings in all directions, rubbing elbows with all sorts of people, especially with the hustlers, the dispensers of paid love, and other regulars of debauchery and trickery. So much so that he arouses the sympathy and interest of Maroleau, the director of the bank of thieves who associates him with his business.

---

12. To a colleague who asked him for biographical information, he replied: "I have not been able to understand until now, what the private life of a writer could have to do with the publication or the representation of one of his works".

This life of adventure and pleasure without the constraints of the ordered and policed world of the State Leviathan appealed to Darien. When the amnesty, following the crushing of his fellow illegalists, allowed the return of the exiles, he remained in London. At most, he was seen from time to time in Belgium or Germany, where he frequented the same circles and engaged in mysterious transactions.

These materials, gleaned over the years and from his wanderings, were used to compose *Le Voleur,* which appeared with P.V. Stock in 1897. If François Coppée, a poet rightly forgotten but who made and unmade reputations at the *Journal,* devotes three pages to vomit on this human larva of Randal, this anarchist bandit otherwise more constructed and formidable, literarily speaking, than Ravachol, Vaillant and other propagandists by the fact, because likely to lead souls not subjected to prejudices to the infamous anarchy, *Ernest La Jeunesse* is inflamed. Declaring himself bewitched by the novel, "*book of serenity without this nightmare of after indigestion that one calls the remorse, without this flower of prison that one names repentance and perfumed of this perfume of truth and courage that one catalogs under the denomination of cynism".* The great Rachilde understood that behind this novel and its characters stood a man, passionate, and his thought, intractable.

But the era was one of great rallying of the proletariat, of democratic consensus orchestrated around the Dreyfus Affair. This is why Darien's book goes somewhat unnoticed.

He also abandoned the project of a novelistic cycle organized around the characters of Le *Voleur*. Instead, he published *La Belle France* (1901), one of his best works and a pamphlet of rare violence. He had more trouble publishing *L'Epaulette,* which did not appear until 1905.

But he was disillusioned and turned again to political action, with Emile Janvion saying of him:

"What a singular figure of refractory! And what a beautiful writer's temperament," he was to write later. "*The style was the man: thin lips, slanted mouth, sharp eyes, ginger cat's moustache, thick hair, tight jaws, athletic waist, wrestler's torso and muscles stretched under the skin. The gentleman, not convenient, of Calvinist mentality, with ideas of steel, and who preferred to prolong Biribi in the civil rather than to bend before 'all the doglit of the arrivisme in livery'".*

The little he knew of his life and career made him even more worthy of respect and sympathy:

"Superb figure of a rebel and a failure. But the magnificent loser, the voluntary loser, about whom Clemenceau wrote, in *Les plus forts,* this painful truth: *'The loser! With the missed lives, is made in pain, the genius of the whole humanity.'"*

He publishes *L'Ennemi du Peuple,* a newspaper intended to prepare the anti-militarist congress of Amsterdam. Thrown wholeheartedly into revolutionary propaganda, he turned this free sheet, terribly alive, into a weekly of ideas and combat. His articles, moreover, cause a sensation. They are, says Victor Meric, *"Of a crazy vehemence, enamelled with puns and wild metaphors".* For example, he calls for war as a means to precipitate the revolution. At the same time, he collaborates with Gustave Hervé, Urbain Gohier, Laurent Tailhade, Miguel Almereyda... One of his targets is the anarchism that is already in order and aspiring to recognition (always).

But it was also through the theater that Darien sought action. Between 1906 and 1910, he wrote numerous plays, only a few of which were performed and without much success... with the exception of an adaptation of *Biribi* in 1906 (coupled with *Chez les Zoaques* by the beginner Sacha Guitry).

"The Darien of the heroic era, lean, dry as a boner, has become enormous. The thick neck, the blood in his face, the furious voice, he seemed always ready to explode" (Voléric). This did not slow down his debauchery of activities. In 1910 he founded the Union Syndicale des Artistes Dramatiques and created various leagues, publishing apostrophes and manifestos, brochures and newspapers, organizing numerous conferences to defend his great idea of a single tax taken from the physiocrats of the eighteenth century France. If L'Union Syndicale had some success, of agitation more than of recruitment, La Ligue pour l'impôt unique did not captivate a public, not very familiar with certain utopias.

It ceased all activity in 1913, the utopia became a nightmare with Caillaux and his progressive income tax.

Darien left the anarchist or revolutionary milieu, he distanced himself from those he called *"the geldings".* He even joined the radical socialist party (that of the aforementioned Caillaux) of which he was the unhappy candidate. However, he continued to write for the theater, a great melodrama on the Steinheil affair, and even a novel, *L'Epaulette*, in which he somewhat disavowed his former antimilitarism. His only success, which his temperamental nature quickly turned into a debacle, was a play based on his novel *Biribi* at the Théâtre Antoine.

After the great world catastrophe of 14-18, his signature can be found in *Le Rappel* where he develops an agrarian socialism inspired by the theses of the American Henry George.

He then tried to reconnect with some of his companions. Georges Pioch of the *Journal du Peuple* saw him again: *"I saw Darien. Ah, the poor man! I saw a finished being, broken, despairing of everything. He no longer has the strength or desire to work.*

A few weeks later, on August 19, 1921, he was dead.

For epitaphs we will recall what he wrote to Janvion:

> *"Is all independence forbidden to us in this cavern of goinfers?"*
> *"To have the right to pass, one must be registered and classified in a party, a lupanar, a brotherhood. Be a black Jesuit or a red Jesuit, or die! Well! I will pass and proudly on the guts of all this scoundrel."*

Léon DAUDET (1867-1942)
The Royalist Accuser, the King's Manant

Léon is the son of Alphonse Daudet, who cannot be forgotten by anyone who remembers being a child. He was born in the Marais on November 16, 1867 at the Lamoignon Hotel. It was the time of Offenbach, whom he hated, a symbol of the modern Babylon that was the Paris of the Second Empire. A persistent smell of decay emanates from it, which makes the bed of the ideologies of the recovered revolt which are born from the decomposition of the traditional society. Daudet father is a royalist. He was the private secretary of the Duke of Morny, who had just died, an emblematic figure of this period reconciling aristocratic distinction and bourgeois baseness.

Daudet father wrote some novels that can still be read with profit today: *Sapho, The Immortal.* He knew the prints of a writer of great renown and Léon adored him, as he adored his mother. He was an excellent student and pursued solid classical studies at Louis-le-Grand where he imbibed the spirit of latinism which was to be the basis of Maurassism. However, his father was his best teacher, of whom he would say much later: *"I was brought up from an early age by my father, who was a great educator, with the idea that if one wanted to write, one had to have the most regular, normal and tranquil life possible. Alphonse Daudet was in favor, for the novelist, for the philosopher, for the journalist, of the family, of its shelter and refuge, and after a youth that he had had rather stormy, of the regular conduct of life".*

He lived his childhood surrounded by a lot of love and among the best minds of the time. The salon of Mme Daudet was indeed the center of the Parisian spirit where the "Tout-Paris" of literature and arts, from

Flaubert to Goncourt, passed by. "*At that time,* says Léon Daudet, *at least for France, the political question was not what it is today and the men of various opinions dined together, elbowed each other, and even discussed, without reaching the degree of acrimony where the things would come today if one still formed similar meetings...*

My father and mother entertained in Paris and in Champrosay. The Thursdays of Champrosay remained famous. That day, the table was set for twenty-five or thirty people, and anyone who wanted to come from Paris would come. If the audience was larger, an extra table was set. The two protagonists of these meetings were my father, Goncourt and Drumont. But we also saw Zola and the whole naturalist school."

In these salons and country parties, Mirbeau, Rosny Aîné, Hugo and the whole world of scientists of this rationalist era, which he would later describe in his memoirs, rubbed shoulders and appreciated each other: Charcot and Berthelot, Taine and Potain. From all this substance he feeds himself. He gathers and organizes this material which will nourish his life and his work. It will be, according to the word of René Joseph, "*the masterpiece of Alphonse Daudet*". Although he was made, from his adolescence, to write, according to the wish of his father who intended him to teach, he became a doctor.

No doubt because of his bulimia for knowledge but also because of his father's illness, the syphilis that will be the leavening of 19th century culture.

The doctor is then considered with respect, he enjoys in the opinion an incomparable prestige that confers him the scientific Dogma substituted to the religious Dogma in perdition. Like the shrink-something of today. The doctor of then is solemn and peremptory. He asserts and he vaticinates. The only thing he lacks is television.

Of these "*executioners of the sick flesh*", Léon Daudet said, clear-sighted and prophetic: "*Too spoiled, too adored, both those of the drug and those of the scalpel, abused the situation: financially, by exploiting their clients or their dupes; intellectually, by extending their professional fatuity to philosophy, by claiming to regulate the minds*".

In 1885 he enrolled in the Medical School. He lived a real life as a rifleman, the opposite of the dryness of body and soul that propriety suspects in any right-handed man.

But he will always be very faithful to this training of the mind and the will, which he will say is the best school of "*altruism and non-laziness*".

He will also always keep the respect of his masters, coupled with the most pronounced critical acuity. But he is not one of those monomaniacal interns who ignore everything that is not of their discipline. He is a *polygamist of culture* and during these seven years he continues to frequent literary circles and certain politicians, such as Clemenceau and Camille Pelletan. He also read everything and listened to music, all the music that was available at the time. The French, of course, but also Nietzche and Wagner, Ibsen and Strindberg, Dostoyevsky and Tolstoy... But also "*we had a lot of fun too, in a noisy and sometimes scandalous way - considering the habits of the bourgeoisie -, but perfectly normal and healthy... Having said that, we loved women and even - proh pudor! - madly. But these relationships with city girls with joking eyes or with country girls who were quickly dried out, did not involve, I repeat, any coarseness or even, on their part, any greed.*"

In short, the classic life of a student, since the 12th century, and perhaps even before. He is also a good student; even if he fails the internship, he will still be a temporary intern.

And then one day, it is the overflow of sufferings and misfortunes, he escapes. And it is journalism that welcomes him in the person of the already known Francis Magnard who publishes in *Le Figaro* an article signed by *a modern young man*. This article will be followed by several others and soon Mrs. Adam publishes her first essays in *La Nouvelle Revue*. Finally, in 1895, when he was twenty-eight years old, his first novel, *L'Astre noir (The Black Star), appeared*. It tells the story of a great man - one thinks of Hugo, who had recently died - who, dominating his century, reduced his family to servitude.

Finally, the great storyteller will attack, it is his first pamphlet, the whole body of doctors. It will be *Les Morticoles* dedicated to Edmond de Goncourt where his truculent genius and his accomplished style evoke Swift and Rabelais.

He expresses there "*finally the contempt and the nausea accumulated by the sight, by the hearing, by the pores*". The theme: a certain Felix Canelon disembarks with a whole crew in an imaginary kingdom, the kingdom of the Morticoles, where the doctors, absolute masters of everything: justice, administration, police, parliament... tyrannize the dumbed-down people of men who are admittedly sick or who ignore themselves.

For all eternity, the cutishness of the masters is pinned down and the spinelessness of the impetuous summarized by the foot-licking ceremony. *Shakespeare's Journey,* which follows shortly after, plunges us into the world of the sixteenth century, so dear to the author. In this book, which has the appearance of a novel, the different material, intellectual and spiritual forces of this century, the preface of the modern world, are put on stage. Humanists, Protestants and Catholics clash arguments in the middle of violent or debauched scenes and scabrous stories with as a guiding thread "*the healthy invective [which] is, like the beautiful color, made with the vilest materials*" (Pierre Dominique). And always this abbot of Meudon of whom he tells us that having chewed from his youth the herb of vehemence whose taste makes all iniquity intolerable, he is an admirable man. Beautiful evocation of the ideal of the self...

When the event of which his father spoke to him mysteriously occurred, Drumont was preparing "*an enormous bomb*". Léon Daudet was 19 years old when *La France juive* was published on April 14, 1886. The young pamphleteer had always loved and admired his elder brother, whom he saw "*as a 16th century character, retouched by a 20th century scholar, a clinician and an outstanding historian*." When *La Libre Parole* appeared in 1892, he was twenty-five years old. He was listed under No. 8, and, out of admiration for Drumont, he joined the anti-Semitic league.

Is he, according to the criteria of the time and beyond any anachronism, an anti-Semite? Yes, if one considers that he distrusts the Jews, and no, if one considers that he has no feeling of superiority, and that his thought is strictly political. "*To persecute Israel would be impolitic and odious. It would be a good thing, even a very good thing, to set limits on propriety and political action, the moral benefit of which would soon be reaped... many intelligent Israelites readily acknowledge this and ask not to be confused with those whom they generically and contemptuously call "the leviticus", that is to say, the eternal malcontents, the eternal agitators. Many intelligent and far-sighted Israelites are also beginning to feel the need for order, an order that would cordially but firmly put them in their place and in their plan.*"

During fourteen years, Daudet lives a little in the shadow of the "*gruff magician*" (Bernanos). He learns his trade at his home and, after the assault, the white wine. When he publishes *Au pays des Parlementeurs,* a merciless and furious satire against parliamentary democracy, he dedicates it to Drumont. At Drumont's request, he collaborated with *La Libre Parole,* but he did not give up his work as a novelist and continued to write articles for Le *Gaulois,* Le *Soleil* and Le *Journal.*

In 1896, *Suzanne,* histoire d'un inceste (*Suzanne,* the story of an incest) was published in serial form in *Le Journal and was* a great success.

He also published other novels, *Deux Étreintes, Le Partage de l'Enfant,* which confirmed his success.

During the Dreyfus Affair, he fought behind Drumont, Barrès and Maurras and in 1899 he was one of those who created *the Ligue de la Patrie française* under the presidency of François Coppée. His political commitment deepened and in 1900 he agreed to write the Sunday lead article for *La Libre Parole,* a regular collaboration that would continue until 1908, when *L'Action française* quotidienne was founded. He had matured and this change of century completed his evolution. For several years he had become a Catholic and had detached himself from the Republic. He was not yet a royalist and his commitment to Drumont was a kind of right-wing Blanquism. He also married his cousin, Marthe Allard, in 1903[13] and settled down in life.

He assiduously frequents F. Lemaître and his muse Mme de Loynes as well as the staff of the Patrie française. The Syveton affair, named after this deputy of the league who, after having slapped, in the middle of a session of the Assembly, General André, instigator of the anti-clerical denunciation cards in the army, was committed suicide on the eve of his appearance in the court of assizes where he was supposed to make revelations, completes Daudet's enlightenment on the impotence of this nationalist league devoid of program for lack of opinions or point of views.

The time had come for this meeting that would decide the rest of his life: "*Now,* says Léon Daudet himself, *there was however at that time (1900) a man equal to the first among the greatest French politicians and thinkers, ardently patriotic, of a cold lucidity, of an unshakeable judgment, surrounded by a very small number of followers writing in a little-read newspaper* La Gazette de France *and whose name, unknown to the mass, made the embroidered vest salonnards like d'Avenel or politicians, even subtle ones, like Dausset, shrug their shoulders. Lemaître, raising his*

13. He was married in first marriage with the granddaughter of Victor Hugo, in a simple and civil marriage.

finger, said of him: it is the first, and by far, but I would not say it in front of Syveton... Then, after a silence: he is even the only one. Déroulède said of him: we will have to have a very serious, very complete debate together... Jaurès and Clemenceau said of him, since a certain famous article which had turned a compromised situation around: he is a sophist. This man carried in his mind, constructing and hierarchizing, the way to avoid the worst misfortunes and knew the remedy to the numerous evils. This man carried in his will what to raise all the altars and all the hearts. When the idea of his country held him, he did without eating and sleeping and, for lack of action, he wrote twenty hours in a row, without breaking stride, immortal pages and fiery advice of wisdom. He was born in Provence, under the sun. He lived in the haze of Paris, insensitive to anything other than the pre-eminence of the French name between his books and a few faithful followers.

His name was Charles Maurras."

Maurras is his junior by a year. He has written magnificent books and is about to publish *L'Enquête sur la Monarchie.* Daudet, still at *La Libre Parole,* sees the weaknesses of Drumont, a leader of the pack rather than a party leader. He also saw, and this seduced him, the coherence of a political-philosophical system that rejected point by point everything that stemmed from the revolution of 1989: *"From 1906 to 1908, I went, frequently at first, and then assiduously, to the political meetings held at Maurras' home, in his small apartment, cluttered with books and newspapers, on the rue de Verneuil. Later on, this will be a historical place that will be depicted with more or less accuracy by the Lenôtre of the future. The appearance alone of the audience gave the impression of an intellectual conspiracy for the service of the fatherland... It was there that I met Léon Montesquiou, Jacques Bainville and Lucien Moreau, then Robert de Boisfleury, and Delebecque, Pujo, Lasserre and all those who made up the steering committees of L'Action française.*

I noticed that these men, these writers, these military men, these academics, of different backgrounds, coming from diverse milieus, converged and joined together in one point, which was the thought of Maurras, the doctrine of the King. One can imagine the powerful atmosphere that all these personalities brought together to swirl around Maurras' home and the cramped office of the Revue d'Action française on rue du Bac. But, whereas at the French fatherland, everyone was shooting up and down, here all thoughts and efforts converged under the immediate influence of our brilliant leader. We left there comforted and full of hope for the future."

In short, Daudet found there a school, a doctrine, at the center, a school leader and around, a party. When in 1905 *the Ligue d'Action française* was founded, he was one of the partisans of "*integral nationalism*". The attempt to bring together *La Libre Parole* and *La Revue d'Action française* having failed, and some funds having been providentially available, on March 1st, 1908 the journal *L'Action française* appeared with the epigraph of the Duke of Orleans: "*Everything that is national is ours*". Among the editors, Henri Vaugeois, Léon Daudet, Charles Maurras, Louis Dimier, Léon de Montesquiou, Jacques Bainville... Daudet was editor-in-chief and gave a mood piece and echoes that he signed Rivarol. Among the episodic contributors, Lemaître and Bourget are included.

Around the newspaper a nebula of organs and organizations: *La Revue universelle, L'Institut d'Action française, La Ligue d'Action française,* the *Action française* students, and especially the *Camelots du Roi.* In short, a political machine of such power that only the communists, later on, will be able to match it.

Daudet was not only a journalist of extraordinary verve but also an exceptional orator of eloquence and clarity; he quickly became the tribune of the team. In addition to the article he offered every day to the 200,000 readers of *L'Action française,* he wanted to reach out to the general public. He believed in the necessity of imposing himself in the street. So he was one of those who, at the time of the Thalamas Affair (named after a Condorcet professor who had made fun of Joan of Arc), imposed the annual procession in favor of the Saint, which for years saw the Camelots and the police clash.

He was also involved in all the battles of the time against those whom *Action Française* suspected of betraying the interests of France to the benefit of foreigners: the German, the Jew, the English, the Russian, etc. And never has the conspiracy view been more widespread than in this period when the spirit of revenge was married to the desire to expand the outlets for national production.

Clemenceau is one of the heads of the polemicist. He nicknamed him *the Killer* since he ordered, or tolerated, the massacre of the workers of Draveil. He also calls him "*the old scoundrel*" and makes fun of "his fake head of mongoloid". The one who had "*a taste for all false ideas*" was probably reproached for not caring enough about the rearmament of France.

Caillaux, the inventor of the progressive income tax, was another of his enemies. He reproached him for being a pacifist and, as Minister of Finance, for having cut back on the army budget. But the main fight was materialized by a book entitled *L'Avant-Guerre (Before the War)* which gathered all the "studies and documents on the German Jewish espionage in France since the Dreyfus Affair". The book and articles made a huge noise denouncing the German penetration in France. That is to say, *"penetration of an economic or cultural nature, or other"*.

In sum, Daudet denounces from a nationalist and reactionary point of view what Hilferding and Rosa Luxembourg denounced from an internationalist and revolutionary point of view: the process of globalization of the capitalist economy (in its imperialist phase). Thus he discovers that the French forts in the East are supplied with German coal, that the lubricating oil used by the army's automobile service is German, and that the port of Dielette, in Normandy, where iron was mined, is home to the German industrialist Thyssen, supplier of the Krupp factories.

In reality, he was protesting against the rampant colonization of French soil and subsoil which, if war broke out, which he did not doubt, would weaken and weaken the country.

Then comes Friday, July 24, 1914, when Austria's ultimatum to Serbia announces the war that breaks out on the morning of the 26th. With the exception of a few harmless skirmishes, the proletariat, which was supposed to fraternize over the borders, drunk without shame on the fumes of war. The patriotic storm sweeps everything away and Jaurès is assassinated. The few demonstrations of popular anger that broke out then were nothing more than a flash in the pan.

On August 2, Daudet, who had an automobile accident, was quite severely injured. This avoids him the palinody of an engagement which, at his age, would have led him to a more glorious office and a subjection to the Republican government.

Where Charles Maurras had seen in the future *"500,000 young Frenchmen lying, cold and bloody, on their poorly defended land,"* the four years of war would count 1,300,000. *"The class of 1914,"* he wrote, *"was, as was to be expected, the most cruelly tested (85,000 dead out of 292,000). It was the generation that came into the world at the time of the*

Dreyfus Affair, a generation sacrificed almost in its entirety to the bloody chimeras that had presided, like bad fairies, over its cradle." During this war, after having been muzzled by the censorship, *the Action française* will energetically commit itself around the ministry Clemenceau, the enemy of yesterday. It was Léon Daudet who was the first to see in him the man of action, the man on whom one could count for the continuation of the war. It was *L'Action française* that brought down the Caillaux-Malvy ministry, whose two accomplices were tried before the High Court. Daudet played the ugly role of "*king's prosecutor" in the* words of his opponents.

The action of Daudet, and of Maurras, will be decisive. The dictatorship of Clemenceau, from November 1917 to January 1920, led to victory in the war and defeat in the peace according to the Maurrasian doctrine. (In fact, the Treaty of Versailles never seemed to please anyone and was the cause of the second world conflict). Of the peace, signed on June 28, 1919, Daudet will write in *Excelsior* "*And it is finished. The peace is initialed. After the ratification of the Assemblies, it will become enforceable. Muller and Bell (the two German signatories) hear the cheers that resound outside, as the sheepish people take pride in foolishness. Where do their thoughts go? To resignation, to revenge? Neither their composed faces nor their automatic gestures betray anything. But, perhaps, as they left the Hall of Mirrors, they said to themselves "we are a great people of sixty million men. The imperial unity founded here in 1871 remains. We no longer have an emperor, but we keep the Empire, the source of our past greatness. Who knows, with this instrument of power, what the future may bring us*? And Maurras spoke of the peace in these terms in *L'Action française* of October 3: "*The armistice was mediocre; the treaty is bad. Most of the evil came from the absence of preparation for peace. Among the many characteristics of our peace of threat and war, we can consider four decisive points: 1) It leaves at our feet the whole immense problem of Eastern Europe and Russia, insoluble by the presence of a great Germany. The problem would have lost nine-tenths of its gravity with a Germany that had returned to its divisions. 2) The condition of our security is placed outside of us, in the hands of our Anglo-Saxon allies. 3) The League of Nations is the expression of this foreign peace. If we pass over the more or less utopian nature of the goal, it remains that the means adopted to reach it unquestionably presents all the aspects of a chimera. 4) This warlike peace necessarily remains an armed peace. We have stated here more than once our deep desire to see this immense benefit: the abolition of compulsory military service. This is what the French are missing with the good peace".*

But the war was an opportunity for Daudet, in the moments of respite that his passionate commitment allowed him, to write. It is a diversified production which includes essays: *Devant la Douleur, Salons et Journaux* and novels of which the famous *L'Hérédo* which deals with hereditary servitude and the psychological and physiological basis of moral responsibility. He develops the thesis according to which *"Each man carries within him the possibilities of a masterpiece, or more exactly of the masterpiece here below. The blossoming of his own conscience, out of the congenital fetters".* A hymn to freedom tempered by effort and will... This book appeared in 1917 by its audacious thesis on the self and the self evokes the great psychoanalyst Carl Gustave Jung.

On November 16, 1919, Léon Daudet was elected as a royalist deputy for the third sector (left bank and 16th arrondissement). A lifelong anti-parliamentarian, he saw this mandate as a lever to try to reconstitute a state by relying on Clemenceau who, although a democrat, despised parliament. But Clemenceau, after an ignominious maneuver, was removed from the presidency of the chamber and entered into retirement. Then for almost five years, Daudet, sitting in the front row, will constitute the only opposition worthy of the name. That is to say, free, free of all the schemes and maneuvers thundering and fierce, without prejudice and insolence. He creates or provokes, indifferently, the heckling, so much so that a certain Noblemaire will shout at him: *"Mr Daudet, let us work".* For he is neither complacent nor complicit and affirms that one should have no human respect for the adversary *"and to take it on ad hominem".* For him, the platform is a continuation of the fight for control of the street. *"Nature has gifted me,"* he says, *"in terms of the volume of my voice. When I have to deal, as was the case in the House, with a few hollers, I begin by exhausting them, by exciting them, by naming them, by not caring about them, by replying to insults and jokes with other insults, and to jokes with other insults and other jokes. Then the president would intervene, scold my insulters and call them to order. My friends would shout and protest... Most of the time, the session was suspended. Pretty white arms, swans' necks left the galleries and the stands, at the request of the ushers. During this time, I rested, I drank a glass of wine, and the return of the president and his hat found me ready and cheerful again."*

And despite this tireless parliamentary activity he published almost frantically: *L'Entremetteuse* (novel), *Le Stupide* XIXe *Siècle* (essay), *Les Droits et Pronostications d'Alcofribas Deuxième* (Rabelaisian parody) and *Sylla et son Destin* (historical essay). It would be necessary to quote everything, but one can read everything, of these works of the great maturity. So failing that, these two extracts as an appetizer. "*It is necessary that our country has a solid head,* says Daudet, in his book, *to have resisted to such lights, and to have drawn from it with a minimum of five invasions in thirty years. With drivers and pilots fed and soaked with Hugo, Michelet, Quinet, Rousseau, etc., we were entitled to an invasion every ten years. Stupidity is more cruel than wickedness*" and "*It is a touching and unanimous refrain that humanity has never reached such a high degree of civilization, perfection and culture. The further the century advances, the more this state of mind becomes accentuated. When I entered high school in 1870, our teachers (who were excellent and highly educated, by the way) congratulated themselves and us for coming to such a time in history when progress was reaching its peak... Later, at the School of Medicine, I found the same state of mind. From the intern to the associate professor, there was an extraordinary smugness, the persuasion that we held the definitive truth, that, on several essential points, science and, even better, knowledge, were definitively fixed ne varietur.*"

And in 1922 the ultimate drama for a father: the loss of a child. His eldest son, Philippe, was a runaway. He may even have some behavioral or personality problems. He was fourteen and a half years old and was found fatally wounded by a bullet in a cab. There is talk of suicide, but the father refuses this easy version. The story is as follows: Philippe would have contacted the anarchists of the *Libertaire* and proposed them to commit an attack on an important personality. Faced with their refusal and his father's rejection of the ideas he professed, he could only consider suicide.

For Léon Daudet, the affair was fabricated by police provocateurs introduced into anarchist circles in order to compromise him. Daudet was sued for defamation for his accusations and sentenced to five months in prison.

In 1928, a new blow for this man who was mortally wounded by this dramatic disappearance but who remained standing: *L'Aquitaine,* the newspaper of the diocese of Bordeaux, published a letter from Cardinal Andrieu directed against *L'Action française,* which it accused, among other ignominies, of wanting to re-establish slavery and of using the Church as an instrument, whereas Maurras was an atheist. L'*Action française* responded in an address signed by its Catholic leaders, including Léon Daudet. But the affair took on worrying proportions and Pope Pius XI wrote to Cardinal Andrieu to give him his support and on January 9, 1927 *L'Action française* was condemned by the Church. For the readers or members of the Action française this meant exclusion from the sacraments and burial on the sly. This great suffering did not deprive L'*Action française* of the support it enjoyed in Catholic circles but, on the contrary, testified to its moral and political influence in France at the time.

Under the impact of the conviction by the court of assizes, Daudet learns of its confirmation by the court of cassation. He locks himself in the offices of the newspaper with its director, his wife and Maurras. But Daudet did not want the blood to flow for him and went to the prefect Chiappe. He is incarcerated.

And one day, while he is at the table, a guard comes to announce his release. A cab was waiting for him, with an Action Française supporter in the driver's seat. Soon after, he realized that it was an escape organized by the Camelots. They had installed a bypass on an official line that ran under the premises of their newspaper. And the order, addressed to the director of the prison and saying "*This is the minister's office*" was issued from *L'Action française.*

On August 1st, 1927 Daudet is in Belgium and France bursts into laughter. He will stay there for more than two years. He continued to write articles for *L'Action française* and published nearly twenty books, including *Le Courrier des Pays-Bas* (4 volumes) and *Écrivains et Artistes* (7 volumes). This man did nothing but write, passing from high-flying literary criticism and testifying to an exceptional culture, to medicine and politics. Without complexes.

And in his political or literary writings, the same inventiveness, the same formulas, the same joy of writing: "*Bergson, little Hebrew rat of the creative evolution*", "*Zola, the fecal bowl*", "*Viviani, Algerian wave pushed in the poop of the Little Republic*", "*Blum, a kind of Hebrew greyhound, simpering and haughty with easy speech and pedant"*... The list is long and no one escapes the ferocity of the satirist, from Caillaux, nicknamed *"blood clot"*, to his wife called *"the killer"*, through the idol of France at that time, Poincaré, called *"the dwarf of Lorraine"*.

In 1930, eleven books were written, including *Les Nouveaux Châtiments* illustrated by Sennep. In the latter, besides Poincaré and Barthou *"the guard of fools"*, it is Briand, *"the thug of passage"*, as Clemenceau called him, who is pinned down and, through them, the political thuggery of the time.

But the great affair of Daudet, and of the Maurrasian school, is Germany rising again, and a corporal who is agitated. Concerning the so-called Barthou, Daudet wrote in a strange prophetic vision: "History will tell how, having allowed the German-Russian conjunction, Barthou was the architect of the new conflagration which in 19... the Germans and the Russians surging on Poland, then the first, reassured by the Eastern front, on France" and already before, in 1928, he wrote in *Ronde de Nuit: "A Dutchman of great spirit, to whom I asked what he thought of the current state of mind of the German people, whom he frequented for his business, answered me picturesquely: it is a bull locked in a buffet. He is still only shaking the walls of the buffet, disjointing the boards. But, in a few months, he will break everything".* And finally, in 1933, in an article in *L'Action française* of September 15: *"How can Germany raise its finances, since it no longer has any colonies, no more indigenous labor, no more of those natural riches which feed the stock exchanges of the other great nations: oil, sugar, rubber, coffee? - Germany can only raise its finances by its industry, and especially its heavy industry. It must therefore manufacture stocks of cannons, mortars, machine guns, airplanes, in general war machines.*

- But how do you dispose of these stocks once they are manufactured?

- By going to war. This is what happened in 1914. If it had not gone to war, Germany would have been bankrupt.

- Germany, from 1911, was looking for a pretext for war. In the course of 1913, there was the baroque campaign of the German press against the Foreign Legion, a campaign that was clearly inspired. If it had not been for the police attack (Sicherheitspolizei) in Sarajevo, the Germans would have been looking for something else. They want to play the card of possible casus belli."

At the same time, he returned to literature, singled out the young writer Louis-Ferdinand Celine and wrote *Un Amour de Rabelais, a* vibrant eulogy of the *"first of the French polemicists",* the physician (like himself and Celine) François Rabelais.

At seventy years old, he pays homage to the one he calls *"his boss",* according to the term in use at the faculty, and to the sixteenth century, the century of all ideological mutations, this reform which anticipates and prepares the gigantic movement of the value which knows its assumption in the twentieth century, and which Daudet already qualifies, *"of German".*

Then it was February 6, 1934, and this massive and undifferentiated revolt of the people who demonstrated against *"the thieves"* in front of the Chamber where they met under the name of deputies. *L'Action française* and Daudet furiously called for this insurrection of common sense and honesty, but the communists were also there, as well as all the leagues or parties that harbored the rebels.

Democracy had the unarmed people shot, 28 people were killed. The insurrection was only an eructation of anger as the nationalists lacked leaders and a program... But it will give birth shortly after to the *Popular Front.*

Daudet then saw the catastrophe that was coming and in *Ciel de Feu* (1934), he predicted the coming war in a novelistic way. Then in 1935, in *Hitler et l'Hitlérisme,* he wrote about *Mein Kampf: "the hatred of victorious France, the passionate desire for immediate revenge bursts out on every page of this bitter and furious book. Its purpose is not in doubt. It is Germany, mistress of the universe after having taken revenge for its terrible defeat in 1918."* He makes the Hitler movement *"a second Reformation".*

"The Führer," he says, *"is indeed the bearer of Germanism as was the German man Martin Luther in the 16th century"* and *"the second German Reformation wants to hold souls as well as bodies."*

In short, Daudet criticizes Briand's pacifism, which disarms France both materially and ideologically, and solemnly announces the war to come. In 1939, he published *Deux Idoles Sanguinaires (Two Bloody Idols),* sending back to back the two great purveyors of massacres of the century: Hitler and Stalin. With Maurras and *L'Action française,* he tried to prevent a war that the master of Martigues said was "lost in advance". But nothing stops the people on the road to the slaughterhouse where the bad shepherds lead them.

After the defeat, which was another tragedy in his life, he took refuge in Saint-Rémy-de-Provence and then in Lyon, where *L'Action française* had retreated. He supported Marshal Pétain without being fooled by his "*national revolution*". But the illness was there, which first manifested itself in 1940 with a stroke. He fought and regained his dignity as a fighter of the spirit. He writes again, having tamed his trembling and rebellious hand. This book is *Rescuers and Arsonists, a* summary of the mistakes that led to the catastrophe.

Then, on December 17, 1941, an article appeared in *L'Action française,* which we feel was the last word of the old fighter struck down by illness. His last words are "*Long live the future of intelligence*" (title of Maurras' best book).

He died on July 1st, 1942 in the heart of Provence, where he was buried in the heart of the Félibréenne and Occitan land that he had loved so much.

Camille DESMOULINS (1760-1794)

The apostle of liberty or the polite genius

It is in Guise near Cateau-Cambrésis in Picardy that the eldest son of Mr. Desmoulins, lieutenant of bailiwick, was born on March 2, 1760. This modest function had become a little vain because of the fall in disuse of the feudal right and left some leisure to this royal officer that he occupied to write a work of right and, what his son congratulated him later, perhaps rightly, perhaps to create a legend, "to write against the subaltern oppressors, a life always militant against the oppressions of any kind". Later the lieutenant general and his wife had two more sons and two daughters who completed the family but increased the burden.

At the age of seven, he was a child who was a little soft, distant, and uncommunicative with his brothers and sisters. He learned the rudiments of everything in a religious boarding school in Cateau-Cambrésis.

If he is a little soft, but perhaps this is an effect of his withdrawal or lack of confidence, Camille is intelligent and gifted. His father obtained a scholarship to the University of Paris and he entered the Collège Louis-le-Grand in October 1771. This college was located in the Saint-Benoît district at 123 rue Saint-Jacques. It was surrounded by other colleges but, having become in a way the chief town of the University by letters patent of November 12, 1763, it was the first of all, if not the oldest. It owed its name to the protection of Louis XIV under whose patronage the Jesuits had placed it. After their expulsion, it had been assigned to the University of Paris, where the nursery of teachers needed by the State was trained. This is why the scholarship students were housed, fed and educated until they obtained their law degree, their bachelor's degree in theology or their doctorate in medicine.

Like his fellow student who had arrived two years earlier, Maximilien, the future incorruptible, Camille was therefore a scholarship holder. However, scholarships were not won through competitive examinations, but were granted by protection, and they were few in number, as the college archives testify. The mystery of their attribution to two of the main protagonists of the death of the monarchy is not cleared up. But if one remembers Camille's homage to his father and adds that Maximilian's father abandoned his profession of lawyer for months at a time, left, returned, and then left again, can one not think that the revolution was not a sudden storm but the long-term work of multiple networks promoting the same ideological corpus? Louis Blanc himself said of Robespierre père: "*What motive, what instruction did he obey? Wasn't he one of those travelers who were seen staying in the cities on the eve of the Revolution and whose presence, purpose, and fortune were so many problems?*" Finally, is it not strange that Desmoulins père, an obscure character, obtained 297 votes out of 298 voters in the primary assemblies of 1789?

In this college, therefore, where religious instruction had become secondary, the students were offered as models Brutus, the Graccians, and Marius.

The cult of Antiquity had become a true religion and these children, who owed their education to the monarchy and were called to form its personnel, were taught the pride and honor of a republican life and the contempt of a Church that had become an office of lies, allying itself with tyranny in order to dumb down the people.

Many of the prelates who headed the institution took part in the revolutionary events, competing for the odious and the ridiculous.

Camille was a good element there, distinguishing himself by his assiduity at work and his will to succeed, for his ambition burned in his soul and he only loved the city and what it seemed to promise of success and pleasure. It was with gloom that he returned to Guise, his parents and his brothers and sisters during the vacations. In fact, his correspondence speaks only of himself, his needs, his recriminations. Not a word of affection for anyone, does he even have a mother, and when his father reminds him that he has other brothers he replies: "*Yes, but there is this difference that nature has given me wings and that my brothers cannot feel as I do the chain of needs that holds me to the earth.*" He was already ready to trample on his family to get on the stage and be admired because he likes to hurt, mock, humiliate. He is a swordsman, he has guts but no heart. Scandal is his goal, but this goal is only a means to seek brilliance and new ideas as weapons to achieve it.

In September 1784, he obtained a bachelor's degree in law, and in 1785 he was sworn in as a lawyer the same year in the Grand Chamber of Parliament. The future opened up before him, filled with certainties even more than hopes.

But he could not find any case to defend, the Order of lawyers, these "*hoggers of all causes*", blocked his way. Of course, he fears that his lack of pronunciation will also hinder his success, but he refuses to return to Guise where his father could have provided him with a position.

He remained in Paris without money, without furniture, without even a fixed address. He wandered from one garni to another and worked at making requests for the prosecutor, copying rolls, transcribing rulings, and sending out large bills. He thought of becoming a jurisconsult but hardly had time to resume his studies.

So he thinks, like many others, of having a good marriage, of having a good business. But he is poor and ugly and less certain of his future than before. Of course, there is this lady Duplessis, whom he met in the Luxembourg garden and who is the wife of a first clerk of the General Control. An enviable situation even if the husband was an old fool. He had established a platonic relationship with her, which was to remain so, but she had two daughters and one of them, Lucile, was so beautiful, although so young, that Camille was convinced that he was in love with her. But the mother, undoubtedly disappointed that the gallant tribute turns away from her, convinces her husband to reject the suitor.

This disappointment, added to all the others, discourages Camille who lets himself go to the debauchery. This is how he meets the owner of the *Petit Almanach des Muses* to whom he sells his pen and enslaves his soul in the attitude of a journalistic valet who assures him a full bed and a full plate. But the affair was short-lived and he was soon dismissed by his patron, which forced him to return, head down, to Guise. He was admitted to the bar but his bad reputation was so persistent that he was left without a cause. The Estates General, prelude to the Revolution, will tear him from anonymity and project him on the front of a stage where the curtain is not the only one to be red.

When Louis XV, fed up with the hostility of the Parliaments to any reform policy, dismissed them, he substituted magistrates stipended to work on the desired reforms.

But Louis XVI, who succeeded him, either through foolishness, political blindness, or scruples, restored them to their privileges. And again the Parliaments had opposed the reforms, deliberately. Then the king had convened an assembly of notables, magistrates and privileged of the fortune who refused in their turn any reform and forced this one to appeal to the dreaded arbitration of the States General. The letter of convocation was sent on January 27, 1789. Camille, a candidate, was not elected and was deeply hurt by this new failure, especially since his fellow student Maximilien was chosen by the college of Arras. He therefore went back to Paris.

It is there that he applauds Mirabeau, this aristocrat deputy of the Third, whom fifteen letters of seal and various pamphlets had made famous. Mirabeau, who was looking for collaborators for his new newspaper, received the young man with his usual generosity, held him over for dinner and seduced him: "*I find myself to have become the commensal of this one...*" and repeats to whoever wants to hear that he loves her "*with idolatry and like a mistress*". And this dear friend invites him to all the dinners and provides him with a "*patriotic situation*".

Camille has gained a foothold in this world of dear deputies and powerful people of the day, this world will be his from now on if he wants it and he wants it. Then as "*it is necessary to show itself in democracy*" it speaks in the coffees, the clubs and the crossroads. He becomes the usable patriot, Mirabeau's aide. His day of glory, according to the happy expression of Raoul Arnaud, is Sunday July 12. He is at the Royal Palace on this day of social combustion, when all the brains are heated. Desmoulins stirs up the crowd:

> "*I was moaning in the middle of a group about the cowardice of us all,*" he wrote to his father, "*when three young men passed*

by, holding hands and shouting: To arms! I join them; one sees my zeal, one surrounds me, one presses me to go up on a table; in the minute, I have around me six thousand people: 'Citizens, I say then, you know that the nation had asked that Necker was preserved to him, that one raises a monument to him and one drove him out! Can one defy you more insolently? After this blow, they are going to dare everything and, for this night, they arrange perhaps a Saint-Barthélemy for the patriots.' I was suffocating with a multitude of ideas that besieged me; I spoke without order. 'To arms,' I said; 'to arms! Let us all take green cockades, the color of hope.' I remember that I ended with the words, 'The infamous police are here! Well! Let them watch me! Let them watch me well! Yes, it is I who call my brothers to freedom.' And raising a pistol: 'At least, they will not take me alive and I will know how to die gloriously; only one misfortune can happen to me, that is to see France become a slave.' Then I went down: they embraced me, they smothered me with caresses.

'My friend,' each one said to me, 'we are going to make a guard for you, we will not abandon you, we will go wherever you want.' I said that I did not want a command, that I only wanted to be a soldier of the fatherland. I took a green ribbon and tied it to my hat first."

And the insurgents beat the pavement all night long, helped by the rallied French guards, pushing back the royal army, which, having been ordered not to fire on the people, retreated to Versailles.

On the morning of the 13th, the insurrection was in control of Paris, and the government did not react.

The next day they march to the Invalides and take weapons. There is talk of marching on Versailles, where Desmoulins wants to lead the people to end it all, but a cry goes up: "*To the Bastille!*" and they rush towards this almost empty symbol of tyranny. Desmoulins is not there, but he has taken the platform and will not come down.

From then on, he published his first pamphlet *La France Libre* that Momoro, the future enraged[14], offered to publish, which made him

14. And whose wife personified on the altars the goddess Reason.

the *"first printer of the national freedom"*. Text devoid of originality of ideas but prodigious of intelligence, vivacity, sharpness of thought and elegance of style. Let us draw this praise of the freedom:

> *"It is not lowly that we adore her,* he writes. *She has a public cult everywhere... and, as Rome before Caesar was already enslaved by her vices, France before Necker was already liberated by her lights... Yes, my dear fellow citizens, yes, we are free... Listen to Paris and Lyon, Rouen and Bordeaux, Calais and Marseille... Our provinces are filled with comminatory cockades... Paris, like the rest of France, calls with great cries for freedom... We have an army enrolled and ready. This army is of more than 1 million 500,000 men!"*

But here is another text worthy of attention where our polemicist is emboldened:

> *"Brave Parisians!*
>
> *What thanks do I not owe you? You have made me forever famous and blessed among all the lanterns. What is the lantern of Sosie or the lantern of Diogenes compared to me!... Every day, I enjoy the ecstasy of some English, Dutch or Dutch travelers, who contemplate me with admiration; I see that they cannot come back from their surprise that a lantern has done more in two days than all their heroes in a hundred years. So I don't stand at ease and I am surprised that they don't hear me exclaim: yes, I am the queen of lanterns."*

Who's vaticinating like that? It is a lantern that our journalist puts in scene, the one where the first victims of the Revolution were hung. It was located at the corner of the Place de Grève and the Rue de la Vannerie above a grocery store bearing the sign *"Au coin du Roi"*. On July 14, it saw Major de Launay, heroically stabbed in the back, fall to his death, and at his feet, Mr. de Flesselles was hit in the head by a pistol shot. Then she carried in saltire the minister Foulon and the baker François.

Songs glorified her:

Ah that will do, that will do, that will do,
The aristocrats at the lantern
Ah that will do, that will do, that will do,
The aristocrats will be hanged

odes incensed him

Avenger of the French nation, avenge us
Scarecrow of villains, avenge us
Fear of the aristocrats, avenge us

This idol of the Revolution is the object of a real cult of the populace and this is why Desmoulins seizes it and gives as a title to his pamphlet *Discours de la lanterne aux Parisiens*. In this abominable pamphlet, he jokes about the gallows and joyfully proclaims himself a purveyor of death. He calls himself, with indecent joy and scoundrel frivolity, the Prosecutor of the lantern. He complains that it is left idle:

"How many scoundrels have just escaped me," she scolds. "Why was the Marquis de Lambert released? Coward, you will not escape the lantern. Why release again the abbot of Calonne, the duke of Vauguyen and so many others. The aristocracy still breathes".

As Hébert does in his *Father Duchesne* or the one he calls the divine Marat (sic)[15]: *"he marks the victims by laughing at death, he uses without truce this denunciation of which he says: 'I try to rehabilitate the word of denunciation... We need in the circumstances that this word of denunciation is an honor'"*. In that he is the faithful echo of this people of which Lamartine will say *"The people were thirsty of denunciations. Desmoulins lavished them on them. His name had risen with the anger of the people... He maintained this anger to remain great".*

For he showed his strength and many of the new political staff paid tribute to him: Robespierre, of course, but also the Abbé Sieyès, Monsieur de Castillane, de Montmorency and dozens of deputies.

15. Who will say to him one day of brutal frankness: "My poor Camille, you are the Paillasse of the freedom", *the Friend of the People* of May 5, 1791.

But this is not enough for his happiness: "*With virtues, talents, love of work, a great character and great services to the Fatherland, I can't achieve anything. I continue to sigh after a home, an establishment... Here I am thirty years old and have no other lodging than a hotel!*"

Also taking advantage of the notoriety acquired by pamphlets he decides to create a newspaper. The first number of this one appears on November 28, 1789 in the form of booklet of three sheets in octavo and is entitled *The Revolutions of France and Brabant*. It begins with a cry of triumph: "*Consummatum est!*" All is consummated! The king is in the Louvre, the National Assembly in the Tuileries, the channels of the traffic are unblocked, the market is full of bags, the national fund is filled, the mills turn, the traitors flee, the cap is on the ground, the aristocracy expires... the patriots have overcome!

It is a real popular newspaper with the right amount of vulgarity and indecency. The first one, it calls the king Louis Capet and "*that which so many grimauds call the queen, the Austrian*". Prosecutor of the lantern he requires "*in each of the 83 departments, the descent of a comminatory lantern so that the people can see the dried skeletons of their enemies and rejoice in the salutary oscillations of this pendulum*".

For he "*swore to purge the land of brigands*", sometimes "*despicable priests*", sometimes aristocrats and moderate deputies whom he asked "*to be physically killed*".

But he also called for looting "*never has a richer prey been offered. 40,000 palaces, hotels, castles, two-fifths of France's property to be shared...*"

And if the program inspires some repulsion, but the time wants it so, the writer is nevertheless, according to Geruzez: "*the most richly gifted of our pamphleteers. No one has more verve... and it has that of single, that it handles the erudition with grace*".

As for Thiers, he will say of him that he is "*the most remarkable author of the revolution, one of the most spiritual of our language*".

In fact, no one has surpassed him in mockery and repartee, in the inventiveness of his invective, the wit of his apostrophes.

And this weekly pamphlet, he writes it alone or almost, only Stanislas Fréron, the one of the *Orator of the People*, agrees to give him from time to time of the copy. And this solitude weighs on him. Moreover since he made a name for himself, is it commonplace, the Revolution seems to him close to its end.

He only wished for a seat in the new order. Now success had brought Desmoulins back into the Duplessis' salon. Madame's grievances had vanished and Monsieur had become a fervent supporter of the libellist. As for Lucile, she was now interested in him because he had that witty and lively ugliness that appealed. Above all, he was famous and like many young girls, she was sensitive to the charm that fame gave. So Camille is a serious suitor for this theatrical soul and credible for parents attentive to the happiness of their child.

The wedding took place on December 29, 1790 in the presence of Robespierre, Brissot, Pétion and Mercier in a joyful and good mood. Everyone swore to be faithful friends and eternal attachments, all unaware that the future would throw them against each other in a fight to the death.

A life of happiness began for the couple, for Lucile being well endowed, ease now organized the existence of the fiery revolutionary. But finally they loved each other so much that soon that alone seemed to count and Desmoulins announced in no. 86 that he *"solemnly gave his subscribers his resignation as a journalist".* For him, therefore, who was wealthy in 1791, the Revolution was over and he thought that *"the constitutional kingdom would last longer in France than the despotic kingdom".*

In the meantime, he plans to resume his place at the Palace, and in the meantime he leads an idle life in the Cordeliers district with his friends Pétion, Manuel, Momoro, Billaud, Danton, Chaumette, Fréron, Fabre d'Eglantine...

It was with them, when in May 1790 the districts were abolished, that he created the *Society of the Friends of the Rights of Man and the Citizen,* which became famous under the name of the *Club des Cordeliers.* The meetings of this circle composed of lawyers and people of letters often took place in the salon of Lucile, with whom many were in love, or in the charming country house of the valley of the Bièvre where these formidable agitators showed another face.

There they had given themselves candid names, Camille was Boubou or Bouli-Boula, Fréron, Lapin, Lucile, Rouleau and Mme Duplessis, Daronne. Fabre sang *"Il pleut, bergère"* (*It's raining, shepherdess)* and they all played innocent games and enjoyed country parties.

But this quiet happiness was no longer enough for Desmoulins. It was not so much writing that he wanted to do again, but to get out of the shadows. For this he had to find a patron. It will be the bookseller Duplain, one of the familiar ones of the parties of campaign which agrees to make itself "*contractor of truths*". He will thus be able to "*draw the pen of the writing board*" in company of Fréron under the banner of *the Tribune des Patriotes* which follows the number 86 of the *Revolutions.* But the style is toned down and one feels Robespierre's cockroach tutelage that curbs the polemicist's ardor.

The Tribune had four issues and its survival did not exceed one month.

Then came the day of June 20, when the people invaded the Tuileries, and those of August 9 and 10, when the deputies of the insurrectionary Commune came to the Assembly to demand the deposition of the king and the dissolution of the Assembly. It was granted to them the suspension of the monarch and the next meeting of a national convention to regulate the final form of the government.

From then on, with the Assembly out of the picture and the king isolated in the convent of the Feuillants, the way was clear for a government in which Danton and his followers occupied the leading positions "*carried (to power), according to the word of Desmoulins, by the grace of the cannon.*" Having become Danton's secretary, Desmoulins and Madame moved to the Ministry, Place Vendôme, in order to make the most of the luxury of these palaces, whose desire for enjoyment was at the origin of so many revolutionary careers. And in fact the Cordeliers, and more widely the elite of the sectionaries, had put the hand on the country and one saw them in all the posts. Buonarroti, Babeuf's companion, summed up the affair in one formula: "*Once the battle was won, they intended to offer themselves all the advantages that the nobles of the old regime had enjoyed.*"

Desmoulins, however, does not only enjoy the occasion. He works to place his friends, but he also plays with power. He is also the only editor of the official journal of the ministry, which is called *Le Compte rendu au peuple souverain.*

And the prisons were filled with traitors, real or supposed, priests, relatives of emigrants, and simply anyone who had the misfortune to displease a powerful person of the moment, or of the moment, only to be emptied a few days later in a sort of orgy of massacres, tragic outlets like those produced by the former Great Revolution.

Desmoulins in his Compte rendu makes a real apology for the crime and tries to drag the province along. In the elections that followed, the success (of the cutthroats of the party of the cutthroats and of their sponsors) was complete: Robespierre, Danton, Marat, Robert, Fréron, Fabre, Philippe Égalité, and of course Desmoulins were elected.

Such is the Convention, this idol of mud so revered since.

This election is the opportunity of glory so much awaited by Desmoulins but he does not know how to seize it. He is too much gentrified, we would say today, and knows only how to lead a life of sybarite encouraged by the futile Lucile. The new bourgeoisie of blood aspires to enjoy the power and its benefits, also one dines, one suppers, one rejoices, and one goes to the theater. In short one lives in the world.

Then the king's trial became the fashionable entertainment.

For Desmoulins: "*It is a crime to be a king*", he votes for death and attends the execution noting in his diary: "*Today Capet is killed. Everything happened with perfect tranquility*". Then he celebrated the execution with his friends by dining on a leg of venison that Fréron had killed in a royal hunt.

But he had to pay for his situation and Robespierre put the pen in his hand. In the fight against the Girondins, the next meal of the revolutionary Saturn, he launches his virulent pamphlet: *L'Histoire des Brissotins*. Thousands of books are distributed. It was a great success and very effective. It is true that Desmoulins found all his verve and his sparkling style and this irony which tears and leaves its victims alive. On May 31, 1793 the game is played and won.

It is the Dillon affair that begins the decline of the star Desmoulins. This one, a seductive general and former count, is indicted at the Convention. Desmoulins, who was a friend of his, he was infatuated with him, in a different way but with the same passion as Lucile, took his defense and obtained his release. But he had been afraid for himself in front of the suspicion of the revolutionary cagots telling him: "*You have become a suspect*".

When Brissot and his followers were condemned to death by the Terror that he had inspired and nurtured, Desmoulins cried out, "*It is I who kill them*". He knows, he feels that the Terror, barked by the excessive, exaggerated or enraged, Hebert and Cloots, Chaumette, Varlet and Roux, will turn to the indulgent ones, of which Danton, mellowed, had become the leader. Then by conviction, to protect his friends, Dillon again threatened, and himself, flattered by Robespierre who knew he needed this formidable pen, Desmoulins "*decides to leave his cabin and his armchair to take up the panting pen of journalism*" and on December 5, 1793 (15 frimaire) appears the number 1 of the *Vieux Cordelier*. The success is enormous of this newspaper whose author commits himself to "*offer to his colleagues montagnards the lessons of the history*".

And in the number 2 where the inspiration of Robespierre is sensitive, the attack against the Brissotins is renewed, but this time it is the party of Hébert which is aimed. With the same weapons *"Cloots is Prussian... Hébert is sold to Pitt".* One could think one was reading the *Humanité* of the great Stalinist era.

But number 3 is completely broken. What happened to make Desmoulins shake the yoke of Robespierre? Could the lightness of spirit of this man be a sufficient explanation? Here he lets his rebellious pen run freely, "*it is the most beautiful writing of the Revolution*" will say Éd. Fleury. For in this number 3, he draws a picture of this dreadful time without any artifice.

But for that he appeals to the manna of Tacitus, who criticizes the Roman Empire subjected to the yoke of bloodthirsty and misguided Caesars:

Let's read it:

> *"Everything gave the tyrant a bad name,"* writes Camille, *"speaking of Tiberius, Nero or Domitian. Did a citizen have popularity? Suspicious. Did he stand by the fire? Suspect. Were you rich? Suspicious. Were you poor? Suspicious. Were you dark, melancholy or sloppy? Suspect. Were you distressed that public affairs were going well? Suspicious. Was a citizen virtuous and austere in manners? Suspicious. Was one a philosopher, an orator or a poet, it suited him well to have more fame than those who governed? Finally had one acquired reputation with the war? One was all the more dangerous by his talent: Suspect, suspect."*

"The courts, protectors of life and property, had become butcher shops where what was called torture was only murder. One was struck down because of his name or that of his ancestors; another, because of his beautiful house in Alba; Valerius Asiaticus because his gardens had pleased the empress; Statilius, because his face had displeased her; and a multitude without one could guess the cause.
Denunciation was the only way to get there. One could find a host, a friend, a son, as a murderer. One had to show joy at the death of one's friend if one did not want to perish oneself. One was afraid that fear itself would make one guilty."

Certainly Desmoulins ironically warned his readers that this issue is only a literal translation of the historians. But the Incorruptible is not fooled. Nevertheless, he still needs him and he limits himself to admonishing him:

"It is necessary, he says, *to consider Camille Desmoulins with his virtues and his weaknesses... We have seen him successively the friend of Lameth, of Mirabeau, of Dillon... I urge Camille Desmoulins to continue his career, but not to be fickle and to try not to be mistaken any more about men who play a great role on the political scene."*

Number 4 is inspired by the same unknown demon, the incarnation of fate. Pushing the analysis, Desmoulins writes, neatly:

"I think very differently from those who tell you that terror must be left on the agenda, I am certain, on the contrary, that freedom would be consolidated if you had a committee of clemency... Clemency is such a sweet word, so completely forgotten! Freedom is happiness, it is justice, it is reason... Open the prisons to these 200,000 suspects, because in the Declaration of Rights there are no houses of suspicion, there are no suspicious people, there are only defendants of offenses fixed by the law!"

For the bloodthirsty icon of the republicans it was too much. He believed himself, a privileged creature, the regenerator of the human race. So he had Desmoulins attacked at the Jacobins by one of his friends and clients, the printer Nicolas.

And if the journalist, sobered up by fear, naughtily retracts in numbers 5 and 6, it is too late. He had become a suspect and would remain so. Denounced everywhere, in all the forums of the Commune to the Cordeliers who declared him *"lost child deprived of his trust and enemy of the people"*.

On 18 nivôse he was arrested as such at the Jacobins. And Robespierre, like all tyrants, asked that the issues of his newspaper be burned:

> *"It is very well said Robespierre,"* he replies; *"but I will answer you as Rousseau: To burn is not to answer."*

On the 24th of Ventôse, Hébert, Cloots, Chaumette and Momoso were arrested and led to the torture on the 5th of Germinal. On the 10th of Germinal, following an indictment by Saint-Just, Desmoulins, Danton, Delacroix and Philippeaux were arrested in their turn. They were joined by the hilarious Fabre d'Églantine.

In court, only Danton shows courage, head high and laughing, ironic and threatening. Accused of being a sellout, he replies *"a man of my caliber is unpayable"*. The other defendants are more or less pitiful. No doubt they are too familiar with the outcome that so many of their victims have experienced.

And indeed, without debate, without witnesses, without closing arguments and even less pleading, at the fourth hearing the death sentence was notified.

Desmoulins showed no heroism when he was taken to the scaffold. He had to be carried in the cart that was waiting in the courtyard of the conciergerie. Along the way, the people reviled their idols and Desmoulins contemplated, frightened, the vile crowd that he had so often stirred up. It is while staggering that he climbed the steps of the scaffold.

A few days later, Lucile followed him to the Place de la Liberté, where the executioner was officiating; in the cart where she was standing upright, she did not cease "to *talk and laugh with a young man who was standing next to her*."

The republican ogre finished devouring those who had sighed so much after him.

Édouard DRUMONT (1844-1917)
Or the Last Frenchman

In his *Anthology of Journalism,* Paul Ginisty reports that Abraham Dreyfus assured him that Drumont was a co-religionist and that his name was actually Dreimund.

The anecdote is pleasant, but when it comes to presenting or understanding the ideas and actions of a character who lived in another era, one must be careful not to be anachronistic.

Drumont should also be considered as the herald of a then vigorous current, *National Socialism,* which had its origins in the French Revolution. In the early days of the industrial era, this current attacked the evils of the feudalists of financial capital and defended small family property against the excesses of capitalism (*sic!*). Presenting his book *La France juive* to the public, Drumont said *"capitalism is to property what Cain is to Abel".*

Who was this man whose writings were so much in the news at the time?

On May 3, 1844, in Paris, in the home of Arnaud Drumont and his wife Honorine Buchon, Édouard Alphonse was born, the second child of the couple after a daughter. His paternal and maternal ancestors were "*from our region*"; the first from the North, Hainaut, and of modest origin, one finds workers, craftsmen or gamekeepers; the second from Berry and of rural origin.

After starting his life as a college tutor, then as secretary to the Chartist historian Paul Huchon, whose sister he married, he became an "*employee of the Hôtel de Ville*". He became the principal clerk, office manager of

Henri Rochefort who paints an affectionate portrait of him in his book of memories *Les aventures de ma vie.*

The family, living modestly in an apartment near the Tuileries, the real estate not yet democratized allowed then similar follies, the main distractions of the childhood of Edouard are the bright parties of imperial Paris:

> "*My young years,*" he says, in the chapter of memories of his *Last Battle, "were full of visions of balls, guessed from the street: the brilliantly lit castle, officers in great uniforms, superb, happy to be alive, believing themselves invincible, and making their steps sound under the arcades of the Rue de Rivoli, rows of carriages with crystal lanterns waiting their turn, and letting us see ballroom toilets, shoulders covered with diamonds, embroidery, gilding; in the middle of the roadway crews of ministers and ambassadors passing by, fast, raising a fine dust.*"

At the end of the Bonaparte and Charlemagne high schools where he studied, his father fell ill and did not recover until his death in 1870. The young man, who was not yet twenty years old, found himself with a heavy family burden. So he applied for and obtained a position as an employee at City Hall. But he did not have the soul of a bureaucrat and after six months, he left without any plans to return. He was tempted by journalism, the world of the Parisian newspapers being less tight than it became later, and the cronyism less sectarian, he will multiply during years the collaborations. First of all, there will be *L'Univers* of the great Louis Veuillot, Le *Nain Jaune* and Le *Bien Public* of which he is one of the most appreciated columnists. Then Girardin called him to *La Liberté.*

At the *Petit Journal,* he provided for ten years reports on highly prized salons: *"he proved to be a flexible and wise art critic"* (the *monthly Larousse).*

He is also a writer for Le *Monde, a* critic for *La France théâtrale, and a* writer for Le *Contemporain* and *La Revue du monde catholique.*

After a difficult start where he was irregularly paid and charged with tasks that were sometimes not very gratifying, his situation improved and he made enriching encounters. He became a close friend of Alphonse

Daudet, whom he met at the *Bien Public* in circumstances that he wrote about with delicate humor:

> *"It was the flowers that united me to Daudet. Spring was bringing its first joys to the streets of Paris. On my way to the newspaper's offices on rue Coq-Héron, I had bought a bunch of hyacinths, fresh from the market, of those beautiful hyacinths that have the shine of certain women's flesh with lustrous reflections, supple and brilliant. Daudet shouted with envy when he saw these flowers, still wet with the tears of the dawn, and which entered like poetry into this dark entrance hall, where everyone was already making copies: 'The magnificent bouquet,' he cried. - Would you like to take it away and give it to Madame Daudet? - This is how we became friends."*

At the same time he composed several works, including *Richard Wagner* in 1869. The war of 1870 and the defeat leave him with a deep feeling of humiliation and revolt. During the siege of Paris he joined the Garde Mobile. After the capitulation and during the Commune, he did not leave the city. He attended the Bloody Week after having witnessed the burning of the Tuileries and the Hôtel de Ville.

Then he resumed his collaboration with *La Liberté* and his chronicles and continued to devote himself to bookstore works of a popularizing or historical documentation nature. He published, on order of the director of *L'Illustration,* an opus on the National Festivals in 1879 which followed shortly after *Mon Vieux Paris* (1878), a small volume illustrated by Gaston Coindre's vignettes where the nostalgia of an irretrievably bygone era is exhaled.

He even wrote novels that are not remembered: *Le Dernier des Trémolin* (1879)*, Le Vol des diamants de la Couronne au garde-meuble* (1885).

We are at the time of the Republic of the Republicans, the Republic of the Jules. It is the triumph of the bourgeois spirit, whose motto launched by Guizot is *"get rich!"* The old dynasties and those resulting from the Revolution copulate with a decadent aristocracy. The industrial and financial capital imposes itself to the land rent and all the ideological derivations struggle to hide the sad realities of concussion of exploitation, agiotage, skulduggery, uprooting of the men and destruction of the nature (that we are going to call soon environment).

The Israelites, as they used to say at the time, the Camondos, Reinachs, Hirschs, Rotschilds, Pereires, etc., are numerous among the financiers of this opportunistic republic and, above all, they are conspicuous.

Moreover, since the defeat, the climate has been one of nationalism and the Israelites bear foreign and Germanic-sounding surnames, which makes them ideal scapegoats, since it is true that evil is necessarily foreign.

Drumont sought to understand the disarray and disorder of this unstable and unstylish regime and found a relevant answer only in the penetration of the great business Jews into the nerve centers of the system. All the more so since he was directly confronted with what he perceived as an infiltration aimed at a takeover. Girardin's *Liberté* was bought out by the Pereire brothers in order to use the title for their economic and financial interests.

At the same time, after having suffered a broken engagement, he married a woman six years older than him, he was thirty-eight years old, who died after three years of marriage of cerebral congestion on March 8, 1885. He lived quite well at the time, thanks to his income from *La Liberté.* He moved into a beautiful apartment in the rue de l'Université and continued his research in social history, as he put it, with the sole concern of not exposing himself to the vindictiveness of the censors.

It was the death of his wife, by relieving him of a responsibility, that gave him the audacity to publish his work *La France juive.* Completed in 1885, it will represent two volumes of five hundred pages each, so much so that a publisher, Marpon, associated with Flammarion, will agree to publish leaving all the manufacturing costs to the author. During the first days, twenty-five copies are sold. Then on April 19 in the *Figaro,* Magnard, probably solicited by Alphonse Daudet, devotes an article half-figures half-rejects to this work:

> *"I urge M. de Freycinet to have some excerpts read to him from a singular book by M. Drumont,* La France juive, *in which convictions that are sincere to the point of fury and sometimes fiery eloquence*

are combined with a childish credulity that welcomes without choice the flattest gossip.
The minister will see in it the kind of fanaticism that breeds persecution, and he may find in it some food for thought. M. Drumont is a scholar who has long been a distinguished contributor to La Liberté *and who has recently become editor of* Le Monde. *He seems to be prey to a particular obsession which makes him see the Jew everywhere that other monomaniacs see the police, the Jesuits or the Masons. Also, considering them a danger to France, he calmly asks for the confiscation of all the property of the Israelites, bankers or spyglass merchants. With the billions that this confiscation would produce, M. Drumont would like us to try, for the benefit of the workers, great enterprises of cooperation and participation. This is purely savage, and I see no reason to discuss such conclusions, but I would like to note that M. Drumont justifies his theory of confiscation on the Semites by that of the Republicans, on the expulsions of the religious and on the still vague projects which also threaten confiscation of the property of the freehold. It is from this point of view that his book seems threatening to me and that I see in it the germ of a Catholic socialism which would call the unfortunate to the rescue against the rich, Jews or Republicans, as the Republicans excite them against the clergy and the budget of the cults.*
I am well aware that the ideas of Mr. Drumont are his alone: however, it is impossible not to notice that Le Monde, *of which he is the chief editor, is considered as the quasi-official newspaper of the archdiocese of Paris, inspired by Father d'Hulst, vicar general and rector of the Catholic Institute. It would be extraordinary if Mr. Drumont had not consulted his friends in the archdiocese before launching a book which is not an improvisation, but a thoughtful and long-winded work. There are there the symptoms of a state of mind that will not escape anyone except our rulers who have eyes to see nothing and ears to hear nothing - FM".*

This cunning and careful article triggers the sale of what one journalist calls a "*pamphlet pillar*". This article was relayed by the great names of the time: Schall, Mermeix, Geffroy, Anatole France... In addition, two duels gave even more resonance to the advertising hullabaloo. The first one, with Charles Laurent, director of the *Paris* newspaper, forced Drumont to resign from *Le Monde, as* the Church did not allow the duel. The second with Arthur Meyer, director of *Le Gaulois,* had a great impact. Meyer seized Drumont's sword in his hand and angrily forked his own, wounding him severely. Returning sheepishly to the *Gaulois* he piteously confesses his misconduct:

> *"Gentlemen, don't applaud, I have been quite incorrect... To make people forget that, it would take a big war.*
> *"Poor Meyer,"* sighed that viper Gyp, *"he killed himself in a duel.*

Drumont, a little-known forty-four-year-old journalist, suddenly becomes famous, is consecrated as a writer, hated by some and venerated by others. Beyond the monomania that Magnard emphasized, the work multiplies the prophecies.

> *"The expropriation of society by movable capital is taking place with as much regularity as if it were a law of nature. If nothing is done to stop it, within fifty years, or at most a century, all of European society will be handed over, bound hand and foot, to a few hundred bankers."* Or again: "The Jew *Lassalle has seen how thin the intellectual base of the bourgeoisie is, whose opinions are fabricated by the gazettes."*

> *"He who reads his newspaper today,"* writes Lassalle, *"no longer needs to think, to learn, to study. He is ready for all subjects and considers himself to dominate them all. Sixty years ago Fichte, in a kind of prophetic vision, painted his readers, who no longer read books but only what the newspapers say are books, and to whom this narcotic reading ends up making them lose all will, all intelligence, all thought and all faculty of understanding".*

In spite of the declarations of many Israelites testifying *"that in spite of the attacks, we feel flattered by the publication of a work which pays homage to our tenacity, our cohesion, our strength of resistance, and which challenges our final triumph and our conquest of Christendom",* which was a good thing, what we retain is Drumont's statement on the Jewish invasion. Especially since he intended to publish a work entitled *L'Europe juive (Jewish Europe)* in which he would study it at the level of the subcontinent. This work never saw the light of day, but *La Fin d'un monde* (1889), *La Dernière Bataille (*1890) and *Testament d'un Antisémite* (1891) were published successively.

In these works, the anti-capitalist dimension is affirmed and Drumont appears as a precursor of the struggle against the "*Two hundred families*" which include many Jews, of course, but also Catholic or Protestant, royalist or republican bourgeois dynasties that he does not spare. He harshly criticizes these big people who crush the small ones: "*the great feudal system was constituted at the expense of the owners of small fiefs; the great industrial and financial feudal system was similarly constituted at the expense of the small bourgeoisie (...). The world has seen many strange regimes and burdensome tyrannies, but it has never seen anything like this: ruined peoples blessing those who ruin them, those who have raised their prodigious fortunes at the expense of millions of workers: kings honoring financiers who have devoured the nation over which these kings had the mission to watch over.*"

And with regard to this conservative bourgeoisie, he adds, "*they were not content to put themselves in the property of those they were slaughtering. They put themselves in their legend*", thus shedding light on the true meaning of the French Revolution: the replacement of a dominant class (aristocracy and clergy) by another (the bourgeoisie) and demystifying, in the company of a few others, the misleading formulas (Liberty, Equality, Fraternity) and the fallacious ideologies (those of the Enlightenment).

After the sudden and immense sales success of his *France juive,* Drumont's situation changed. If he remains bohemian and faithful to the fashion of the time of the literary gent, the overabundance of hair and beard, he becomes, thanks to his new resources, a landlord, and gives up his journalistic collaborations. He acquires in the forest of Sénart, near Daudet's house, a residence known under the name of "*house without windows*" because the wall giving on the road is blind. He stays there during the summer months and writes his books.

These are welcomed almost without reserve by a part of the press. Émile Berr, in fact, wrote in *Le Figaro* of October 19, 1888, "*one can regret, one can even hate his books, but I defy anyone to leave the home of this devil of a man without being moved by all that one has heard. One would like to say insults to him. And compliments come to your lips.*"

He was not part of the Boulangiste adventure because of his reservations, and therefore his clear-sightedness, with regard to the followers of the Brav'général and even to the latter, in whom he saw a clumsy replica of the Bonaparte of Arcole; he even published a paper in *Le Figaro* entitled *"Les coulisses du Boulangisme" (The backstage of Boulangism),* in which he recounted the maneuvers, the fiddlings and the other intrigues which disqualified this party. Among these is a young and curious character, a *condottiere* and adventurer in the noble sense of the term (explorer, entrepreneur in the Far West and the Far East), the Marquis de Morès. He founded an anti-Semitic league that offered to defend the masses against the oligarchies. Its general delegate was Jacques de Biez. To the former is dedicated *La Dernière Bataille,* to the latter *Le Testament d'un Antisémite.* Drumont became the president of the league in question. Then, in 1892, and in the name of the league, he returned to his first love, the press, and on April 20, he launched a daily newspaper with a large circulation, *La Libre Parole,* whose subtitle was a program entitled "*France for the French*".

Notwithstanding his daily collaboration with the newspaper for which he writes the lead article, the editorial, he continues to publish. Half a dozen volumes were published: *Figures de Bronze or Statues de Neige, les Héros et les Pitres, De l'Or de la Boue et du Sang* and *Vieux Portraits Vieux cadres* for the best known.

De l'Or... is entirely devoted to the Panama affair, a financial scandal involving a large part of the political personnel of the time, and to the Anarchists. This work is dedicated to Séverine, to whose charm Drumont succumbed, to the point of offering her and her companion Georges de Poildebart de La Bruyère a column in his newspaper.

In fact, it was in *La Libre Parole* that Séverine[16] launched, after Vaillant's execution, a subscription in favor of the anarchist's daughter, who was

16. An amusing anecdote, it was Séverine who inherited Drumont's copyrights and after her, Bernard Lecache, founder of the Licra, who married her granddaughter.

left without resources. The public of the newspaper is as diverse as the participants of the League's demonstrations.

The members of the Jockey-club brought by Morès rub shoulders with the butchers of La Villette of Jules Guérin. Priests and old communards were mixed together in the newspaper, whose manager, Millot, was himself a former member of the commune. The affair went well, but the audience seemed too small for the intended purpose. It is indeed a question of nothing less than creating *"one of these great currents of ideas which transform the world"*, *"we are,"* he adds, *"Catholic anarchists, demolitionists and revolutionaries. There is no need to improve this regime, which is only an emanation of international finance. There is only to undermine and destroy it... and to build in its place the true French republic".*

Drumont animates with his particular ardor all the anti-bourgeois and anti-conservative revolts of the time. The Burdeau affair is a great moment. This Burdeau, deputy of Lyon, is the rapporteur of the project tending to renew the privilege of the Bank of France. The Bank's regent was M. de Rotschild, who was very interested in this project, which was also defended in the gallery by Léon Say, who was known as the baron's front man. Drumont, Morès and Guérin organized a big meeting at the Tivoli-Vauxhall to protest against the vote on the project. This was too much for Rotschild who pushed Burdeau to sue for libel for the article, signed by Drumont in *La Libre Parole, "Burdeau and Rotschild"* in which he denounced the financial subjection of the elected official to the great financier. During a sensational trial, the court of assizes condemned Drumont to three months in prison, multiple insertions in the press and a heavy fine. This decision was taken by the president Mariage against the opinion of the jurors who signed a petition for mercy which remained without effect and denounced, without success, the breach of trust of which the president was guilty. On November 2, 1892, he was incarcerated in Sainte-Pélagie with the anarchists Michel Zévaco, Lucien Pemjean and many others. In his cell he deciphered the names of the curious tenants: Barbès, Béranger, Blanqui, Armand Carrel, Clemenceau, Paul-Louis Courier, J. Guesde, P. Lafargue, Lamennais, Richepin, Raspail, Rochefort, Taine, Vallès. In short, the gotha of free thought.

There he wrote his daily articles for *La Libre Parole,* which he signed Sylvio Pellico.

It is under this name that he will lead the campaign against the Panamists, these robbers where "*one sees in action all that has a social role: Parliament, Magistracy, Press, Learned bodies, from the Academy to the body of the Bridges and Roadways, High Bank, small savings. Among all these forces set in motion, not a single man was found to prevent the ruin, not a minister enlightened the country, not a shareholder, emerging from the crowd, organized a meeting to denounce the situation.*

You will see there the decay, the dilapidation, the incoherent functioning of all the social springs, a frightening number of newspapers having as a result to put absolutely the truth under sequestration, engineers of the Ponts et Chaussées, infatuated with themselves, exclusive, looking at themselves as the first mustard makers of the pope and unable to say a useful word in a question of works, a government of pretended discussion, of light, of control, summing up in a ministry which supports a project of lottery of 600 millions by saying: 'The government has no information, it does not want to have any.'

What will dominate, I believe, in your reflections, is the feeling of the complete irresponsibility of all those who make the big moves. Beyond one million, it seems to be the case law that one should not prosecute. As in times of deep crisis, there is a kind of lack of justice. The social machine is so out of order that it backs down in front of the big works. The victims are aware of this situation, they do not even complain."

It tells the story of this dreadful swindle whose promoter, Ferdinand de Lesseps, was beatified by an oblivious history in *La Dernière Bataille,* published in 1890. The Panama Company and the small savers who contributed their modest savings to it were plundered by the financiers Reinach and Cornelius Hertz and their supporters in the opportunist and radical parties. In *La Libre Parole* the article "*Panama, Panama!*" launched the campaign of accusations. It appears during this one that everybody touched: the politicians Rouvier, Constans and Clemenceau, among the most famous, some, besides this Lesseps, such as Gustave Eiffel... While awaiting the work of the commission of inquiry, *La Libre Parole* denounced each day a sold-out deputy. The end of this affair resembles all the others, present and past if not future, of democratic regimes. The few corrupt people who went to trial were acquitted, the others were dismissed. In his book *Leurs figures,* Barrès drew the portraits of the panamists of the Chamber and elsewhere. Nothing is more topical than this volume.

But despite the work of agitation and the effect of awakening on the readers, Drumont is not satisfied with the result. So he decided to add to his tribunes the one of the parliament. For this reason, Drumont decided to enter the Palais Bourbon. In 1898, he was elected deputy for Algiers. Three other "*anti-Jewish*" deputies were also elected in Algeria.

Drumont was an average deputy. He regularly attended the sessions but did not speak much, except to denounce the influence of financiers, Jews and others, and the manipulations of President Grévy's son-in-law (Wilson affair). This earned him an expulsion from the Chamber, carried out *manu militari,* with temporary expulsion, for having qualified, pleonasm, two politicians as "*crazy men*". He also energetically defends freedom of expression, at a time when it is still threatened, by declaring: "*I am really in favor of freedom of thought and I absolutely blame the prosecution of writers and books.*" This earned him applause from the left. The same applause when he denounced the abuses of the indigenous regime in Algeria and condemned "*the penitentiary of Tadzmith, where unfortunate people are treated like dogs*".

Following an article that seemed to excuse the assassination of President Carnot by the anarchist Caserio in Lyon, Drumont took refuge in Brussels. It was there that he learned of the condemnation of Captain Dreyfus, which seemed to prove him right.

In 1897, the resumption of the affair which saw France divided into two resolutely opposed camps marked the end of a certain *Libre Parole.* It became the fortress and the center of the antidreyfusard party. Séverine and Labruyère passed to the other camp, Urbain Gohier too. In front of the newspaper's headquarters, every evening in January 1898, the battle that took place during the day in front of the Palais de Justice continued. Cries of "*Down with Dreyfus, death to traitors*" were answered by cries of "*Down with Barbapous*", and the Dreyfusard gangs confronted those of the anti-Semitic league and Jules Guérin's Grand Occident.[17]

17. Whose symbol in reaction to the three points of the Grand Orient is the two points... "the two fists in the mouth", says Guérin.

It is this one who will be at the origin of the famous episode of the Fort Chabrol. The fact of being a deputy does not give more strength to Drumont's campaigns. The electoral obligations moreover knocked him out. But some Algerians had a dream: to see him as a senator and why not as a president. Drumont himself believed in the Élysée Palace. But the quarrel with Guérin and the fraud dissolve this illusion and in 1902 the dream of the Elysium is dissipated forever.

Drumont's friends urged him to run for the Académie Française. The novelist Marcel Prévôt was elected in the second round on May 27, 1909. Drumont was thus disappointed again.

Four years later, in 1913, he was chosen by a large majority of his fellow journalists, of all stripes, to sit under the dome. From Doctor Cabanes, the famous historian, to Laurent Tailhade, passing by the radical Édmond du Mesnil and Fernand Divoire, the inventor of the *Courrier Littéraire,* the list established by Robert de Jouvenel after examination of the votes, gives the following names in this order: Drumont, Maurras, Gohier, Maret, Clemenceau.

It was with Maurras' team, the one of the future *Action française,* that a project to buy the *Libre Parole* was envisaged. It did not succeed and it was a certain Denais who bought the title. He and his associate Bazire were Pioutists, i.e. Christian Democrats[18]. *La Libre Parole* was abandoned by many of the editors of the old guard and by its readers.

In the meantime, Drumont had met a woman divorced from an architect who wrote a fashion column by India. She had replaced Séverine in his heart and ended up getting married.

Almost blind and seventy years old Drumont does not go to the newspaper anymore. He retired near Moret in Seine-et-Marne and sent his papers to *La Libre Parole.* Ruined by the bankruptcy of the Levasseur Bank, which managed his small fortune, he can only live on the freelance work of his newspaper.

In a volume published by the editor Crès in which some of his writings are gathered, Drumont writes: "*It is not surprising that I could not succeed in a society that does not resemble the society of the past, which lives only for money.*"

---

18. From the name of Jacques Piou, creator of the Action libérale populaire.

In 1917 he came by cab to Paris to undergo a commonplace operation for his diseased eyes. He died the same day he entered the clinic where he was admitted, at the age of seventy-three. The man of whom Jules Lemaître said that he was, with Fustel de Coulanges, "*the greatest French historian*" is buried in Père-Lachaise. In front of his tomb, a red marble tomb on which is engraved a name: Stavisky!

Dessiné par Ch. N. Cochin 1770. Gravé par Ch. E. Gaucher 1771.

à Paris chés l'Auteur, de l'Academ. des Arts d'Angleterre, rue St. Jacques, maison des Dr. de la Visitation

Avec Privilège du Roi.

Jean FRÉRON (1718-1776)
Or the illustrious critic

It is a paradox, but one can see it as a divine joke, that the illustrious critic was born on January 20, 1718 in Quimper. Especially since the night had already fallen when the third child of Daniel Fréron and Anne Marie Campion was born.

Third child of the couple but fifteenth of this devil of a father who will have sixteen in total with three wives. If Anne Marie is a Breton from Pont-L'Abbé, Daniel is from Agen. He is a goldsmith by trade and of a rather modest social rank.

At first, little Elijah is not noticed for his intelligence. At school, he was even described as backward, stupid, just good at guarding turkeys. He himself would say that his childhood was not marked by any vocational trait, except to consider that the supervision of a band of turkeys entrusted to him by his parents predestined him for literary criticism. As a student at the college of Quimper, he finally learns to shine and leaves it to complete his humanities at Louis-le-Grand, an establishment in which he will then teach as a regent of the sixth form. He was not yet twenty years old.

Things then accelerated as he left teaching to enter the novitiate but left just as quickly at the age of twenty-one. What happened? Voltaire's bad tongue would say that he was "*expelled because of his misdeeds*". More simply, Fréron, who did not have the vocation, appeared in secular clothes at a performance of the French Theater. Perhaps he also showed too much independence, but we don't know and *the Anecdotes on Fréron* published in 1764 and attributed to La Haye but of which Grimm, the one of the tales, said "*that one recognizes perfectly Monsieur de Voltaire by his style, and by this particular talent that he has to say insults",* are subject to caution.

However, it is a clergyman, but again out of the ordinary, who will decide his career.

This man is the abbot Desfontaines. For this one posterity was not tender, the contemporaries either. He had a detestable reputation in the world and many see in him a forger. Gayot de Pitaval, author of collections of judicial anecdotes, denounced in a *Faux Aristarque reconnu* (1733), the errors, implausibilities and barbarisms of Desfontaines. He refuses him any original work and denounces his plagiarism: "*Mercury the God of Plagiarists is his patron*" he writes venomously. For Desfontaines' work is varied; literary critic, he is also a political translator (*Histoire du détrônement d'Alphonse VI, État de la médecine, Explication abrégée des coutumes et cérémonies observées chez les Romains, Les Bucoliques*...). Diderot will say of him: "*This journalist could have been successful during his lifetime because his malice contributed to the initiation of public malignity, but today that the aptness of his epigrams does not remain any more, who would want to waste his time to read his sheets?*" (*Correspondance littéraire,* III *386-387,* July 1st, 1757). But for Antoine Sabatier de Castres in 1778, Desfontaines is "*the Boileau of our century, who would have stopped the decadence of our Literature if Pergama dextra defendi pessent*". As for Fréron himself, he makes of him "*the Aristarch of our days*" more effective than Boileau already quoted in his enlightened criticisms of the decadence of the letters and an emeritus translator if not original novelist.

Such is the master of criticism of Fréron who, when this one goes to visit him, engages him to try himself in his periodical collection, "*Observations on the modern writings*". And our Fréron could not hope for better because the abbot knew thoroughly all the secrets and all the resources of this new art.

When the priest died in 1745, he took over and launched his first periodical. He was twenty-seven years old. His journal is called "*Letters of the Countess of****", a very mundane title for him, which he later substitutes with "*Letters on some writings of the time*".

But this early success led to a persecution which was just as much. And after having been immediately flattered, honored and praised, he was just as much chastised, threatened and even interned at the Château de

Vincennes under the pretext of not having paid a pension of a thousand ecus which he owed to some abbot.

But what was the program of the heir of the abbot Desfontaines?

It was simple: to react against philosophers in the name of religion and monarchy, and to bring back literature to the severe traditions of the 17th century. But in order to fulfill this role, he needed support. If that of the clergy was naturally acquired to him, it remained the court to gain. But the courtiers and the favorites of the queen are acquired to these new ideas, this black stream which carries all the hatreds dedicated to the old world, undermines its foundations and prepares its agony. Then Fréron turns to the queen Marie Leszczynska, wife of Louis XV to whom he arrives by his father the king Stanislas. For he is the commensal of the court of Lorraine in Lunéville and will remain so until the end despite the accusations and slanders of which he will be watered until more thirst. The king and his daughter knew all about them, they did not believe anything. And their patronage was exerted in all forms, until holding on the baptismal font the son of Fréron.

It is this protection that earned Fréron the indulgence of the king when the hatred of the beaux esprits pursued him. It was this protection that got him out of Vincennes. From then on, nothing hinders his ascent and in 1754 he founds his review *L'Année littéraire*. It will be the work and the glory of his life.

But who says Fréron thinks Voltaire and as soon as Fréron appears, Voltaire stands up.

It is to begin a small compliment of condolence to Marmontel:

"*I could not prevent that one reads in front of me the reading of a sheet which one says which appears every week, in which your tragedy of Aristomène is torn from one end to the other. I assure you that this sheet excited the indignation of the assembly, as did mine*[19]*!*"

With d'Argental, Voltaire was freer and more at ease: "*Why allow this rascal Fréron to succeed this bastard Desfontaines? Why suffer Rafiat after Cartouche? Is Bicêtre full?*"

This is the beginning.

Voltaire is in a way the enemy of the human race, but among all his enemies, Fréron is the favorite of his bile and he attacks him with a jab and a stroke, in prose and in verse:

---

19. *General correspondence*, Paris, May 1749.

"The other day, at the bottom of a valley
A snake stung Jean Fréron
Guess what happened
It was the snake that burst."

Why this hatred? Because Voltaire knew how to detect in Fréron an implacable opponent of the modernist mire. And then this kind of literature is also a genius of bad faith. And when Fréron mocks his bad comedy *La Femme qui a raison,* Voltaire writes this to the *Journal encyclopédique* in a letter whose every word must be savored:

> *"Satire in verse, and even in beautiful verse, is decried today; all the more so satire in prose, especially when one succeeds all the more poorly when it is easier to write in this pitiful genre. I am very far from characterizing here the author of* the Literary Year, *who is absolutely unknown to me. I am told that he has long been my enemy. That's a good thing! No matter how much they tell me, I assure you that I know nothing about it. If, in the crisis in which Europe finds itself and in the misfortunes that desolate so many States, there are still a few lovers of literature who are amused by the good and the evil that it can produce, I beg them to believe that I despise satire and that I don't do it."*

Then Voltaire had *Le Café ou l'Écossaise,* his new revenge play, printed and performed at the Comédie-Française on July 26, 1760.

This bad piece is as low as a police report, of which it has the spirit, for lack of the style which remains ample, and of a texture to stir the meninges. Fréron is present and if he mocks the mediocrity of the text, he affirms "*it is not me that one immolates on stage, it is the freedom of examination. To want to stifle a voice, one risks a principle*".

A fine lesson in freedom of thought and judgment addressed to one of those whose descendants will proclaim the fateful adage: "*No freedom for the enemies of freedom*". Because it is about this play, which is above all a bad action, that the father of the Enlightenment, Diderot, said: "*It is necessary to exterminate all the enemies of the Encyclopedia*". Only

Crébillon fils saved the honor of the intellectuals, who left the room saying: "*I don't like Fréron, but this show lifts my heart.*"

The latter retorts in *L'Année littéraire,* but there again, the imbecile censorship, it is a pleonasm, mercilessly strikes out his slightest banter. And it is a mutilated charge which leaves their hands. One guesses however the spirit of it by seeing there a philosophical Senate gathered to bray a Te Voltarium. But so that this simple replica appears, it is necessary that Fréron begs Malesherbes who gives his authorization by inciting the censor to "*indulgence towards this poor Fréron*".

But in one of these allusive articles in which he excelled, Fréron also pinned the Clairon of the Comédie-Française, who, although not playing, had worked hard for the success of this play. Immediately, this one, that all tyranny revolts otherwise, threatens to withdraw from the theater if one does not make justice on the spot of this "*vile pamphleteer*". Then an order of incarceration is taken against the editor of the *Literary Year* and it is necessary the intervention of the queen in person so that it is raised.

Here we have to look at Fréron, a man who one would tend to believe that in order to be so hostile to those who constituted the first league of intellectual virtue, *the Encyclopédie,* he had to be a bad man, bilious and even worse a cockroach. But Fréron was a merry fellow who lived a high life and made a feast. He was as fat as Voltaire was thin. And far from being the pusillanimous devotee that one imagines he had, before being married, lived scandalously with his wife who was none other than a very poor niece.

At his table, which he kept open, all sorts of people were attracted by his wit and good food, and an anecdote told by Marselet attests to the spirit that presided over the meals.

> *"Palissot, who was then working on* L'Année littéraire, *went one day to Poinsinet's house, to invite him on behalf of Fréron to his feasts, the most delicious in Paris. The little Poinsinet, enchanted, was full of pride and did not ask for anything better. The day is taken: in the morning, Palissot arrives at his house, his eyes gloomy, his face elongated; he announces to him that Fréron is quite ill, but that he does not want the dinner to take place any less; that he intends to give him the sceptre of criticism and to declare him his successor, in the presence of the whole society. So much tenderness and such*

a deep knowledge of his talents bring tears of sadness and joy from the eyes of the future journalist. He promises to go to the mournful ceremony; he arrives, led by his introducer. As soon as Mr. Poinsinet is named, everyone rises and shows the greatest veneration for his person. It was night then; the room, like that of a sick person, was very weakly lit; he could hardly distinguish anyone; everything marked consternation. He approached the bed of the dying man; a doctor assiduously felt his pulse and announced that he did not have long to live. A dull noise goes rolling: the doctor explains to the candidate this language; he says that M. Fréron shows his sensitivity to see him. The heart of the young poet tightens; he becomes tender, and expresses as much as he can his gratitude. He looked at the face of the dying man, he found no vestige of human form there. - What a deplorable state this great critic has been reduced to in so little time! - It is a hemorrhoidal eresipelas, retorts this one, accompanied by a hiccup; it is a frightful puffiness; his eyes, his nose disappeared; his tongue, embarrassed, cannot return any more but inarticulate sounds. I can only explain them, by the great habit I had with him, and especially by that of seeing sick people of this kind; but the head is very healthy.

From time to time, some whistles were heard, which the interpreter returned to him: they were always obliging things for Mr. Poinsinet, who, distressed with pain, answered only with his sighs. Finally after a few minutes of this interrupted conversation, deeper sounds having been heard, the esculapian testifies to the poet that the patient, feeling faint, wants to embrace him, to give him the hug, and to make him recognize for the heir of his talent to all the spectators. The designated heir bends down, and wets with his tears the cheeks of the dying man, singularly inflated. - Illustrious critic! he cries, may I fulfill with dignity the job you entrust to me! may I deserve the suffrages of the respectable company! may your last breath, passing in my soul, transmit there this powerful genius which animated you! While he pronounced these words, everyone had surrounded him; a very great brightness having spread in the apartment, and a general laughter having burst from all parts, the mystified one suspects some trick. One approaches the lights, he looks, he sees... And what? the ass of Fréron which was still sprinkled with his tears. This one gets up at once; he embraces him cordially, and on the good side. - It is done, he says to him, great poet! Here we are linked of an eternal friendship; you are of ours. Forgive this joke to a custom established among us; there is no initiate who does not undergo such a test. Purify your hands and face, and let's go to the table."

Fréron lived like his enemies, the philosophers, and this is what makes them sorry. For *L'Année Littéraire* was a success in the cultured circles and ensured the fortune of its founder.

But Fréron, in 1762, lost his first wife and was left alone with his daughter and son. In 1766 he returns to Brittany to take a second wife. She is again a relative, a cousin raised in the ignorance of libels and epigrams, of new ideas and philosophical debates. Annetic is the daughter of a tax prosecutor of Pont-l'Abbé. He is forty-eight years old, she eighteen. He is madly in love with her to the point of forgetting lunches in town and literary dinners.

He continues his activity tirelessly but the wheel turns and his adversaries do not disarm. And then yesterday's friends disappeared one after the other who protected him. Finally a lawsuit opposes him to the husband of his daughter Louise. Then, his enemies, headed by Voltaire, decide to strike the final blow and buy the messenger who carries Fréron's articles to the censor. The latter keeps them in his pocket and returns quietly to say that the approval is refused. And this infamous game lasts four years. Four years of late issues, of whole pages to be redone, in the urgency and of a lesser interest sometimes. And the disaffection of the public that follows. And the dwindling revenues. And the creditors who rush because the prodigality of Fréron does not weaken.

But the worst is yet to come. Fréron was at the Comédie-Française on March 10, 1776 when he was told that the Garde des sceaux had withdrawn the privilege of his journal. The threat was known, that Annetic tried to ward off by imploring in the antechambers of the palaces. But he did not dare to believe it. By carelessness and also because he was a fighter, valiant and passionate.

Then he takes the blow and the gout, which was the price of his intemperance at the table, overwhelms him. The same evening, he died, even though his wife had finally obtained the withdrawal of the fatal decision. He was fifty-five years old. It is the real father of the French literary criticism which disappears but also the long unequalled model of the polemicist. Certainly he is a cold polemicist, a little haughty whose palette is a little monochrome. His articles all have more or less the color of irony. But what mastery of it, what skill in its handling, what gradations of tone! And what a breath! Because his intellectual adventure lasted thirty years, not one less, in spite of everyone, and the censorship and the apostles of the freedom for oneself inclusively and exclusively. And what an adventure too, for he recognized Rousseau and Buffon, and even appreciated Voltaire like no other, and understood Shakespeare like few Englishmen.

Since the privilege of *L'Année Littéraire* was restored, it was his son Stanislas who continued it until 1790. At first he defended the memory of his father by drawing on the latter's correspondence. Then he was victim in his turn of a caprice of a theatrical cuistre named Desessarts.

For having been called a ventriloquist, the latter demanded an exemplary punishment: retraction or suspension. Rather than submit to the command of the fat histrion, he was very fat, the young Fréron, summoned by the magistrate who asked him to remove his sword, replied: "*I prefer to give back my sword than my pen*". He was then forbidden to sign in *L'Année Littéraire* which passed under the control of the abbé Royan, brother of Madame Fréron bis.

When in 1790 this newspaper became *L'Ami du Roi*, Fréron fils, who had been the college classmate of Robespierre and Desmoulins, created *L'Orateur du Peuple* with this explicit epigraph:

> *"Let the earth wake up to the sound of my voice!*
> *Kings, pay attention, People, listen!"*

L'Orateur du Peuple (The People's Orator), a horrific supplement to *L'Ami du peuple (The People's Friend)* by the immoral Marat, is an organ of denunciation and calls for murder. This earned Fréron fils a prison sentence for excessive republicanism, while his mother was imprisoned in the Abbey for excessive royalist zeal. Released, he was appointed deputy to the Convention, voted for the death of Louis XVI, and condemned the Girondins to oblivion. He became commissioner of the army and was sent to Marseilles to re-establish the republican order, where he became the executioner. Such success made him appointed to Toulon where he redoubled his murderous abjection. Such massacres, at a time that knew how to appreciate them, earned him the title of "*the savior of the South*" from the Jacobin society.

His notoriety frightened the worthy Robespierre who had his case discussed by the Committee of Public Safety, Fréron fils saved his head by participating in the plot of the 9th Thermidor which brought down the Incorruptible and put an end to the Terror. Sent again in the South to stop the royalist reaction, he shows himself more indulgent, undoubtedly disgusted by the memory of the blood he had spilled. For a while he was promised to Pauline Bonaparte, but the future ogre and emperor of the French refused to accept him as a brother-in-law.

His political life was over and he fell back into obscurity, obtaining from the First Consul only a tiny place in the administration of the hospices. In 1802 he embarked on L'Océan, a ship that sailed to Saint-Domingue. On board he found, ironically, Pauline and her husband General Leclerc.

He disembarked in Santo Domingo and died there shortly afterwards under obscure conditions. His life illustrates the adage that no man is accountable for his posterity.

Urbain GOHIER (1862-1951) or absolute independence

His real name was Urbain Degoulet. Born in Versailles on December 17, 1862, this peasant's son was quickly orphaned. He was taken in by Mr. Gohier, who gave him his name and his chance. After solid studies at the Stanislas College where he would later teach, he became a professor. Gifted as much for law as for literature and history, he also taught at the École de Saint-Cyr. Although he was exempted from military service, he joined the cavalry... which he left after a serious fall from his horse. He then became a lawyer and journalist. Although he was close to the communards, and to the miscreants, it was a royalist, Orleanist newspaper that welcomed him. His collaboration with *Le Soleil* allowed him to lead vigorous campaigns that ended with books with evocative titles: *Contre l'argent (Against Money), L'Armée contre la Nation (The Army Against the Nation), Le Nouveau Pacte de Famine (The New Family Pact).*

The editorial staff of Le *Soleil* was headed by Édouard Hervé, a supporter of the so-called "*Count of Paris*," but the editorial staff welcomed writers of all opinions, from the legitimist to the radical republican.

This explains the apparent mystery of publishing such radical prose in a conservative organ. It is true, too, that *Le Soleil* was the first major political newspaper to charge 0.5 cents.

In *Contre l'Argent (Against Money),* which will later be incorporated in the book *La Révolution vient-elle?* he writes a few lines, a manifesto of his life to come:

> *"You want to live? To live is to act; and gold is a powerful lever. Misery also gives independence.*

He is strong, the man who has a few millions. But he is formidable, the man who has no needs, who has no ties, who has no fear, and who keeps a firm soul, a lucid thought, the right eye and the prompt hand. Stay poor.

If you are deprived of the opera girls, of the mocking greeting of the lackeys, of the obsession of the parasites, of the envy of the faquins, of the betrayal of your friends, you will not miss however some satisfactions.

You will feel the invigorating jolts of anger and the strong enjoyment of contempt."

The Dreyfus affair will be the great affair of his life as a polemicist. He was thirty years old and had unmitigated ideas. He will be a Dreyfus supporter and will defend in this affair "*the truth, justice, the right of the individual, the French Honor against the Reason of State, against the traitors, against the forgers...*"

Then, after fifteen years at *Le Soleil,* he joined *L'Aurore* where he met Clemenceau. Clemenceau was jealous of his qualities as a polemicist, which overshadowed him. And then the Vendean with the mongoloid features is envious of his elegant silhouette and moustache of musketeer.

Having no more platform, he tries an individual adventure by launching *Le Cri de Paris,* which will end after a few issues.

Having signed the famous *Red Poster,* he was brought before a court of assizes and sent to prison.

After having collaborated with various daily newspapers such as *Le Matin, L'Intransigeant* and *L'Œuvre,* he launches with his accomplice Jean Drault the weekly pamphlet *L'Œuvre.* Then it will be *La Vieille France,* also weekly.

These pamphlets which welcome some famous signatures, La Fouchardière, Gustave Tery, Robert de Jouvenel... testify of the disconcerting independence of their promoter. So much so that some people wonder about his commitment to the right or to the left, given the positions he took.

He answers superbly: "*I have not changed. It is my neighbors who have changed because men change as they approach power... Having no Coterie, having with nobody a community of calculations and interests, I found myself simply the companion of those who at this or that moment supported the ideas that I always supported... In fact, I have never obeyed anything but logic and the passion of justice, which are foreign or even odious to all parties."*

He adds: *"I was a man of the nineteenth century, which animated the cult of freedom, first of the individual freedom; I cannot adapt myself to the morals and the gregarious aspirations of the new century. Between the generous soul of the 19th century and the brutal soul of this century, there is an abyss."*

So much so that after the war he took part in the journalistic adventures of the billionaire banker François Coty, *L'Ami du Peuple* among others, which were wildly successful... and had a dramatic fate since his financier died alone and mysteriously. During the Occupation he wrote for the collaborationist press, *Le Pilori* and *Je suis partant*. Judged during the purge despite his old age, he died shortly after at his sister's home at the age of ninety.

> *"Freedom, freedom dear!, poor old woman, fight with your defenders...*
> *Where the hell are they?"*

F. Bonneville del.
E. Bovinet sculp.

Jacques HÉBERT (1757-1794)
The guillotine convulsioner

Hébert is the anti-Robespierre. And the difference is not only theoretical, it is one of character, of personality, of human texture, one could say. As much as Robespierre is cold and calculating, a formidable politician according to some, a laborious tartufe for others, as much as Hébert incarnates the man of the apparatus, identified with his cause, feeding it unceasingly but living from it. And if both played an essential role in the victory of the French Revolution, both had a numerous posterity. At the end of the portrait of our hero we will have some words for his successors.

Jacques-René was born in Alençon on November 15, 1757 into a wealthy and esteemed family of the city. His father was indeed a master goldsmith, former first judge consul, alderman and lieutenant of the bourgeoisie. From his childhood we will remember what Triden wants to say about him, he was a *"kind and gracious child and a lazy and mischievous schoolboy".* Jacques-René was a schoolboy when the event occurred that an analyst would say polarized his existence. An apothecary and a doctor argue about a very accommodating widow. The argument degenerates into a fistfight and blood is spilled. Jacques-René, whose house is next door to the apothecary's, runs over and intervenes to separate the rivals. Hébert's testimony is decisive and an agreement is reached between the parties. But the aggressor, the doctor, does not keep his commitments, Hébert and the apothecary write a pamphlet, anonymous, which abuses the man of art. A complaint was lodged; Hébert and his accomplice were condemned to a heavy fine for these defamatory placards. Hébert became, in the time of the trial which lasted four years, a clerk in practice at a prosecutor's office and was ruined, and his family had to sell all its properties to settle this lawsuit. He will keep from this bitter defeat a resentment which will be the leaven of his natural sensitiveness.

Leaving Alençon where he was not retained, he went to Paris where he was attracted by the hope of a quick success. He then tried a career as a playwright which led him to a modest job as a box-office worker in a theater. There he rubs shoulders with those that *Father Duchesne* will later name "*the mirliflores with narrow breeches and square clothes and the pretty naughty girls*". Jealousy, jealousy.

While he was working at the *Variétés Amusantes,* his mother died (January 28, 1787). A last liquidation plunges him even more completely into misery. In *the "hotel of frugality",* he suffers *"from hunger and cold and lives on the alms of a friend*[20] *and on odd jobs*". Because he left his job... chased away as an indelicate cashier will say Desmoulins, with the regrets of the company will retort Hébert.

While he was thinking of committing suicide, a doctor offered him to write one of his works. *A Life of Marie-Antoinette,* more libel than biography, and introduces him to one of those factories of pamphlets against the Court which constituted the satirical background of the time. And his first writing is called the *Magic Lantern or the Scourge of the Aristocrats.* We are in 1790, Hébert is launched.

During Lent, he launched a campaign against Abbé Maury, whose role in these first months of the revolution was decisive. It is *Le Petit Carême de l'abbé Maury.* His style and system are still in their infancy, but we read things like this: "*To isolate oneself in the middle of the world, to renounce the pains of society, to live in absolute privation, such is the fate of the poor. Desires which are themselves pleasures, turn into regrets for him; the earth offers nothing, which can be his; he hardly snatches a black bread which prolongs his life and his troubles. His days are dark, his nights are dreadful; death is the only good he has a right to hope for.*"

In April 1790, he began to publish a magazine that would have four issues, *Le Chien et le Chat, a* journal in prose and verse where his republican positions were affirmed.

Towards the end of the same year, the first issue of *Père Duchesne* followed. Hébert does not have the paternity of this title. The expression

20. And the little people of the Maubert district where he lived.

Duchesne was already in the common language. Like Jocrisse or Pointu, it evoked a puppet with a vigorous language and a populace look, a potter of earth or a merchant of furnaces.

In 1789, the theater seizes it and the first publicist who exploits it is Lemaire who publishes *Les vitres cassées by the real Father Duchesne, deputy to the States General.* Big success, plethora of imitators. Lemaire then founds *Les lettres b*[21] *... patriotiques du Père Duchesne.* There will be 400 numbers.

Hébert's appeared in August, at first very irregularly with his *Grandes Joies* and *Grandes Colères,* then more regularly twice a week. He then inaugurates a kind of great reportage, which he calls his *Grandes Visites* and are some kind of commented pastiches of interviouves of great people of the moment: the countess of la Motte, Talleyrand, Lafayette...

Hebert at the time is moderate, respectful of the person of the king and even attacks *"the rascal who swore to lose me by unreasoning, to say of expert, under my name which he usurps..."* Indeed, the Father Duchesne incriminated by Hébert professed very advanced ideas.

It is after the adventure of Varennes, the attempt of escape of the king, that the Father Duchesne gives free course to his fury: *"What are we going to do,* he cries out, *about the imbecility of Gilles Capet, this big pig, who only gets drunk?"* And the old merchant of furnaces also attacks, and even more viciously, the queen *"This Messalina, this infernal fury",* the monarchs united against the Revolution:

"The Prussian Mandrin swore on his moustache that, if we wanted to pay the costs of the war and give him a few hundred millions, and two or three provinces, he would soon bring Louis Capet back in triumph over the ruins of Paris...

But we will not come to that; all the peoples will do justice to themselves. Before ten years, there will not be a king, a sovereign in Europe..." and to the National Assembly which did not pronounce the deposition of the king. After the days of July 1791, and the bloody repression of the Champs de Mars[22], during which he did not play any role, perhaps because of this moral agoraphobia of which he was affected and which others call cowardice, Father Duchesne softens his tone and moderates his polemic. It is true that he began to gain importance and was

21. Once and for all, "f" stands for "fuck" and "b" for "bum".
22. Wanted by the constitutionals and Lafayette to break the popular movement.

entrusted by the printer Tremblay with the editing of a *Journal du soir* sans réflexion and *Le Courrier de la Capitale.* And this newspaper was of moderate tendency because he had once again plundered the title, and the ideas, from a competitor. In addition, he founded with some colleagues a translation agency that produced a comfortable income. Finally, he married, he said, "*a young lady of excellent character and kindness*" who had "*quite a fortune*".

Françoise Goupil, whom Prudhomme calls "*a big spider*", was very ugly and older than her husband. Raised in a convent, she had taken the veil and when in June 1790 the law abolished the monastic vows, she left the cloister alone. Hébert met her at a meeting of the Société fraternelle des deux sexes, a revolutionary club based at the Jacobins. She was well-to-do but he was in love with her. The 600 livres annuity she received and the 700 livres pension given to secularized nuns allowed them a very honorable lifestyle.

But this marital happiness does not disarm him. During the Tuileries day of June 22, 1792, when the riot under the direction of Santerre violated the Tuileries palace and put the red cap on the king after having massacred the Swiss, he wrote that it was necessary to fill the staffs with "*good bastards like Santerre*" and invited the "*blond general*" (Lafayette) to fight the Jacobins. Because the day of June 20 showed that the palace was not inviolable; as for the person of the king it was desacralized. Also Hébert calls with all his wishes the catastrophe, moreover imminent. Hebert also reveals in his press his ideological corpus. Collectivism, in the sense of state socialism, rabid atheism and patriotic internationalism (all nations are sisters, but one must listen to the big sister that is France) define his theoretical triptych.

The tension grows between the king and the Chamber and all the parties decide to come to the hands to break with this intolerable situation. The outcome of the anti-monarchic campaign is the insurrection, not spontaneous, of August 10. In fact of insurrection, one should rather speak about conspiracy, where one finds the d'Orléans, Danton, Marat, Pétion, Robespierre, etc.

Hébert will write: "*Everything was concerted for this insurrection. The faubourg Saint-Antoine, at midnight of the night of August 9 to 10, gathered and shouted: To arms, citizens! The sections soon resounded with the same sounds and cries.*"

The victory of the insurrection sounds the death knell of the monarchy - Louis XVI is suspended! This allows the accession to power of Danton and the Montagne. The first act of the insurrectionary Commune is "*to round up all the rascals who surround Monsieur Veto...*" (*Le Père Duchesne* no 163). The second, under the inspiration of Hébert and Marat, of whom Taine said that he was "*the director of conscience of the New Commune,*" was to eliminate "*the public poisoners,*" the royalist and moderate newspapers. Freedom of the press lived.

Hébert became the inspiration for the Commune. The latter maintained the insurrectionary climate that led to the September massacres. It was an execution committee under the orders of Marat that organized the killings decided by the Commune to terrify the external enemy. Hébert did not participate directly but he wrote: "*the arm of the people has purged France of all the scoundrels recruited to slit our throats*" but also: "*Great detail of the execution of all the conspirators and brigands detained in the prison of the Abbey Saint-Germain, the Conciergerie, the Châtelet, the hotel of La Force, Bicêtre and other places, etc.*"

After recalling that Louis the traitor "*forced the people to turn their arms against him*" and that after the extermination of "*his infamous satellites*" he was taken prisoner with "*his impure race*", Hebert points out "*the indications of a new plot to excite a counter-revolution in Paris*"...

"Before leaving and rushing like a torrent against the enemy, the people wanted to purge Paris of the brigands who were infecting it. Irritated by the slowness of the judges to punish the crimes of August 10, they took justice into their own hands and massacred all the counter-revolutionaries".

"At the Abbey... all the others were torn to pieces; among them were the valet de chambre Thierry, the intendant de Bouillé, the Swiss officers, the justices of the peace Buob and Boquillon, Sainte-Palaye commanding the battalion of Saint-André; in a word, all the leaders of the League and the most deadly enemies of the people, said to number 288.

The popular arm crushed at the same time more poisonous snakes; more than 150 refractory priests were immolated in the house of the Carmelites of Luxembourg where they were confined".

This day of August 10 however sounded like a response to the provocative manifesto of Brunswick that the royalist sheets themselves vigorously condemned. But this answer did not seem sufficient in the eyes of the people who were indignant by such summons. Of the people and especially of its leaders who demanded the irreparable, that is to say the death of the king. Hébert is of those which claim the annihilation of the race of the kings and it devotes itself with enthusiasm to the mission of jailer and executioner, so much the stake seems to him determining, with his usual ferocity.

"We must reduce these man-eaters to beans and potatoes... We must raise the little cub at Mercy so that he loses the memory of his royalty; we must make a seamstress or a groomer of the little pimbêche, formerly royal, and make him know that it is much more beautiful to earn his living by the sweat of his brow than to be a posh princess...".

And, as if the spectacle of such abasement had given him only an incomplete satisfaction, Hébert asks that after the judgment by the court of August 10 "*of the tiger Capet and the guenon of Austria*", their children be struck with a punishment, of which it was reserved to the revolutionary courts to make thereafter such a broad application:

"Let that little snake and his sister be thrown into a desert island. I do not know any other reasonable way to get rid of them. My turn has come," he writes, "*to guard the menagerie of the Temple, as a municipal.*" He compares Louis XVI to "a *rhinoceros foaming with rage*" and Mrs. Veto has taken on the treacherous figure of a cat...

"The little sapajous, sired by this guenon, do little jumps and gambols to amuse those around them... but these naked b... know that we must suffocate the species, if we want freedom and happiness to reign on earth."

"This Convention so praised, walks like crayfish; a handful of rascals throws the disorder there, instead of making the happiness of the nation. It is going to give it the coup de grace, if the nation does not rise again to exterminate all the traitors. The hardest thing to skin now is the tail. Now that there's no turning back, and that the drunken Capet must be made to jump, all the capons are bleeding from the nose. What! they say, we would judge a king! What would the other nations say of us if Louis the traitor is cut short?"

Hébert became one of the official oracles of the Paris Commune. He was the substitute for Anaxagoras Chaumette, the prosecutor of the Commune. And this is an essential function in times of revolution. For he finally wins his case. The king will be executed, as stipulated in the decrees of January 15, 16, 17, 19 and 20 of the Convention. In the "*Funeral*

Oration of Louis Capet, last king of the French", but comparing the tortured monarch to a criminal, Hébert writes *"he was firm and devout until the last minute"*. But the satisfaction of Hébert is not complete: *"His wife and his b... of race still live, you will have rest only when they are destroyed"*.

His hatred of the monarchy was such that he submitted to the Commune a proposal to authorize any citizen to stab anyone who supported the restoration of the monarchy.

By virtue of his functions, Hébert influenced the Commune, which he intended to use as a political weapon in order to take power in the Convention, after eliminating the Girondin federalists, of course, but also his momentary allies from the Montagne. For the ideological corpus, which was going to identify the Hebertist fraction, is still only imperfectly distinguished from the whole coming of the republican ideas and the social practice of the most extremist of the sectionnaires gathered around Varlet and Roux. It is the theme of the constitution of a revolutionary army to exterminate the enemies from within that will be the occasion and the battle horse of the future Hebertist current. The enemy is real and the Catholic and royal Grand Army is a serious threat. But for the new bourgeois power, torn between its two tendencies, Girondine and montagnarde, another threat hovers, that of the proletariat agitated by the enraged who demand social and egalitarian measures. The men of the state apparatus and the new ruling class cannot but agree on a project that will divert the attention of the people from their own objectives. Moreover, Hébert already sees himself as general-in-chief of this army which, after having crushed the Vendeans, will be able to *"return to do the same to the Brissotins"*. But in these struggles of apparatus, after having tried to reach the Mountain in the person of Marat, it is through Hébert that the Gironde strikes again. He was arrested for six issues of *Père Duchesne*, along with Michel, Marino and Varlet, who were guilty of provoking the people to insurrection. A battle then began between the Committee of Twelve (Girondin) and the General Council of the Commune, with the Convention as arbiter. From the depths of his prison, Hébert joyfully witnesses the events of the battle.

"His great anger at being forced to whistle the linnet at the Abbey, by order of the Committee of Inquisition of the National Convention". In the same issue, he addressed his thanks to *"all the good sans-culottes who had taken his defense, and his good advice to defend their*

liberties and raze the new bastilles that one wants to raise to enclose all the Jacobins and the defenders of sans-culotterie." It was both an indictment of the Committee and a *pro domo* plea. He spoke about Isnard and his threats, about the plot lent to the sans-culottes, of which *Father Duchesne* would be the instigator: "*They say that I am a factious because I discover the factious ones...; that I am a man of blood, because I have long moustaches, me who would not want to hurt a chicken... Have I not always told you that you must respect all the members of the Convention, even the Brissotins? Let them make me appear, if they dare, before the revolutionary tribunal, I will drag them through the mud and I will come out like Marat...*"

Hébert, and his co-accused, will be freed and this one will be crowned with a crown that "*some enguenillés sans-culottes brought to me*" will say Chaumette while giving it to him. It was a triumph.

This was the announcement of the agony of the Gironde and the seizure of power by the Montagne. Hébert and the Commune were jubilant. Father Duchesne wrote in his no. 242 of the Girondins: "*They will in turn whistle the linnet*" after the arrest of dozens of them.

From January to June 1793, which saw this triumph, Hébert led the "*wide life*" that Jaurès would later claim, and hosted an epicurean society at his home, presided over by his wife. He kept an open table, where one could taste refined dishes and drink great wines. He also dined or dined out and sat in the restaurants of the Tuileries and the Palais-Royal.

And in the last days of 1793, Father Duchesne exclaims (no· 246): "*The Convention, in the end, gives birth to a good Constitution that will put an end to civil war and ensure the Republic... The law will defend the properties of the rich and will assure work and subsistence to the poor. There will be no more beggars*".

This was not the opinion of Varlet, Leclerc and Roux who, in their Central Club, called for the continuation of the Revolution. Hébert chooses his camp, he recommends "*to put himself with the Republicans who protect the property against the plunders that the Enragés organize*", but he continues his campaign against his rivals of the state apparatus concerning the direction of the armies of the Republic.

The death of Marat, assassinated by Charlotte Corday, gives him the opportunity to claim the succession and to push it to his advantage. Thus, as a worthy pupil of the master, he denounces everything and everyone at the General Council, at the Jacobins, at the Cordeliers and in the *Père Duchesne.* At the Jacobins he exclaims:

"If a successor is needed to Marat, if a second victim is needed, it is all ready, it is me. Provided that I take with me in falling, the certainty of having saved the fatherland, I will still consider myself too happy; but, no more nobles! no more nobles!"

The situation was serious. The riots continue in Paris where the famine is severe and the defeats accumulate in Vendée and in the borders (capitulations of Magence, Condé and Valenciennes). Then Father Duchesne enjoins the Convention to take henceforth its provisions so that "*not one [of the traitors] escapes the national razor"*:

"As the aristocrats have resumed their pranks in the bakeries, it is necessary that the bandits who make up the staffs of the armies be recalled and put in a place of safety, that the suspects be arrested throughout the territory of the Republic, that they be locked up in cellars or in churches, as I have already requested, and that the cannon, loaded with machine-gun fire, be fired in all the places where they will be detained..."

At the same time, Hébert denounced to the General Council a new plot of "beings with *silver marc*", to expel from the sections the true sans-culottes. They have on them lists of proscription; and, what is to be feared, it is their gold, their money, their daggers, their poisons and especially "*their affected patriotism*".

It is in this spirit and context that Hébert applies for the ministry of the interior after the resignation of Garat. His competitor Paré is preferred to him with 118 votes out of 222 voters. From then on the great anger of Father Duchesne will be unleashed against the Convention or more exactly the Montagnard faction. And to ask, the situation it is true is desperate, Toulon is given up to the English and the muscadins, young royalists, parade in Paris, the creation of a revolutionary court.

"When Rome had traitors in its bosom," he cried, *"did it use forms to drag them to the Tarpeian Rock? We want a revolutionary tribunal, but we want it to judge without forms. There are two parties in France; it is necessary that one succumbs and that the other triumphs. Let us thus form a revolutionary court in the public places... The guillotine will be placed beside the court, the sheep will be raised, the razor will shine to cut off the head, either of the guilty, or of the judge who would dare to forgive the crime."*

And the Convention submits to the demands of Hébert and the Commune, "*the Convention will be worthy of the people*" says Robespierre sententiously. This is one of the greatest joys of Father Duchesne, who shouts that the granaries of the hoarders will be opened "*by the virtue of the holy guillotine*" and that the revolutionary army will rain down on the muscadins.

Terror was the order of the day with the law on suspects, which affected all those who did not have a certificate of citizenship issued by the Paris Commune, the law on foreigners, which stipulated that in order to remain in France they had to present certificates of hospitality, the certificate of residence for religious people, etc. It even became, according to a famous word, *suspicious to be suspicious.*

During the trial of the queen, Hébert added to the ignominy, accusing her of incestuous relations with the Dauphin. For this, resolutely modern, he based his accusation on the interrogation of the unfortunate child entrusted for months to the filthy cobbler Simon. In the words of Louis Blanc, this accusation made Marie-Antoinette great by trying to degrade her, and even Saint-Just had to say:

"This imbecile of Hebert, it is not enough that she is really a Messaline, it is necessary that he makes of it still an Agrippine and that he provides her, in her last moments, a triumph of public interest".

After the queen, came the trial of the Girondins. The twenty-one appeared before the Revolutionary Tribunal even as Hébert urged the executioner to "*grease his pulleys promptly in order to make Brissot and his cohorts do the rocking*". They were, of course, sentenced to death and guillotined.

After the elimination of these, the fight to the death is prepared between Hebert and Robespierre. One of the pretexts is the atheism. Hébert encourages the phenomenon of deprecation which extends to all the departments but he does not limit himself to fight against the skullcap, he wants to replace the Christian cult with the cult of the reason. Chaumette asks that the metropolitan church be officially dedicated to this new cult. And one saw in France the multiplication of the bondieuseries of a new kind while a systematic destruction of the objects of old worship took place. And this is opposed to the cult of the Supreme Being that the deist Robespierre, to whom atheism is repugnant, wants to impose.

But the direction of the armies and the problems of supplies oppose even more vigorously the two comrades who exchange at best the accusations of concussions.

Robespierre speaks out against Heberism in terms that clearly target it with accusations of being blood-drinkers and fanatical atheists.

"What right do men, unknown until now in the career of the Revolution, have to come and seek, in the midst of these events, the means of usurping a false popularity, throwing discord among us, disturbing the freedom of worship in the name of liberty, attacking fanaticism with a new fanaticism, and degenerating the tributes paid to pure truth into ridiculous farces?"

"He who wants to prevent mass from being said is more fanatical than he who says it. There are men who claim to make a religion out of atheism. Any philosopher, any individual can adopt in this respect the opinion which pleases him; he who would make him a crime would be a fool; but he would be a hundred times more foolish still, the legislator who would adopt such a system... It was not in vain that the Convention proclaimed the Declaration of the Rights of Man in the presence of the Supreme Being..."

" ... Atheism is aristocratic. The idea of a great being who watches over innocence and punishes the triumphant crime is quite popular".

The authority of Hebert is strongly shaken and he growls like a lion in cage, drunk of impotence: *"Do not fear to put down the idol of the day... it is a crime not to unmask the traitor who covers himself with the mask of patriotism... a true republican must denounce his best friend, his father when he has reproaches to make to him".*

But he is afraid. He feels that Robespierre is only sparing him because he feels he is still too powerful. He understands that by attacking Anacharsis Cloots and by having him removed from the Jacobins, it is he who is targeted through one of his main supporters.

Then comes *Le Vieux Cordelier* by Desmoulins, whose no. 2 attacks Hebertism in the face. Desmoulins is a close friend of Robespierre and it is this one who inspires him.

Are then struck the hébertists of the ministry of the war, Ronsin, Vincent and Maillard, at once imprisoned.

At the end of 1793 and the beginning of 1794, the situation became clearer and the struggle, which had begun on the terrain of principles, shifted to that of personalities. On one side, Hébert and his followers, the

Commune, the popular societies and the sections, on the other side, the Dantonists and, further back, as observers and arbiters, Robespierre and the other members of the Convention.

Le Vieux Cordelier in its number 5 goes even further.

"*The muscadin Hébert, who knew how to disguise in such an originally grotesque way in his leaf of Père Duchesne, is one of those who draw at discretion from the national treasure under the benevolent auspices of the monarch Bouchotte. In the month of September alone, he received 60,000 livres to praise himself and his clerks. It is natural that Mr. Hébert earns his money, but the people will not be long fooled by this hypocritical juggler, who digs into his purse to raise a pedestal to his oppressors and executioners; horrible veils will be torn and Mr. Hébert will go to the guillotine.*"

And Desmoulins calls Hébert "a *contractor of counter-revolution*". The latter retorts by calling him a "*long-eared mobster*", a "*pillar of gambling dens, a dehorner of aristocratic dinners, a consulting lawyer for all red heels...*" and other niceties. He does not deny that Bouchotte bought thousands of issues of his Père Duchesne but justifies this as a revolutionary act[23].

After a long period of wavering and procrastination, Robespierre secured his leadership in the Committee of Public Safety and the Jacobin Club.

Thus, when Hébert, sensing that the situation was becoming threatening, launched an offensive in favor of a new purification, the Commune did not follow him and only one section supported him. The street itself did not move. Some sections speak of the hébertists as "*intriguers under the veil of patriotism*" and one even says that he is a hoarder.

Then Saint-Just goes up to the tribune on March 13 (13 ventôse) to read, in the name of the Committee of public salvation, his report in which he accuses the hébertists of preparing a plot against the republic:

Saint-Just has no indulgence for anyone. He investigates the trial of popular societies "*where there are too many officials and too few citizens*". Today, letters spread in the Halles ask for a king. Another class of corruptors, it is the "*household of the civil servants*". And, by this transition, he arrives at Hébert: "*What merit do you have, when you are filled with goods, when a pamphlet brings you thirty thousand pounds*

23. Bouchotte paid Hébert 60,000 livres for 600,000 copies, of which only 17,000 were to be delivered.

of income, that you oppress the citizens, that you are free and powerful?" Then he adds:

"A writing without naivety, but dark and stilted, where, by a trap set perhaps for a long time, freedom is burlesque, is it then all the merit of patriotism?... It is the foreigner who tends to the destruction of the present government in order to substitute a unique leader".

And, as the young tribune wielded willingly, on occasion, the double-edged weapon of sophistry: "*The factions*", he said, "*were a good to isolate despotism and to decrease the influence of tyranny; they are a crime today because they isolate freedom and decrease the influence of the people*".

The Hebertists and their leaders are arrested the same evening. And the people rejoice in the misfortunes of their former idol.

The indictment of Fouquier-Tinville is a masterpiece of baseness and servility. The theme of the conspiracy is served up in abundant detail to those who have exploited it so much. The conspirators wanted, by starving the people, to incite them to the massacre of the deputies defenders of liberty and to make them acclaim a tyrant whom they nicknamed the Great Judge. The English government of Pitt and the coalition powers were the leaders, Hébert, Momoro, Vincent, Ronsin and some generals, the executors. Nobody laughs to the listening of such a monument of cretinism. And on the 1st of Germinal, day of the opening of the trial, the crowd, the same one that salivated at the trial of the queen, of the Brissotins, etc., the peat and the dregs of the revolutions, in a frightening tumult filled the galleries of the Palace. Hébert, crushed, only defends himself with difficulty, but Momoro, Ronsin and Vincent are mocking and sneering. The accusation is used of all and of all the small vilenesses and basenesses which punctuate the life of Hébert (like those of all the men). The outcome is known to everyone even before the judgment is pronounced.

The condemned were supplicated on the 4th of Germinal (March 24) on the Place de la Révolution where most of them had already sent so many victims. On their passage a crowd, vibrating with joy, was pressed.

Hebert was taken to the guillotine in a state of quasi-prostration.

After the executions the crowd throws its hats in the air and shouts "*Long live the Republic*". The victims change and will change again, the cries of the rabble remain and will remain eternally ignoble.

Jules JOUY (1855-1897)
The whining poet

Émile Pouget announced his death in the *Père Peinard* of April 11, 1897: "*One of the most shapely songwriters of the last twenty years, Jules Jouy, a prolo, has just given up the ghost. Already, for two years, he had been intellectually dead; the madness of grandeur, engendered by the sipping of too blue purées, had killed his verve. He remains nevertheless one of those guys who gave a rich note of revolt. Also, as his songs are too little known, Father Peinard will have a hell of a time putting some of them under the noses of the good guys*".

The good people of that time have disappeared and those of today cultivate their revolt in private plots. Some aging music lovers and various monomaniacs may remember that his songs were performed by the greatest stars of the time: Yvette Guilbert, Rejeane, Polin, Fragson, Paulus, Marguerite Dufay, Aristide Bruant, and played on the most beautiful stages: *L'Eldorado, La Scala, L'Éden-Concert, À Ba-ta-Clan.*

But Jouy is not a simple chansonnier, even of a vigorous proletarian vein, he is much more. He is a polygraph of genius and his palette is rich in all styles and genres: the political song competes with the social song, the patriotic songs, the anti-militaristic songs, the nursery rhymes, comic songs, poems, articles, advertising texts, etc.

This pillar of the Montmartre song that his colleagues of the Butte called "*the song made man*" has truly embraced his time in its diversity, its complexity and even its contradictions.

His premature death at the age of forty-two did not allow him to experience the joys and torments of recording, which did not help to reduce his posterity.

In 1813, his grandparents, butchers in Coulommiers, settled in Bercy. His father, Jules Théodore, married in 1843 a young girl of fifteen years old, like himself, who was a butcher, and set up as an offal dealer. Louis-Jules was born on April 27, 1855 in Bercy, which was still only a village and would not be attached to Paris as part of the new 12th arrondissement until 1860.

He will live a modest, even miserable childhood, full of suffering and deprivation, which will form the humus of his talents and his revolts. After elementary school, he became a butcher's boy but did not cease to submit to his passion for reading, which would follow him all his life, with a singular curiosity for medicine and technical works.

The Commune, as for many others, will crystallize his belonging because he will never abandon his fidelity to *the Red,* making this fidelity a compass that will save him from certain ideological wanderings.

While working, Jouy writes songs that he performs in the evening in various goguettes. He eventually left the butcher's shop and worked at various jobs before offering his first texts to Léon Bienvenu's newspaper *Le Tintamarre.* From 1877 to 1879 he continued his apprenticeship and his pen became bolder. He also frequented the singing society, *La lice chansonnière* and animated its banquets by interpreting the texts of his songs.

In September 1878 he is associated with the foundation of the *Sans-Culotte,* of the draftsman Alfred Le Petit. He publishes poems, jokes and texts which beat the measure of his polemical verve. His targets are the enemies of the Republic but also the calotins and, by extension, the bourgeoisie and its failings.

It was at this time that he met Paulus[24] and obtained from him the incorporation into his repertoire of the song *"Derrière l'omnibus"* set to music by Louis Raynal. This song will be a huge success and will make Jouy a lyricist appreciated by the great interpreters. Appreciated, but not

24. Paul Habans, known as Paulus, was born in 1845. After having held several jobs he came to Paris in 1868. Author of the song "*En revenant de la revue*", which glorifies General Boulanger, he is the first singer to become a big star and to demand big fees. He was the owner of *L'Eldorado* (Nice), *À Ba-Ta-Clan* (Paris), *L'Alhambra* (Marseille). He died in 1908.

enriched; having given up his last job as a porcelain painter, he lives in precariousness despite various courageous undertakings such as the creation with the composer Marcel Legay (who is also J.B. Clément's) and the journalist Gérault Richard (the boss of the *Chambard*) of a publishing house, Aux Auteurs Réunis. While waiting for the bankruptcy, the storage shed shelters the nights of Jouy.

Jouy frequented some of the circles of the intellectual and artistic bohemia of the time, the Cercle des Hydropathes which welcomed Paul Arène, François Coppée, André Gill, Francisque Sarcey, Sapeck, and published a journal of the same name which had thirty-two issues before dying out. The Hirsutes will succeed the Hydropathes in 1881. In the same register, more political, if not more serious, Jouy and Sapeck founded in 1881 *L'Anti-concierge, an* official organ for the defense of tenants. It will have only seven issues, written by Jouy and illustrated by Sapeck. Its manifesto is the following:

"WIPE YOUR FEET. PLEASE. *When they're really dirty, on the janitor: put thumbtacks in her butter and itching powder in her bed; sow fulminating peas in her alcove and pepper in her wife's snuffbox; throw scornful glances and flowerpots in her face; Tie up by the tail twenty furious cats and a few dozen hydrophobic dogs that you will release at night on the stairs; pour salt in his coffee and sprinkle sugar on his vermicelli and tapioca; spread slanderous noises on his account and orange peels and apple peels on his path. Finally, do to him all the miseries that your indignation as an oppressed tenant can suggest to you."*

Such is the program that *The Anti-Concierge* submits to its countless readers.

One of the participants in the Hirsutes meetings, Rodolphe Salis, founded in 1881 an artistic cabaret that would become famous, *Le Chat Noir.* Wishing to organize poetic evenings, he called upon his fellow members as well as the Fumistes, another circle of the same tobacco. He also created the newspaper *Le Chat Noir* in 1888, of which Jouy was a faithful editor one year later.

It is this same year that Jouy who collaborates with the cartoonist Eschbach in *La Gazette Grivoise* founds his first title: *Le Journal des Merdeux.* A single placard will appear, which we reproduce below:

OUR PROGRAM : SHIT
Political bulletin

There are some who are for the tricolor flag.
There are some who are for the white flag.
There are some who are for the red flag.
There are some who are for the black flag.
We are for the noble standard where the noble colors of the shit shine.
The golden yellow of healthy babies' shit;
The sorrel green that characterizes the crap out of sick kids;
The asphalt of the shit of the solid men at the post ;
The Yellow Brown of Teenage Shit;
The soft brown of the ladies' shit;
The black of the dog shit,
The yellow green of goose shit;
Etc...
As for our political views, they can be summed up in these two words:
THE THRONE!
The throne, there is only that!
But not one of those unkempt thrones in one-eyed houses. No, a small, clean mahogany throne, where you can sit without getting dirty, with rabbit skins hanging on the wall, to gently wipe yourself when you're done.
Just talking about it makes our mouths water.

Jouy, who performs his own texts at the *Chat Noir,* has some success and meets Aristide Bruant with whom he writes several texts (*La fille à la mère Michelle, L'Enterrement, Mademoiselle écoutez-moi donc*) and whom he attracts to the cabaret.

It is in this same cabaret that he meets Jules Vallès, editor of the *Cri du Peuple,* who offers him to collaborate. He publishes songs under the pseudonym of Titi and Gavroche such as this *Chanson du Bourgeois*:

"(...) When we shoot the fireworks,
Not to lose a firecracker,

In the world I slip in and out,
But I always arrive too late;
I feel extreme discomfort
In the middle of the assistants ;
I don't see anything, but I'm keeping it all the same:
That's what I spend my time on.

I don't talk, lest I bite myself
After the revolutions,
I'm still on the side of order
And for all's feedback.
In Paris, as in Versailles,
To spend a few moments,
I'll see the scoundrel die
That's how I spend my time."

(*Le Cri du Peuple,* November 10, 1883)

It is also at the *Chat Noir* that Jouy will meet another dreamer of the absolute: Achille I, king of Araucania, descendant of Orélie-Antoine de Tounens, ex-avoué périgourdin and founder of the kingdom. Jouy is inducted as a Knight of the Crown of Steel.

But Jouy's great affair was Boulangisme, which he treated in *Le Cri du Peuple* de Séverine, which succeeded Vallès, in 265 texts, from December 1886 to March 1888. All the followers of the apprentice dictator, but also everything that embodies the established order, bourgeois respectability, and the brassiness of the people, are torn apart, ridiculed, etc. Nevertheless, when in 1888 part of the editorial staff showed sympathy for Boulanger, Jouy was part of the split that continued the campaign in the journal *Le Parti Ouvrier* of Jean Allemane, leader of the Revolutionary Socialist Workers Party.

There are 150 texts, almost 150 calls to murder, which testify to the author's hatred for the Bonaparte of operetta (vaudeville). No one better than Henry Barrès has said what should be thought of this literature:

"(...) He sings as the orator speaks, as the journalist writes a chronicle or an article; each of his songs is a small poem of a strange

and strong flavor that delights me. He really has the bitter, ironic and combative note; the primitive, violent, audacious and populace inspiration that comes out of the marrow of the race; he is the bard of the great vile, of a complicated, corrupted civilization, of a unique milieu, thirsty for art, emotions and enjoyments, of a society in decomposition and in fermentation.
(...) This strength of invective, this power of satire, this audacity of verse, this picturesque invention, this fighting inspiration, Jules Jouy has just brought them to a new newspaper, Le Parti ouvrier, *to a raging campaign against the dictatorship and its leaders. The fame of the general was made in songs: it is by virulent, audacious, inspired songs that Jouy works to destroy it. Can we still repeat the old saying that everything ends in song?"*

For all that, Jouy breaks the ties with some of his former friends such as Georges de Labruyère and Séverine and his long-time enemies such as Paul de Cassagnac, the famous Boulangiste pamphleteer who, in *L'Autorité,* stigmatizes the sinister rhyming of this seed of Marat. This does not disarm our rhymer who calls upon the progress of boulangisme to the ultimate resource of the republicans: the assassination.

And to write paragraph 112:

PREDICTIONS

"The day of the great riot,
In one fell swoop wanting revenge,
The People, sinister pack,
Bondira on Boulanger.
The lackeys, like the master,
All of them will be shot,
Without sparing a single traitor...
And Rochefort will be there."

The success of the Boulangist candidates in the Parisian elections was ephemeral. The announced defeat of Boulangisme coincided, at the end of 1889, with his departure from the Workers' Party for the Journal *Le Paris* where he published his songs day after day until 1891. He continued to write and sing at the *Chat Noir* and published various works including a magnificent children's album entitled La *Chanson des Joujoux* illustrated by Adrien Marie.

Jouy is a tireless worker but also an unlimited consumer of the green fairy. And the first effects of the evil that will take him away can be felt in some texts where cynicism and the macabre tone do not prevent humour.

But Jouy continues to devour life. In 1892, he went on tour with the *Chat Noir* troupe in France, Switzerland, Belgium and North Africa.

In 1895 he collaborated, albeit very briefly, with Drumont's newspaper *La Libre Parole,* to which he gave some vigorously anti-Semitic articles. The following year he took over the management of a cabaret that he named *Cabaret des décadents,* participated in the foundation of the satirical newspaper *Le Rire* and in a tour of the Association of the Chat Noir songwriters, who had fallen out with Salis.

If he knows a certain material ease, in spite of the bankruptcy of his cabaret, which enabled him to acquire a house in Aulnay-sous-Bois, with his companion Marguerite Dufay, Jouy does not think of taking off.

It is the disease that catches up with him in the form of alcoholic dementia and leads him to be interned in a clinic. He died there on March 20, 1897, at the age of 42, after having completely lost his mind, which allowed him to escape the spectacle of the drowsiness of a world that he had wanted to be revolutionary.

Félicité de LAMENNAIS (1782-1854)
Or the Babeuf of the chasuble

Who today remembers Lamennais, Lacordaire, Montalembert?

Do we know that the workers who composed his pamphlet *L'Esclavage Moderne* were, according to Proudhon, in demand of guns and wanted to march at once against the palace?

Have we forgotten the contemporary and "*The country*" of Chateaubriand?

Yes, yes, yes... Well, it's time to resurrect this giant of literary memory.

Félicité Robert de la Mennais was born in Saint-Malo, at seven months old, on June 17, 1782. He was born with a lifelong illness - a considerable depression of the epigastrium gave rise for a long time to serious concerns for his survival - from a family of the old Malouin bourgeoisie. His ancestors were sailors, shipowners, privateers, slave traders and merchants. And through the female line, exiled from Scotland for the cause of the Stuarts and of Religion (i.e. Catholicism).

A brilliant student, he learned Latin at the age of nine, then English, Spanish, Italian, German and Greek. He had a taste for music and enjoyed horseback riding. He says "*I am neither a royalist nor a companion, I am me and that's all*". In short, a young man like many, who, in 1802, wrote: "*the enemy was born in the family, one winter evening*". He then thought of leaving for the colonies to live a more exciting life. But when his brother Jean was ordained a priest in 1806, he abjured his past and renounced his future. He made his first communion, God had caught him in his net. One day he told Victor Hugo: "*I envied the life of a village priest*". So "*the privateer of God*" received the tonsure on March 16, 1809.

The following month he published his first work, a spiritual guide, a booklet of ascetic morals. Many others would follow, which he would write in collaboration with his brother Jean. At that time, he was fully committed to ultra-montanism and fought in its favor and in the name of legitimacy and tradition. The return of the Emperor, the Hundred Days, pushes him to exile in England. He will remain there only a short time, so great is his avidity for apostolic combat.

His first great work, hailed with admiration by Chateaubriand as well as by Lamartine and Joseph de Maistre, was *L'Essai sur l'indifférence en matière de religion,* which Victor Hugo himself said was "*a frightening book for the future*". It is also a great success which allows the apologist to be assigned a unique rank in the clergy which was going to allow him to exercise a real dictatorship in the Church of France. A second volume appeared in 1820 which defined the bases of a regenerative theology which postulated a philosophy of faith, authority and common sense and opposed Cartesianism and the philosophy of private sense. Moreover Lamennais wrote in *Le Drapeau Blanc* where he proclaimed his contempt for parliaments and abused the words inquisition and intolerance. In 1824, *Le Mémorial Catholique* was published with the aim of spreading the master's thoughts. Then Lamennais went to Rome where Leo XII received him twice.

This was the first of several trips during which Lamennais tried to convince the Holy See of the validity of his theological choices. But his theses offend the authorities and the ministry pursues him. Although defended by Berryer, he will be condemned, the work seized and the copies destroyed. But he continued his apostolate by creating the school of La Chênaie, a place of formation for the Congregation of Saint Peter, a new company created for the service and glory of the Papacy.

In 1829, *Des Progrès de la Révolution* and *De la Guerre contre l'Église* were published. The author attacks the monarchical authority, proclaims his contempt for the charter and invites the Church to separate its cause from that of the kings, proclaiming the supremacy of the spiritual power over the temporal. He declares himself partisan of the freedom of the press and turns to liberalism as answering a "*deep claim of the human conscience*".

It is the beginning of his detachment from the monarchic power. He soon asserts his convictions on the value of freedom in the preparation of a new society, and looks with sympathy at the popular masses that he sees as bearers of the approaching fatal Revolution.

On October 16, 1830, *L'Avenir* appears with the epigraph: "*God and Liberty*". This newspaper will last thirteen months and will have, enormous figure for the time, up to 30,000 readers. This newspaper militates in favor of the freedom of conscience, the freedom of teaching, the freedom of the press and the freedom of association. It was in this newspaper that Lamartine published his famous poem against the death penalty. Lacordaire, Montalembert and Sainte-Beuve give their take to this newspaper.

But the encyclical "*Mirari vos*" of Pope Gregory XVI curses the freedom of conscience as a delusion, the freedom of the press as execrable and liberalism as a heresy. The newspaper is thus threatened and soon the school is closed.

When he arrived in Paris in 1833, the crisis of soul experienced by Lamennais, who called the Sovereign Pontiff a "*cowardly and stupid old man*", made him resign from his position as Superior of the Congregation of St. Peter; he carried in his luggage an explosive manuscript. He renounced all priestly functions and published *Paroles d'un croyant* in 1834. It is a return to deism where he proclaims "*I was mistaken, the crucified is not God, but Jesus Christ is a great figure. [...] the true type of humanity*". Of this work, which a bishop called "*the catechism of insurrection and the gospel of anarchy*", more than 100,000 copies were sold. For a few days near the Odeon, people paid so much per hour to read it, and there was a queue. It was said that this book had "*contributed to stop the modern society in its dissolution and in its atheism*". This book will influence Hugo who transforms from now on the classical satire into lyric and apocalyptic satire, Lamartine and his *Jocelyn,* Veuillot and *His perfume of Rome,* Leconte de Lisle and his *Qaïn.*

In *The Affairs of Rome* published in 1836 the break with the Catholic system is consummated. His faith of the old days is dead forever and the author declares that he abandons the Christianity of the pontificate to follow the Christianity of the human race.

From that day on, Lamennais abandons his particle and decides to be only the moralist, the polemicist of democracy. As director of *Le Monde,* he published his *Politique à l'usage du Peuple, a* sumptuous work in terms of style and a marvelous treatise on social morality. Then comes the pamphlet, in 1839, *L'Esclavage moderne,* where the revolutionary tone becomes more intense:

"Slaves rise up, break your fetters, do not suffer the name of man *to be degraded any longer in you".* Other pamphlets followed, up to *Apostrophes à la foule: "You are sabered, shot, or like the ox at the slaughterhouse, you fall under the bludgeon of paid and patent stunners".* Eight days later, the satire was seized and the author was brought before the Assize Court. He was sentenced to one year in prison and incarcerated.

The evolution continues with *L'Esquisse d'une Philosophie* which follows *Discussions critiques et pensées diverses sur la religion et la philosophie.* Catholicism is for him no more than an ossified system of beliefs whose spectators are the survivors of a collapsed world. The Church is no more than "*the soul of the fable*" which brays for the benefit of governments, which employ it by despising it. He also writes: "*Satan, wanting to parody God, took mud, kneaded it, and then, satisfied with his work, he turned around. What are you doing here? someone asked him. What am I doing? A deputy!*"

The Pelagian of La Chênaie is henceforth a deist for whom a right which would not draw its force from the essential laws which do not die, would be only a shadow without substance and an illusion of the spirit. He proclaims that "*whoever obeys man alone is a slave*" and that "*no law emanating from man alone is binding on man*". Only religion can bind men "to a higher authority". This one must be embodied in the popular sovereignty which gives commission to the power, to administer a temporal society for the general utility. Freedom alone can therefore solve all social problems and Lamennais can declare: "*I am for no one, I am for freedom*".

During his year in prison at Sainte-Pélagie, he received many expressions of sympathy and visits such as those of Béranger and Chateaubriand. He entered prison in January 1841 and left on January 3, 1842. He publishes *Amschapands and Darvands* where he reviews the various forms of government in order to cover them with healing, or to deliver them to execration. He announces the end of all the revealed religions and of all the institutions of the past. He calls himself a Christian socialist or rather a socialist-evangelist.

At the age of sixty-six, on February 27, 1848, he embarked on the adventure of publishing a daily newspaper, *Le Peuple Constituant,* and was elected deputy for the Seine.

After the bloody repression of the days of June by the executioner Cavaignac, he exclaims: "*There is a God who will ask you for an account of so much blood*". And when the bourgeois fear of liberty leads to the obligation of a guarantee for newspapers, indignant, Lamennais scuttles his newspaper in a great cry: "*today we need gold, a lot of gold, to enjoy the right to speak. We are not rich enough. Silence to the poor!*" This last issue of the *Peuple Constituant* of July 11, 1848 appeared framed in black. 400,000 copies were sold.

He then joined the Montagne party and became director of *La Réforme.* In 1851 he left the Assembly, soon dissolved by Bonaparte. From 1853 onwards he did not leave his room. But he continued to work and wrote, at the age of seventy, an introduction to *Dante.* However, in January 1854 he was bedridden by illness. A badly treated pleurisy will be the reason of him in a few weeks.

He died on February 26, having refused the help of a priest and asked that nothing be planted on his grave.

Claude LE PETIT (1638-1662)

The scandalous poet

Little information allows us to trace the life of this libertine poet. He was born in 1638 or 1639 in Paris to a tailor father. After studying at the Jesuit college of Clermont, in Paris, he studied law. He interrupted his studies suddenly after receiving a rather strong correction. While wandering around Paris, he met a young Augustinian novice. Having quarreled one day, he killed him and then fled from France. He travels particularly in Spain and Italy, countries of which he learns the language and is initiated into their literature. He was compared to Ovid for his knowledge of the poetry of the countries he crossed. His business having been dulled by his absence of seven to eight years, he returned to Paris. He then lives from his pen, producing booklets and eulogies of authors, by the dozen, suitable to be put in the form of sonnet or epigram and madrigal, at the head of their works both good and bad. He is, in short, a public writer and a "negro" (before his time) and lives miserably. So he hastened to respond favorably to the offer made to him by a publisher to publish his volume of poems. But the police seized at the printers Eustache and Rebuffé the proofs in some sheets "*which are the beginning of a book which deserves more the darkness than to appear in front of you...*" writes the civil lieutenant Daubray to the chancellor Seguier.

In a few days he was condemned to the stake in the Place de Grève for example, that is to say for atheism and because he mocked the relations between Mazarin and the queen dowager. Among the incriminated poems is *Le Paris ridicule,* so much quoted and so little known, and a small sonnet on the death of Jacques Chausson des Estangs and Jacques

Fabry who had their tongues cut off and were burned alive for having committed the crime of sodomy.

His friend the poet François Colletet writes in his memoirs:

> *"This day, the first day of September, was broken in the Place de Grève, in Paris, after having had his fist cut off, and having made amends before Nostre-Dame de Paris, was strangled Claude Petit, advocate in Parliament, author of L'Heure du Berger, and of L'Escole de l'Interest for having written a book entitled: Le Bordel des Muses, escrit l'Apologie de Chausson, Le Moyne renié and other compositions of verse and prose full of impiety and blasphemy, against the honor of God, the Virgin and the State. He was twenty-three years old and was greatly regretted by honest people because of his beautiful mind that he could have used for things more worthy of reading."*

Few people have read this much-quoted work, but its editions are essentially known for their rarity. It seems that this poem circulates, first in manuscript and from mouth to mouth... so much the edition of this work was risky for the publisher.

The life of the poet would be unknown to us, if the unpublished Memoirs of Jean Rou who was his friend had not been discovered in 1857 in the archives of the State in The Hague. And the uncertainty reigns on the conditions of his death and the date of this one: *"I cannot say if it was in 1664 or 5 or 6, because I made a stay of almost three years in Chateaudun; I lean more for 1664* (Note of Jean Rou). I had known him, by chance, in a rather honest place *(It was at the home of Mr. Vignon, inventor of the angelica, musical instrument, participant of the lute and theorbo".* (Note by Jean Rou).

In order to underline the political and religious intolerance which characterized the second half of the reign of Louis XIV and which found its apogee with the revocation of the Edict of Nantes, we will quote in conclusion the decision of the Parliament of Paris... and the song that Claude Petit had written one year before during the execution of his friend Chausson.

JUDGMENT OF THE PARLIAMENT OF PARIS

"That the said Petit be led naked, in a sulphur shirt, with a rope around his neck, by the executor of the high justice, to the front of the main door of the church of Notre-Dame, where he is, having in his hands a burning torch weighing two pounds and being on his knees, declares in a loud and intelligible voice that, wickedly and impiously, he had composed and written and given to print the writings and libels recognized and mentioned by him in the trial, for which he would ask forgiveness from God, from the King and from Justice...
This fact, let him be led and taken to the Place de Grève, where he will have his right fist cut off, then tied to a post and burned alive with the minutes of his trial and the ashes thrown to the wind!"

(Du Tillet - President - August 31, 1662)

SONG BY CLAUDE LE PETIT

Friends, we burned the unfortunate Chausson,
He sang with a cheerful air the gloomy song
And dressed without fading the heavy shirt,
And from the burning pyre of the burning pile
He looked at death without fear or trembling.

In vain his confessor preached to him in the flame
The crucifix in hand to think about his soul:
Lying under the post when the fire had overcome him

The infamous towards the sky turned its immondo rump
And to die at last as he had lived
He showed his ass to everyone.

The crotchety poet

When you see a man with that gravity
In the hat of clabaud to walk its savate
And the strangled collar of a dirty tie

Arrogantly walking on Christianity,

Bearded like a savage and up to the kidneys crotched
A black shoe top without belt and without tab,
And a few shreds of an old buratte
At all times constantly cover his nudity,

To see each one with a haggard and squinting eye
And chewing in the teeth some fierce term
Gnawing the horn of his fingers to the point of blood,

When, I say, with these features you find a man,
Say for sure: he is a French poet!
If someone denies you, I will go and tell Rome.

Sonnet foutatif

Fucking up the ass, fucking up the ass,
Scum of the Earth and of the Sky
Devil's and thunder's blood
And the Louvre and Montfaucon.

Scum of the temple and the balcony,
Fuck peace and war,
Fucking fire, fucking glass,
And water and Helicon.

Fucking jacks and masters,
Fucking monks and priests,
Fucking up the fuck and the fucker

Fuck everyone together,
Screw the book and the reader
What do you think of the sonnet?

264.85h

Albert LIBERTAD (1875-1908)
Anarchy against the cult of carrion

"Never did he feel more offended than when a delegation of socialists from his district, led by Charles Bernard I believe, came to offer him a candidacy for general councilor in the 18th arrondissement. Very seriously, he asked these men what harm he had done to them so that they felt obliged to come in numbers to bring him such an affront."

Albert Libertad was a controversial figure during his lifetime and his death did not change anything. The ratichos, the pigskin-wearing ratichos, the ink-slingers and other forgers of the revolt attributed to him the most infamous qualifiers for a libertarian.

Jean Grave, the senile anarchist, in frock coat and top hat, refers to him as a provocateur, Henri Rochefort, though otherwise well inspired, makes him a police informer, and the sinister Louis Aragon, that intellectual bloodstain, describes him in *Les Cloches de Bale* as a lawless scoundrel.

Libertad is nevertheless a major character of the anarchist movement of the end of the 19th century and the beginning of the 20th. He illustrates sumptuously the individualist current bubbling with the hope of life and tumultuous revolt, refusing the established order in all its forms, including those of the smugglers of the revolution. In our time of pissy liberalism and chlorotic humanism, to rediscover Libertad is to renew with the free idea.

In 1875, a certain Joseph-Albert was born in Bordeaux of unknown parents. He would be the natural son of a prefect. He was raised in an orphanage, which was then called an asylum. As a high school student, then as an apprentice, and already rebellious, he was expelled and returned to the asylum from which he quickly escaped. From then on, he frequented anarchist circles that had just broken away from the socialists in 1881 and advocated *"propaganda by deed"* that tried to materialize the idea in exemplary acts. No doubt he participated in the Bordeaux newspapers of the time: *Forçat du Travail* and *Bordeaux-Misère* created by the lawyer Paul Boutin who would defend one of Ravachol's companions two years later, and no doubt he was a militant in the Anti-Workers group. In 1894 he became an accountant and was already under police surveillance because of his radical opinions. Times are hard for the anarchists of the time. That same year, Vaillant, Emile Henry and Caserio were executed and the trial of the Thirty began, in which *"anarchist leaders"* were implicated under the charge of criminal association. It is undoubtedly the difficulty of finding work because of his ideas which leads him to take the way of the capital. Rirette Maitrejean tells that he lived there first of all of alms: *"The evening falling, of the delayed passers-by met at the edge of the woods a strange being, agitating enormous clubs, and which asked for charity with a voice so frightening that one hardly dared to refuse it to him".*

It was because he was taken in by a companion, as the anarchists of the time were called, who was sensitive to the destitution of this deformed young man who made his bed on the piles of issues of the *Libertaire* founded two years earlier by Sébastien Faure. He leaves the premises when a passing companion writes to him *"it smells like the court of miracles".*

From his stay the one who was only Albert keeps a name: LIBERTAD.

Starving, Libertad went to the Sacred Heart. Bread vouchers are distributed, but he has to hear mass, and after mass the sermon. As the priest begins his homily, Libertad thunders. Clamor, hullabaloo, intervention of the beadle and parishioners. Nothing happens. The canes make reels and the word swells and vituperates the merchants of the temple. But he ends up being tied up and taken to the station. He does six months in prison: he is launched. Here is the account given by *Father Peinard,* from Pouget, of that day of September 5: *"inside the prayer box, the ratichon Lemius, perched in the gin, was preaching (...). At one point, the Lemius started drooling against the anarchists, calling them Satan's minions, scandal-mongers... and other cockroach-like nonsense. He didn't continue for long! From the heap of the heaps of rubbish emerges a shaggy guy, crutches in his fists, who claims: You are the ones who make scandal and have unhealthy ideas! You have quite a nerve! ... The vaults of the prayer factory, made of wicker helmets, would have collapsed and the bewilderment would not have been worse. The police bedlam, howling and furious, jumped on the crutch and, with as much malice as enraged cops, gave the poor fellow a thorough beating. At the door of the foul turret, the unfortunate man went from the clutches of the bedraggers to the palms of the sergeants. And he didn't find any difference! Taken to the Quarter-Eye, the demonstrator declared that his name was Albert Libertad, that he was an accountant and that he had a crush on anarchist ideas. They put him in the block! And, one of these mornings, the pals, the enjuponnés, will avenge the affront made to the ratichon at Notre-Dame de la Galette. The actors will be changed, but it will always be the same sinister comedy."*

In 1898 and 1899 he collaborated with Le *Libertaire*, which stopped and was replaced by *Le Journal du Peuple*[25], where he found Pouget, Janvion, Matha, Pelloutier, etc. During these years he worked as a printer's proofreader and spent some time in prison. Three months, for example, in 1901 for having shouted "*down with the army*" and in the company of Léon Jouheaux, the future secretary of the CGT then still anarchist. In the meantime he worked at Briand's *La Lanterne*, who, before becoming one of the promoters of *the League of Nations* (the rotten ancestor of the UN that de Gaulle rightly called "this thing") and a government socialist, was still an anarchist, and at the Lamy-Laffon printer's, where he stayed until the creation of *L'Anarchie*[26]. He also began to give conferences, such as the one in March 1900 in Belleville on Guyau's book, *Esquisse d'une morale sans sanction ni obligation.*

In 1903, Janvion founded *L'Ennemi du Peuple* with the participation of Paraf-Javal, Yvetot, the poet Jules Laforgue, Darien, Zo d'Axa and Almereyda, the father of Jean Vigo. Libertad is one of them. In 1905, encouraged by the success of the *Causeries Populaires* that he had founded in 1902 with his two companions, the sisters Anna and Amandine Mahé, he launched *L'Anarchie, an* organ of anarchist philosophy and action. The first issue was a call to the resigned. *L'Anarchie* will be the organ of the individualist anarchists that he defines as follows: "*The new force that will*

25. Created to regroup the dreyfusard anarchists.
26. It is in 1901 that he will be admitted to the Union.

liberate men when they will know how to realize it". This newspaper will never have a director or an editor and will be printed "*in comradeship*". From then on, he was involved in all the battles, writing, talking and contradicting in all the public meetings. During the legislative elections of 1906, two posters and two brochures are published: *Le Bétail Electoral* and *Le Criminel.* Libertad and his companions, Lorulot, Armand, Mauricius, Paraf-Javal, contradicted each other in numerous public meetings and polemicized with Sébastien Faure and the partisans of the haughty indifference to electoral filth. That same year he became a typographer on the day shift of the Imprimerie Dangon. This represents a turning point insofar as this more collective activity will lead Libertad to put a little more emphasis on "*mass propaganda*". Thus, on July 14, to celebrate "*the arch-national holiday*", *L'Anarchie* prints 100,000 copies of a poster *La Bastille de l'Autorité.*

During the Courrières disaster (Pas-de-Calais), where 1,200 miners perished, he wrote "*a company that refused to do anything useful to save the miners still alive in the mine and where one spends one's time in the useless gestures of the cult of carrion, is a judged company. The rescuers would deserve their names, if instead of clearing the carrion that clutters the coal mine on behalf of the shareholders, they would clear the surface of the earth of the carrion that clutters them themselves*".

But this newspaper, curious and combative, also dealt with all the issues of what is commonly known as daily life, because there was little belief in the revolution in the year 2000, and it preached immediate emancipation and the joy of living. These were also the subjects of the articles and talks given by Libertad and his companions. The influence of these ideas in a wide range of circles is striking. It goes from the practical life of free love, which was a great preoccupation of Libertad who lived successively with two "couples" of sisters, to those of processes like the counterfeit money or the burglary, known under the name of individual recovery.

These economic rebels, who refuse to be enrolled in anything, including the unions, which are denounced, with what foresight, as pimps of the labor force, are trying to improve their lot and are supported, with what panache, by the one whose apostle profile and legend are regularly swelling.

But the police surveillance is very heavy. Inspectors followed him constantly. One day, exasperated, he declares to one of them: "*I once knew a poor devil who could not do anything else but work as a garbage collector and had been hired by the corporation. He smelled bad when you came near him, but you see, I'd rather smell shit than smell a policeman! Policing is disgusting. I cannot understand that there are men vile enough to do such a dirty job."* The repression fell accordingly, that is to say heavily, on the phalanstery of the rue du Chevalier de la Barre where was located the print shop of the newspaper inaugurated in 1907. At the end of a meeting, that same year, on the theme of "The Joy of Living", organized precisely to celebrate *"the inauguration of the Machine of the Printing Office of the Popular Talks and the entry of the newspaper* L'Anarchie *into its third year"*, Clemenceau's henchmen charged the crowd attending the talk. Libertad was knocked down, beaten and hit with a saber. The cops, frightened by their own outburst of violence against what they called "*this red nest*" and its leader, left him for dead on the pavement, saying "*he's going to slap us in the hands*". The retort is superb and, during a meeting, Lucien Israël asks about the police: "*Should we kill them*?"

In order to promote the way of life which they advocate, Libertad creates the association of the "*Free Friends*" which founds a living environment in Châtelaillon in Charente-Maritime. Such attempts were numerous at the time, everywhere in Europe where naturist, vegan and raw vegan living environments were flourishing.

In the autumn of the same year he gave a series of lectures in Switzerland on the joy of life and trade unionism. On his return to France, he became involved with the companion Matha, who was accused of having been involved in a counterfeit money affair. In his speech on the "*useful revolts*", he declares "*effectively all that can destroy or lessen the authority, the property, the money, is an anarchist act [...], we accept the direct cousinhood with our comrades counterfeiters*". In this case the case was set up by the police and Matha was acquitted.

The following year he participated with Almereyda, Malato and others in a meeting on the theme of "*Revolutionary Europe in 1908*" and engaged with his usual passion in the anti-militarist struggle on the occasion of the departure of the class. A big anti-militarist conference was organized in September 1908. But the arrests follow one another and alternate with the conference tours and the beatings. It was during one of these, when the cops jumped on his chest and stomach and dragged him down the steps of a staircase, one evening in Montmartre, that Libertad died in the

Lariboisière hospital, where he had been taken, on November 12 of the same year.

This courageous crutch, this Great Pan of Anarchy, was the first to rebel against the catastrophic mysticism of the romanticists of the great night and the sordid agiotage of the electoral socialists.

"Where is his work?" asked Paul Morand one day, one of these hair-splitters.

"His work is colossal. Where is it? But in the fear that seizes you in the belly as soon as one speaks to you about him".

Honoré de MIRABEAU (1749-1791)

Or the thunder of eloquence, the Count of Bourrasque

On March 9, 1749, at the Château de Bignon between Montargis and Nemours, the Marquise de Mirabeau gave birth to a son, Gabriel. A stormy birth, regulated with irons and a worrying result: the child has a twisted foot, an enormous head of hydrocephalus and his tongue is retained by a very short net. He will have difficulty speaking, prophesies the midwife. In short a missed entry in the world and which already displeases the father. This one is a marquis, a Riquetti de Mirabeau, well if one wants to believe the family legend which claims an Italian origin, the Arrighetti of Florence. For the skeptics, the ancestry is that of the Riquets from La Seyne who were schoolmasters before settling in Marseille as manufacturers. It was a certain Lhermite de Sarliers, a genealogy maker, i.e. an artist in historical lies, who created the family links from scratch, at the price of gold.

The father of our Mirabeau let himself be called the Friend of Men. He is a physiocrat of a scientistic sect, whose great master is (was) Quenay, the king's physician, called the Confucius of Europe. At that time the sect has followers and the works of the marquis are sold in the whole Europe. For the ideas were fashionable and took part in the great revolutionary tide that was about to break. Their preaching is democratic and denounces the idleness of some privileged people, but not the privileges, the respect of the legality and the parliaments which are the guarantors of it, the absolute freedom of the trade inside and outside, the extinction of the rents... In short, a bourgeois catechism that seduced the soft-crusted aristocracy.

This father, suffering from post-eromania, a common but rarely harmless disease, had only daughters alive. A little disappointed by the appearance of his successor, he is even more so when the latter catches smallpox, which does not kill him but leaves him bruised like a skimmer, making the marquis say, about his son, *"that he is as ugly as Satan".*

On this, his mother leaves, called back to Limousin by the death of her father, Mr. de Vassan. She will remain there and will fight against the marquis, her husband, all her life. The latter then calls to him his mistress, Madame de Pailly, the black lady, who dresses only in black, whom Gabriel does not love and who does not love him.

He is an intelligent and even brilliant child who exhausts his teachers because he learns with such disconcerting ease. And he learns everything on his own: ancient and modern languages, mathematics, drawing, music, literature and philosophy and, to relax, singing, horseback riding, fencing, swimming and palmistry. Gabriel was sent to Choquart's boarding school in Paris and was thrown out. But he raises his companions and manages to return in grace. It is the first victory of his eloquence. At the same time, this line reported by Pierre Dominique situates the teenager: *"What would you do,"* said the Duke of Conti, *"if I gave you a blow?" "The question would have been embarrassing,"* Gabriel replies, *"before the invention of the double-barreled pistol."*

But as brilliant as he is, this young man suffers from the esteem in which his father is held. This inferiority complex, to the maintenance of which the marquis contributes only too much, is the key to the understanding of Gabriel's youth, if not of his life.

At the age of eighteen, to get rid of him, his father did not buy him a regiment, as was done at the time, but sent him to Berri-Cavalerie, then stationed in Saintes. There begins his real life, that is to say that he makes debts and seduces girls. He even went to war, in Corsica, against peasants who were not afraid of anything and who shot well. But he is not afraid either, and he distinguishes himself, both in battle and in the boudoir.

Then he returned to Mirabeau, where his father did not welcome him, in the hope of obtaining the purchase of a company and a pension. Of course he fails and his father sends him to the Court. Gabriel soon threw himself, like a dog in a game of skittles, into this staid and vain court. He seduces and fascinates to such an extent that Madame de Durfort writes to his father: *"Your son would dismantle the dignity of all the courts, but he is more witty on his own than the whole court.*" But he also works like a madman in the reading rooms, which does not prevent him from visiting salons, cafés and girls' houses.

At that time, one night, on the way back from one of his nocturnal runs, as his carriage, in the rue du Pot-de-Fer, skirted the wall of Saint-Sulpice, he heard a voice calling out to him and saw a young clergyman running up to him, all in a bell. "*Sir, sir*"... Mirabeau yells at the coachman to stop. "*Sir,*" said the abbot, "*may I ask you a favor?*" "*Gladly, Sir*". And the other one: "*I belong to this honorable house. I left it at the beginning of the night without anyone knowing it and I would like to get in, but the wall is very high. If you would be so kind as to have your car parked against it, I would climb it and from there I could easily reach the ridge*". "*Nothing could be simpler.*" And the abbot, with a thank you, leapt from the wheel onto the roof and disappeared like a cat.

No doubt they had told each other their names. The young man was the abbot of Périgord who became Talleyrand, and thus began a friendship which had its clouds and even its storms, but which was to last until the death of the tribune.

After the failure of a conciliation mission entrusted to him by his father and in which he anticipates, he is not yet twenty-three years old, all the richness of his oratory talents, Gabriel finds himself without a future. The career of the weapons allured him but his father refused him any money. Then there remains marriage, if the chosen party brings a beautiful dowry. Such is the case of Émilie de Cavet, daughter of the Marquis of Marignane. In spite of the reluctance of this one, Gabriel seduces the girl and tears off the consent by displaying his nudity on the balcony of the damsel, thus using the scandal as a blackmail to the honor. Marignane yields, but offers only a modest pension to his daughter.

Too modest for Gabriel who very quickly found himself burdened with debts that his father refused to cover. From then on, the only thing left to do is to put the money under the king's hand. What is it about? When a nobleman can no longer pay his creditors, he cries out for help. Then the king seizes him, the nobleman ceases to be free but he can no longer be sued. It is thus a royal guardianship which preserves to him the third of his income, the two other thirds being reserved to his creditors. This was not enough, and he was soon, and forever, placed on the list of the forbidden, at the request of his father. A misfortune never arrives alone and Gabriel must soon face the infidelity of his wife. If he forgives the unfaithful one, he leaves the castle where he was assigned to residence in order to calm down. He thus breaks his ban, heavy fault. Moreover, warmed up by an evening of drinking at a consoling mistress's, he decks the author of a cupboard, rolling in the mud his lady of opportunity. He was arrested and the police officer who came to arrest him found him composing his *Essay on Despotism.* He is locked up in the castle of If on September 20, 1774, he is twenty-five years old. He seduces a canteen girl. Then he is transferred to Joux in the Jura. But the governor of the prison is quickly suborned and Mirabeau frequents the salons of the city, even travels to propose his writings. And of course he seduced women, in particular Sophie de Monnier, the young wife of the senile former president of the Court of Auditors of Dôle. He was not her first lover. With the money from the sale of his *Essay on Despotism,* which had just been published in Switzerland, and in which he called the king "*a state employee*", he fled with his mistress and settled with her in Amsterdam. There he lived by penmanship in a relative solitude that he populated with struggles. But he never ceased to run around the pretence, taking the pretext of Freemason meetings. There is not only pretext there, because he writes on this subject in *The Memorandum* concerning an intimate association, to establish in the order of the Freemasons to bring back it to its true principles and to make it tend truly to the good of humanity; it is a plan of revolution that he establishes black on white. He conceived an international from which only the princes would be excluded and whose followers would commit themselves to collaborate to "*abolish as much as they could, in all countries, the servitude of the peasants, the enslavement of the men to the glebe, the rights of handmaidens... the corvées... the masteries, the hindrances put on the industry and the trade by the customs, the excises... the ecclesiastical jurisdictions, and to restore the freedom of the press and the religious tolerance*". Because, finally, "*provided that a man is useful to the State, what does it matter, to the legislation, what he believes?*"

He also joined his mother in the quarrel she had with her husband, and published anonymous articles against his father in *Le Courrier du Bas Rhin* and *La Gazette Littéraire*. But he is soon arrested and locked up in the dungeon of Vincennes and put in solitary confinement. During his stay he wrote many letters that the conventional Manuel published after his death and which were very successful. In them he described his conditions of detention, his physical and moral sufferings, he analyzed his situation and made numerous digressions on all possible subjects. Even today, whoever reads these letters discovers a man and a thought, a style and a will out of the ordinary.

Fearing, for example, that he might go blind, he learns to write with his eyes closed so that he can play with his handicap when the time comes. And he works, to chase away the madness that threatens, on everything: Greek, Italian, English, morals, hygiene, philosophy, he makes translations of Tacitus, Boccaccio, Tibullus, writes tales, a history of Philip II, two tragedies, a work on the letters of seal, and conceives a summary of grammar.

Then he learns of the death of his legitimate son, little Victor, and his suffering, lived in confinement, is terrible, unspeakable. It will be redoubled when shortly afterwards his daughter, whom he had with Sophie de Monnier, dies in convulsions. He did not know her, did not embrace her and will never embrace her.

After forty-two months in prison, he is extracted. For this, he had to accept the conditions of his father, negotiated by Dupont, the future Dupont de Nemours, which deprived him, among other humiliations, of the use of his name. Soon he regained his head and sought asylum in Switzerland at Neuchâtel. There he publishes his *Lettres de cachets*, which will be successful enough, so that in 1784 they stop putting prisoners in Vincennes, and some writings of less importance. Above all, he met Brissot, but also Chavière, Duroveray, Dumont and Reybaz, all democrats from Geneva in exile, who were to be his future collaborators and with whom he learned about economic questions. He is thirty-one years old and looks much older.

Then came the trial in Aix-en-Provence where he put his wife and her father, M. de Marignane, in the hot seat. This was a big game that would decide the career of Mirabeau. It is true that this is a private affair, but it seems today that it will change his image. Until then he was a son of a ruined family, a fickle and scandalous man, a second-rate pamphleteer. But now he imposes himself, without support of any kind, as a talented orator, a sensitive and painful man, a generous and powerful spirit. Facing him, he has 23 lawyers out of the 24 that the bar of Aix counts, among them the famous Pontalis. And Mirabeau, to ask to plead his case alone. His request was accepted. Then, in front of a huge audience, he will plead several times and for several hours.

When the flights of his bronze voice fall, the rooms weep or shake before the vigor and relevance of an argument, supported by an eloquence without equal. And it is a triumph.

He ridiculed those who tried to degrade him and aroused in the population an enthusiasm that would never waver. He has conquered souls and hearts. But it is not finished. On the evening of the judgment he challenged his wife's lover to a duel. He wounded him in the blood but finding the wound too light asked for a new engagement. M. de Gallifet evades. Then Mirabeau sends him two crayfish with these words: "*They find that they do not move back well enough. They come to you because no one can teach them to back up better than you*".

When the trial ended in 1783, Mirabeau returned to Paris. He had no money, no platform, no resources. But he is combative. He was under his father's guardianship, but he was entitled to the accounts, and they were false. Legal proceedings, trials, he obtains a pension. And then there are always the women, and in particular the young Henriette-Amélie de Nehra, aged nineteen, whom he makes his official mistress. And then, as he always needs money, a lot of money, and action, a lot of action, he puts himself at the service of ministers and in particular Calonne. Then, in conflict with the latter, he fled to Germany from where, through the intermediary of the abbot of Périgord (Talleyrand), he was reconciled with Calonne of whom he became an unofficial agent. Finally, on January 14, 1787, he learned a piece of news that excited him: "*I consider as one of the most beautiful days of my life the one in which you inform me of the convocation of the notables, which will undoubtedly precede that of the National Assembly. I see there a new order of things which can regenerate the monarchy. I would believe myself a thousand times happy to be the first secretary of this assembly of which I had the happiness to give the idea*". In a few words the hopes and the projects are said, the program is summarized, the fights can engage. Six days later, leaving Madame de Nehra in Berlin, he left for France.

Because Mirabeau feels that the times are close. He also knows that his pamphlets have made him known. Some porters had thus called on him to ask for his support: "*There is a man in Paris who will support you, it is the count of Mirabeau. He always takes the side of the weakest against the strongest..."*

From the outset, he commits himself and writes *La Dénonciation de l'agiotage au Roi et à l'Assemblée des Notables (Denunciation of Agiotage to the King and the Assembly of Notables)* and then *La Lettre du comte de Mirabeau sur l'administration de Monsieur Necker (Letter from the Count of Mirabeau on the administration of Mr. Necker)*. And always with a loud voice, insolence: "*no Necker, no foreigners at the General Control*" (Ministry of Finance). And he supports Loménie de Brienne against him. His words are accurate and strikingly topical. He reproaches Necker for making loans without covering them with taxes "*that is called diverting the burden on the following generations*".

In front of the crisis which swells, the riots which burst sporadically, the royal power which wanders, he specifies his thought. He believes France "*geographically monarchic*". He is thus monarchist and wants "*to combine the royal authority with the people against the privileged ones*", "*the war to the privileged ones and to the privileges, here is my motto*".

And he seeks allies. It was at this time, in 1787, when the Duke of Orleans, the future Philippe Égalité, was exiled for having sided with the Parliament against the king, that he contacted him and congratulated him for having defended legality.

In the spring of 1788, in connection with the invasion of the United Provinces (Netherlands), he wrote an *Address to the Batavians on the Statharderat*, a democratic manifesto in which he advocated the government of the people by themselves, for militias against standing armies, in a word for freedom.

In 1789, he made use of all the subjects, he invected, he exploded, he provoked, his name resounded everywhere, his ideas circulated and were discussed. He creates with Brissot the *Society of the Friends of the Blacks*, he acts within the *Society of the Thirty* whose members are all masons (Talleyrand, Condorcet, Lafayette, Lauzun...). There they prepare the candidacies and train the electoral agents, they elaborate the tactics and study the ground in view of the elections to come, this Society is, according to the word of Pierre Dominique "*the school of war of the Revolution*". He knows that in order to play a role he must be a member of the States General. Also he leaves to Aix to carry out campaign and sows the disorder. "*I ask if it is right that the two orders which are not the*

Nation (i.e. the Nobility and the Clergy) prevail over the Nation". The Third Estate cheers him, the others conspute him and call him a traitor and a rabid dog: *"Rabid dog, great reason to elect me, because if I am rabid, the abuses will die from my bite"* and also *"the privileges will end but the people are eternal".*

And he publishes; his *Secret History of the Berlin Court* sells 10,000 copies. The one whom the crowds call the Friend of the People is a candidate simultaneously in Aix and in Marseille. In both cities, and in the villages, tens of thousands of people cheered him.

He was elected in Aix and in Marseille, he chose Aix. He was forty years old and had just applied for the position of State Director.

It was in the ranks of the elected members of the Third Estate that he entered the Estates General at Versailles on May 4, 1789; it was in its ranks that he sat, from May 5, in the Salle des Menus.

Mirabeau's first political act was to found his own newspaper: *Le Journal des États généraux,* without authorization. The government of Necker forbids it. Mirabeau criticizes *"a so-called popular ministry that brazenly dares to put the seals on the thought".* The Parliament supports him, the government gives in. Immediately twenty newspapers appear. He founded the freedom of the press.

Then comes the quarrel about the way to name the Assembly. Sieyès proposes: Assembly of the known and verified representatives of the French Nation. Mirabeau: Assembly of the representatives of the people. But this word "people" offends the bourgeois of the Third Estate who only aspire to inherit the privileges of their predecessors of the nobility and the clergy.

Then Mirabeau thunders:

> *"Yes, it is because the name of the people is not respected enough in France, because it is obscured, covered with the rust of prejudice, because it presents us with an idea of which pride is alarmed and vanity revolts, because it is pronounced with contempt in the chambers of the aristocrats, it is for this very reason, Gentlemen, that I would like, it is for this very reason that we must impose upon ourselves not only to raise it, but to ennoble it, to make it henceforth respectable to the ministers and dear to all hearts... Do you not see that the name of representatives of the people is necessary for you*

because it attaches you to the people, this imposing mass without which you would be only individuals, weak reeds that would be broken one by one? Don't you see that you need the name of the people, because it lets the people know that we have linked our fate to theirs; this will teach them to rest all their thoughts and hopes on us. More skilful than us, the Batavian heroes who founded the liberty of their country, took the name of 'beggars'; they only wanted this title because the contempt of their tyrants had pretended to wither them of it; and this title, by attaching to them this immense class that aristocracy and despotism debased, was at the same time their strength, their glory and the pledge of their success. The friends of liberty choose the name that serves them best, not the one that flatters them most; they will call themselves remonstrators in America, shepherds in Switzerland, beggars in the Netherlands; they will adorn themselves with the insults of their enemies; they will take away the power to humiliate them, with expressions of which they will have known how to honor themselves."

It is the word of *"National Assembly"* which will triumph, proposed in fine by Sieyès, but it is of Mirabeau.

With all this Mirabeau is not yet in front of the stage. A storm was needed, and it broke out on June 23. The king wants to disperse the deputies of the third and other orders and enjoins them to meet as of the following day in the places assigned to their order. Clergy and nobility obeyed. The third order did not move. This is the real beginning of the revolution. Then the king sends M. de Dreux-Brézé to renew his injunction. Mirabeau rushes towards him and thunders: "*Go and tell those who send you that we are here by the will of the people and that we will only get out by the power of bayonets*". The king gives in and surrenders: "*They want to stay? Well, damn, let them stay!*"

His newspaper was very successful and Mirabeau launched his *Courrier de Provence* which reported on the work and debates of the Assembly.

He is in contact with the advances and newspapers of the left (Desmoulins, Danton...) and always pursues his objective: to be called to the ministry to wrest the king from the nobles, the clergy and the parlements. For that, he defends the right to absolute veto of the king because "*he wants to revive the executive power, to regenerate the royal authority and to reconcile it with the national authority".* Moreover this right of veto does not put in question the essential, the constitution, guarantor of the fundamental rights of the people. To that a fundamental reason:

> *"We are not savages arriving naked from the banks of the Orinoco to form a Society. We are an old Nation, and probably too old for our time. We have a pre-existing government, a pre-existing king, pre-existing prejudices. We must, as far as possible, match all things to the revolution, and save the suddenness of the passage. It is necessary, until it results from this tolerance a political violation of the principles of the national freedom, an absolute dissonance in the social order. But if the old order of things and the new one leave a gap, it is necessary to cross the step, to raise the veil and to walk".*

This shows us a wise, temperate Mirabeau, a reformer rather than a revolutionary. As such, he faced a double mistrust: that of the conservatives and the king, and that of the clubs.

Much has been said about the connections between the Duke of Orleans and Mirabeau. If it is assured that Danton is paid by Philippe, if Laclos (Choderlos de) affirms that there is liaison between the duke and the deputy of Aix, and Lafayette, that this one "*was very before in the secrets*" of the Orleanist plot, Mirabeau himself speaking about the duke is very explicit: "*If it is necessary a dummy, as much this idiot as another*". Because he fights for the crown, that is to say for a principle and not for a man. That's why they don't want him at the ministry, especially the queen whose influence on her husband is well known. He frightens some and frightens the others, only the French according to the word of Goethe "*look at Mirabeau as their Hercules and they are perfectly right*". He knows it, even if he refuses to admit it, he will not be a minister and his only power will be the one given by the tribune. So he is admired, adored, listened to like an oracle... except for the royalist pamphlets which overwhelm him: *L'Ami du Roi* by Royon and *Les Actes des Apôtres* by Peltier and *L'Orateur du Peuple* by Fréron and *L'Ami du Peuple* by Marat on the other side.

But he fears so much the despotism of assembly, premonitory sight and that nothing in the continuation of the centuries does not deny, that he pursues his advances near the court.

He was granted on July 2, 1790. Marie-Antoinette is seduced but he is even more seduced: "*Madam, the monarchy is saved*" he cries at the end of the audience. And he believes it. But the libels, anonymous or not, denounce the interview between the "*French Cromwell and the king*", his ambitions and his duplicity and they threaten him with the lantern. No matter, he did not give in and after having overthrown Necker in August, he frankly put forward his candidacy for the leadership of the state. The king hesitated between Lafayette and Mirabeau and then rejected the idea of calling upon Mirabeau. Then this one proposes a secret ministry accentuating his role of occult adviser. They are too badly surrounded and too stupid, they refuse. The king prefers mediocre courtiers, reflection of the nullity of a formerly brilliant monarchy. He is too much afraid, and too much contempt of the new ideas and wants only to finish with the Revolution. Mirabeau has this word: "*Royal cattle*". Mirabeau continues to work: intervention in the Assembly, notes to the Court in the form of political letters very neat, very thorough, immense correspondence and then, always, the dinners.

> *"In my life, I have never had a more pleasant meal than at Mirabeau's. His dining room was unlike any other man's. Of the four sides of this room, one had a rich and elegant sideboard worked with refined taste with antique vases filled with exquisite things. One side was a library of beautifully bound books and rare editions. One side was covered with paintings depicting the pleasures of the table and the fourth side was lined with rare prints on the same subject.*
>
> *Mirabeau, having noticed that meals with the most interesting men often become insipid because of the reserve that one must command by the presence of ignorant and often unfaithful servants, and more often reporting askew the remarks made at table, had imagined a way to protect himself from this misfortune. At his house, one had nothing to fear in this respect, one could give oneself up to the pleasure of the freest conversation and the boldest remarks, because there was not a single servant. When the table was served, one entered the dining room. One sat at the table without ceremony, and between the guests were placed servants with four levels covered with bottles, plates, glasses, services, so that each one served himself at will.*

The first service being eaten, Mirabeau rang the bell and then one suspended the speeches. Three valets would take away the empty dishes in a moment and three other valets would replace them in a moment by as many dishes forming the second service, and the valets would disappear in a moment. It was the same at the end of the second service, for the dessert at the end of which Mirabeau rang again to warn that one prepared the coffee and the liquors and two minutes after one rose from the table to enter another room where, without the presence of any servant, one took the coffee and the liquors".

Mirabeau is sick, a kind of dysentery weakens his body that the doctors of the time abuse even more by bleeding him abundantly. But he continued to fight, to fight and to live. His greatest struggle, in which he testifies to his unwavering commitment to the freedom of the individual, is his fight against the law on emigration. And yet his enemies do not disarm. Marat accuses him of frequenting gambling houses, but he accuses everyone, Bailly, Lafayette, de Cazalès... Above all, the strongest accusation is that he is the king's man. And it is true. In this context occurs a decisive incident. The aunts of the king, Mesdames Victoire and Adélaïde, refusing the masses served by the sworn priests, leave the kingdom to go to Rome. Immediately the rumor spreads that the king will follow. Marat barks that they take twelve million gold and the Dauphin in their skirts. In Paris demonstrations broke out and on the 21st they were arrested in Arnay-le-Duc. Mirabeau declared: "*They were free to leave*". He knew that it was dangerous to defend such a thesis, because the Assembly charged his Constitution Committee with drafting a law against emigrants. Paris is in turmoil. The people try to force the palace, invade gardens and courtyards. The Committee wants to introduce a bill prohibiting emigration. Mirabeau, the "*minister of Paris*" according to the word of Desmoulins, protests:

"One must be happy in your states, Sire; give the freedom to expatriate oneself to anyone who is not held back in a legal manner by particular obligations: give by a formal edict this freedom... A law of emancipation, far from scattering men, will keep them in what they will then call their good country, and which they will prefer to

the most fertile countries; for man endures everything on the part of Providence; he endures nothing unjust on the part of his fellow man; and if he submits, it is only with a revolted heart (a large part of the Assembly applauds). The man does not hold by roots to the ground; thus he does not belong to the ground. Man is not a field, a meadow, a cattle; thus he cannot be a property. Man has a prior sense of these simple truths; thus he cannot be persuaded that his leaders have the right to chain him to the soil."

But the left, supported on the tribunes, is relentless and proposes that a committee decides "*on the right of exit of the kingdom*" under penalty of being deprived of the nationality and of the confiscation of the incomes and the goods. Mirabeau insists, he shouts that the law is barbaric:

"I declare that I will believe myself released from all oaths of fidelity to those who would have the infamy to appoint a dictatorial commission. The popularity that I have aspired to and which I have had the honor of enjoying like any other, is not a weak reed, it is in the earth that I want to sink its roots on the imperturbable reason of reason and freedom... If you make a law against the emigrants I swear never to obey it".

Lafayette will say it: "*Mirabeau was never greater than in this discussion*". The debate will continue in the Jacobin club; there too it raises the enthusiasm but there again it will be defeated. The Revolution shows its new face, it is time that he disappears. On leaving the club on the 28th, he says: "*I have just pronounced my death warrant. It is done with me. They will kill me*". But he continues to live. Brissot tells that a few days before his death he spent a night in the arms of two dancers of the Opera: the Canlon and the Heilsberg. A frenetic night to the great satisfaction of the two Amazons. However, his strength diminished, both physically and mentally.

He has always had a premonition of an untimely end. He is getting heavier. The forces decrease. The face becomes earthy. He digests badly. He is melancholic, discouraged. He asks everyone for epitaphs. He sees things in black. "*They wanted to rule the king instead of ruling by him,*" he says, "*but soon it will not be them or him who rule; a vile fraction will rule them all and cover France with horrors.*"

His agony, in spite of the diligent and impotent care of the great doctor Cabanis, is dreadful. The care of the time was a kind of euthanasia that did not know itself, bloodletting, cantharide sinapisms and other random medications. After several days of such treatments, Mirabeau died. If some suspected poison, there is every reason to believe that he had killed himself from misery, work and pleasure.

He was buried in the Pantheon and enjoyed the admiration of the crowds for months.

But, when seventeen months later, the opening of the iron cabinet reveals his collusion with the king, the Thermidorian Convention, that elegant collection of garbage, on a report of Marie-Joseph Chénier, the brother of the martyred poet, "*considering that there is no great man without virtue*", orders that his remains be removed from the Pantheon to be replaced by those of Marat. So the great Mirabeau was buried in the common grave. This one will never be found. But if he did not have the honor, so dear to the bourgeois, of a marbled grave, he entered history through the hole of the common grave, his memory lying in the hearts of free men.

Octave MIRBEAU (1848-1917)
Son of the Revolution, screamer of insults

Octave Mirbeau was born in Trévières, Calvados, on February 16, 1848, just a few days before the revolutionary days that shook France. His parents were true Normans of good bourgeois stock. His mother was a notary's daughter, and his father a doctor. Shortly after the birth of this first child, two daughters will follow, the Mirbeau couple migrates to Rémalard, the birthplace of the father. He will make a career as a doctor there, but will also be deputy mayor and district councilor. Octave's childhood was that of a hypersensitive and sickly boy, like his mother.

His schooling continued in a posh college, Saint-François-Xavier in Vannes, which served as the setting for his first novel, of which he has bad memories because of the bad treatment he received and perhaps the sexual abuse of one of the teaching priests.

Thus he was excluded and returned to his family to prepare for his baccalaureate which he passed in Caen in 1866. The following year he went to Paris to prepare his law degree. Not very motivated, he leads a bohemian life, goes to breweries and even smokes opium. When the war of 1870 broke out, a derisory and murderous attempt by the dying Empire to restore its image, he enlisted, first as a second lieutenant and then as a lieutenant in the Mobile Guards of the Loire Army. Ill, he did not participate in any combat and was even accused of desertion. Released in February 1871, he returned to the Orne and the despairing notary's office that he called the "*notary's coffin*" of Master Robbe. This explains the commitment of the man who called himself a "*son of the revolution*" and denounced the project of re-establishing military service for all as a return to the *"savage state"* in the army.

Reduced to a "*corpse*" by the notary's office, the war could paradoxically resurrect it.

In the same way, the return is so painful that the proposal of a friend of his father, Henri-Joseph Dugué de la Fauconnerie, is welcomed with relief. General Councillor and deputy of the Orne, this one is, in 1872, at the head of *L'Ordre de Paris*, official organ of the bonapartists. And he is looking for a private secretary. Mirbeau, a proletarian of the pen, thus chose political-literary prostitution over death by intellectual asphyxiation. For more than ten years he will be editor, art critic and drama critic in this conservative organ. With ardor and virulence he supports and promotes the young impressionist painting and castigates Zola, to whom he pays tribute, accused of defaming the people. Then Mr. de Saint-Paul, Mac Mahon's confidant, sends him to Foix to the prefect.

He fights, under the livery of sub-prefect, against the republicans by collaborating in particular to *L'Ariégeois.*

His independence of mind allowed him to keep this position for only a few months, as the paragons of the Moral Order, which summarized the Marshal's government (already!), quickly evacuated him.

After this ten-year experience, Mirbeau, at the instigation of a mistress (he had several with a fairly high "*turn over*"), started a business in the stock market. Then he bought a sardine boat and settled in Brittany. He read and went to sea with the fishermen. But this life is too quiet and when Arthur Meyer, director of *Le Gaulois*, calls him to him, he runs. This newspaper has just passed from Bonapartism to Legitimism, but what does it matter? It is a major national daily and Meyer, fascinated by Mirbeau's "*volcanic soul*", lets him off the hook. He quickly became an outstanding polemicist and made use of all kinds of wood. Bonapartist or monarchist according to the employers and the circumstances, he stigmatizes the forbidding politicians who monopolize the republic which they use instead of serving. It distributes hats to the Throne or to the Altar, pays homage to the empress Eugénie, commemorates the fall of the emperor...

It is in the already well-meaning *Le Figaro*, to which he also contributes, that he begins to express himself. On October 26, 1882 appears "*Le Comédien*", article in which he exhales his contempt for a society which hoists on the social flag the histrionics, scorns the true values and ignores the true talents. This seems to him to be the pathognomonic sign of decadence[27]... After this paving stone in the pond of complacency, he disturbs his bosses Meyer and Magnard whose business cannot be threatened. He is fired.

This time is for him a time of great change. He met Augustine Toulet, an actress under the name of Alice Regnault, who became his companion. He also embarked on an ambitious enterprise, such as all well-endowed journalists have dreamed of, and dream of, creating his own newspaper. On January 15, 1883 was born *Paris-Midi Paris-Minuit*, a bi-daily news paper, without political articles, which lived until April 18. On July 21, *Les Grimaces*, a weekly pamphlet, was born. Its patron was Edmond Joubert, vice-president of the Bank of Paris and the Netherlands. If on the surface *Les Grimaces* is a reactionary pamphlet, beyond the symbols and the republican personnel, it is the whole social order that is challenged. In the evening of his life, Mirbeau confided that he was at the time "*a revolutionary Bonapartist*". Behind this paradoxical term appears the Mirbeau who, beyond his apparent nationalist, royalist, anti-Semitic convictions... testifies to his intrinsic penchant for the spirit of revolt. This is what is meant by articles such as the call to the *Avenging Cholera* or the *Liberating Riot*. They say that it is this world that must be destroyed either by means of a man's power grab or by popular revolt.

The targets are, and will remain, the "*kind escarpes who govern us*", the bias is, and will remain, that of the oppressed of the city and the fields. Prophesying the social explosion to come, in these times that resemble ours, he vituperates the foul charity, he would say today solidarity, in brilliant terms: "*Charity has become the exploiter of misery, the acrobats beat the bass drum on the skin of the victims*".

And this even though his boss Meyer is one of the most assiduous in organizing these weeping masses.

Also his speech displeases more and more the masters of the game who do not like this irregular who, to sweep away this world "*unjust and badly made*", calls for "*the streams of blood*" which will wash away "*the streams of pus*".

Joubert does not finance *Les Grimaces* any more and Meyer expels him from *Le Gaulois*. We are in January 1884. The great turning point

27. What would he say more than a hundred years later about the society of the spectacle that has come to its assumption?

is for soon that announced a letter to Henry Baüer to the publication of *Grimaces: "The policy of* Grimaces *will not be yours, but I can assure you that we will meet more than once, in common hates and in common admirations".* One could not say better.

In the meantime, after a seven-month stay in Audierne, where he was recovering from the disappointments of a love affair, he returned to Paris, rejoined *Le Gaulois,* although he had made amends, and signed a contract with the Republican newspaper *La France.* During two years, at the cost of hard work, he will establish his financial situation and his fame and complete his first two books: *Les lettres de ma chaumière* and *Le Calvaire.* The autobiography *Sébastien Roch et l'abbé Jules,* countless stories and chronicles in the *Gaulois, Gil Blas, Figaro...* will follow. The social question becomes his favorite theme, as well as the rejection of democracy and universal suffrage, sordid mystifications that make the bed of political scavengers. He is also, spontaneously, anti-Boulangist and becomes an adversary and resolute critic of the State. The mutation is completed, he is an anarchist. He then authorized Jean Grave, the pope of anarchism, to publish his articles in *La Révolte,* such as *La Grève des électeurs* which appeared in the December 9, 1888 issue.

He will also be the preface of the work published in 1893 by Jean Grave: *La société mourante et l'anarchie (The Dying Society and Anarchy)* and will be vigorously involved with Jean Grave in the affair that opposes him to the Société des Gens de Lettres.

His commitment is based on two pillars. He considers that "*capitalist society has sown misery: it reaps hatred".* This is right, but also that all power is cursed, as Louise Michel said, and that the role of the State, "*murderer and thief*" can only be criminal. So he feels inclined to justify the anarchist attacks that sow terror in the veiled bourgeoisie. After the execution of Ravachol, he exclaims:

> *"He will be avenged, he will be avenged. One day the horizon, which is becoming more and more obscured by the opaque and heavy clouds of hatred, one day, from all points of the globe, the horizon will be ablaze with the great and red glow of insurrection..."*

And he became involved with the anarchists in the case of the trial of the Thirty, initiated by the government after the passing of repressive laws (in December 1893 all acts of anarchist propaganda were prohibited), multiplying accusatory articles in *Le Journal.*

At the same time, he became the herald of the Impressionists, Monet, Pissarro, Cézanne, Utrillo, the thurifer of Rodin, saluted Gauguin and praised Camille Claudel. This role of art critic was not enough for him, he invested his money in the acquisition of works by Maillol, Van Gogh (including the *Iris* and the *Suns*) and his impressionist friends of whom he had a famous collection of watercolors, gouaches and drawings. He also has his hatreds and pins Cabanel, "*crushed by the speeches, suffocated by the delirious apologies of the critics*", or Meissonnier whose "*hair slides and sabretaches*" he mocks.

This openness and independence of spirit are combined with a sensitivity to everything that lives and vibrates.

The Dreyfus Affair will see him commit himself alongside Zola and Urbain Gohier in the Dreyfus camp. Despite his neurotic shyness, he participated in public meetings with Francis de Pressensé, president of the League of Human Rights, in many provincial cities. He was also involved in *L'Aurore* where he wrote numerous articles analyzing or denouncing anti-Dreyfusards such as Mercier, Drumont and Meyer. His position was close to that of Gohier: it was a question of committing oneself against the injustice of which a man was a victim, beyond all ideological biases.

A passionate and fascinating speaker, a formidable polemicist, he is also a virtuoso animator, whom Léon Blum, the inspiration for *La Revue Blanche,* described as follows:

> *"Mirbeau's violent soul, torn between so many opposing passions, did not give itself away. He threw himself wholeheartedly into the battle, although no natural inclination inclined him to enlist under the name of a Jew, because he loved action and the fray, because he was generous, and above all because he was pitiful, because the sight or the idea of suffering, the suffering of a man, the suffering of a beast, the suffering of a plant, were literally intolerable to his nervous system."*

This cohabitation with the socialists will have a profound influence on Mirbeau.

The ferocious repression against the anarchists and the Dreyfus Affair both contribute, from the point of view of the bourgeoisie, to the same objective: to suppress all consciousness of class antagonism and to drown the proletariat in the abyss of collaboration, under the guise of humanism and solidarity. Any prospect of subversion is thus stopped and the state emerges strengthened from these "*crises*". If Mirbeau ceases to hope in a revolutionary perspective, he does not cease, and will never cease, to be an anarchist and will continue to militate, by default, in favor of a little more justice and humanity in social organization. He thus gets closer to socialists like Blum or Jaurès, of whom he nevertheless continues to be suspicious, denouncing collectivism in these terms:

> *"What is collectivism, then, if not an appalling aggravation of the State, if not the violent and dreary trusteeship of all the individual forces of a country, of all its living energies, of all its soil, of all its tools, of all its intellectuality, by a State that is more compressive than any other, by a State discipline that is more suffocating, and that has no other name in the language than State slavery."*

In 1904, he agreed to collaborate with the young *Humanité in order to make a* large popular audience aware of the social question. He will stay there six months and will be disgusted by the spectacle of the appetite of power of the politicians. However, he used this platform to castigate the militarism of the "*warring souls*" who plundered and martyred the colonized peoples, the clericalism of the soul rotters, and he supported the fight of Emile Combes in 1905 against *the "abominable poison*" and *the "odious lie*" of religion. Finally, he campaigned for the liberation of Maxim Gorky, imprisoned on the orders of the tsar, and against the Russian loan "*stained with blood*".

But he did not stop being a writer and over the years he wrote *Le Jardin des supplices, Le Journal d'une femme de chambre (The Diary of a Chambermaid*) from which the magician Louis Buñuel made a sumptuous film, *Vingt et un jours d'un neurasthénique (Twenty-One Days of a Neurasthenic)* and several comedies that were performed on many stages. He will be moreover, with Romain Roland, the promoter of a popular theater and the initiator of a literature of popular expression which anticipates the proletarian literature of the years 1930.

And as he was primarily concerned with efficiency, he took the initiative in 1907 in *Le Matin* of a campaign against a hospital medical system, which Léon Daudet denounced in *Les Morticoles, "full of dubious science and puffed up with superiority"*, then against the death penalty and for the defense of the right to strike. These are his last fights.

Before the war he still published *The 628 E-8* and *Dingo*, novels, and a play.

Sick and physically diminished, he was then under the control of a cantankerous and possessive companion who literally sequestered him in his house in Triel.

When the imperialist slaughter broke out, which sounded the death knell of his last hopes for a different world, he kept silent. Pressed by patriots and renegades, among whom Anatole France, Rémy de Gourmont and even Jean Grave, he agreed to publish in 1915 an open letter to "*our*" soldiers in which he expressed immense pity and total commiseration for those who were suffering and dying, and hoped for victory. He did not deny himself and said in 1916 to a newspaper writer: *"I am still an anarchist. But at home since the war the anarchist sleeps"*.

On February 16, 1917, he died before he knew about the revolution, albeit bourgeois, that was taking place in the East.

Three days after his death, a pseudo-political will of Octave Mirbeau with patriotic and warlike overtones appeared in the press. Alice Mirbeau and Gustave Hervé are the authors of this "*corpse make-up*". The balloon deflates thanks to some friends. This ridiculous text cannot have for author the one who wrote :

> *"Wherever there is a wound to burn, rascals to unmask, decadence to flog, virtue to exalt, we will not hesitate, despite the calculated indifference of some and the fury of others."*

ALEXIS PIRON.

Alexis PIRON (1689-1773)
The Priape of mating

He was born in Dijon on July 09, 1689 and died in Paris on January 21, 1773. He will be in turn poet, chansonnier, goguetier and dramaturge.

Aimé Piron, his father, is an apothecary and his mother, Anne Dubois, the daughter of the sculptor Jean Dubois. His father was a poet who wrote Christmas songs in patois and competed with La Monnoye in this field.

Having studied law in Besançon. Alexis was admitted to the bar in Dijon, but his father's ruin kept him away from the profession. At the age of twenty, he composed an *Ode to Priape* whose talent was recognized and whose content scandalized. Fontenelle said: *"If Piron has written the famous ode, we must scold him, but admit it; if he has not written it, let's close our door to him".*

The Marquis de Sade cheerfully parodied this ode in *Histoire de Juliette.*

Piron remained in Burgundy until about 1719, riddling the inhabitants of his native town with epigrams. He did not spare those of his rival, Beaune, whom he called the *"donkeys of Beaune"*.

Thus, one day at the city theater, when a spectator was complaining about not hearing anything, he exclaimed *"It is not for lack of long enough ears".*

When he was about thirty, he came to Paris and became a famous author of comic operas (written in the form of monologues because the Comédie-Française had obtained that the shows of the fair [sic!] were limited to one spoken role). His first play *Arlequin Deucalion was* a great success (Piron imagined in it a Harlequin who survived the Deluge and who, as a result, soliloquizes), reinforced by the twenty-one following plays, some of which were written in collaboration with Lesage.

Financially supported by some patrons, he ended up being played by the Comédie-Française and was almost elected to the Académie Française, but Louis XV was opposed to it, as he was shocked (which is not without salt) by *L'Ode à Priape*. As compensation, his supporters obtained a scholarship from Madame de Pompadour.

His wife sank into dementia, Piron treated her with devotion and retired from the political scene. He died a few years later, at the age of eighty-four, and was buried in the church of Saint-Roch in Paris.

If the most famous work of Piron, known as Binbin, is *La Métromanie* (five acts in verse on the stubbornness of rhyming), he is above all redoubtable for his epigrams which he says he "sneezes". His favorite target was Voltaire, but Fréron and Desfontaines (etc.) were not spared.

He mocked himself, writing his epitaph: "*Here lies Piron, who was nothing, not even an academician*".

Sainte-Beuve evokes Piron as being "*gaiety itself, a cheerful man of verve and mimicry. A man whose brilliance sparkles in the memory and deserves that the spirits dive into it*".

THE TEACHER OF PLAINCHANT

An abbess was instructing a young novice
In the community's own song,
On a certain Latin word in a common psalm
That she sang badly out of malice.
This word, as one author says,
Is this one: *conculcavit*.
Hear it well, she said,
Hold this *sucker tight*;
Shrug your *ass*: good for you,
A little higher still; there, it is good.
For the *life,* make it long.
From this elongated syllable,
I know the measure inside out;
Father Blaise, after the sermon,
Has shown it to me more than once.

ODE TO PRIAPE

Nine bitches of the Pindus
Daphne's lover's ass
Whose flask lives on
That by dint of being skated on!
You are the one I call upon to help me
You who in the cunts, of a stiff live,
Throw it in the air:
Priape! Support my breath
And for a moment in my vein
Carry the fire of your balls.

Isn't this Ode to Priape an ode to freedom?

— 186.221
Sauget Emile
168
28

Émile POUGET (1860-1931)
A man against

Pouget was born in 1860 into a middle-class Aveyron family in Pont-de-Salais. Through a succession of family misfortunes, the death of his father, a notary, and then of his stepfather, an employee of the Ponts et Chaussées, whom his mother had married for the second time in 1875, he had to leave the high school where he was studying. Already in the grip of the demon of journalism, he created and directed alone *Le Lycée républicain, a* handwritten newspaper. He was forced to earn his living as a clerk in a novelty store. In Paris, where he went to live, he became an anarchist under the influence of the Narbonne communard Émile Digeon, and was active in an employees' union that he founded in 1879.

Ten years later, with *"a physique like D'Artagnan"*, Charles Malato, a young man of twenty-nine, founded one of the most original newspapers of the period: *Le Père Peinard*, whose subtitle was "*Reflecs d'un gniaff*". He introduces it as "*good fellows, read every Sunday the Father Peinard*". Under this title, every week, the gniaff-journalist publishes his reflecs in which he does not chew their truths to the jean-foutre of governors and bosses. "*The issue contains sixteen pages of sandwiches and costs two rounds*". Initially a weekly in the form of a small sixteen-page brochure, it is decorated with a small drawing of a cobbler writing, leaning against his work table. On the first cover a drawing signed Ibels, Luce, Pissaro or Willette. It has a few hundred subscribers and sells quite well...

Pouget will be of all the anarchist fights. He was one of the organizers of the great demonstration called in Paris on March 9, 1883 during the economic crisis of 1883-1887. That day the police dispersed the unemployed gathered on the esplanade of the Invalides. The demonstration, led by Pouget and Louise Michel, turned into a riot and looting, with cries of "*bread, work or lead*". If Louise Michel managed to escape, Pouget was arrested. At his home, the police found pamphlets entitled "*To the Army*" advocating the methods of propaganda by deed. During the trial Pouget was sentenced to eight years and Louise Michèle to six.

During the same period *Le Père Peinard,* without explicitly supporting the practitioners of individual recuperation, openly advocates direct action. In particular, he pays homage to Ravachol, whose *Le Chant de guillotine* he publishes. Verse VI is explicit: "*If you want to be happy, God damn it! Hang your owner, cut' the priests in two Name of God! Fous les églis 'par terre, sang Dieu et l'bon dieu dans la merde, Nom de Dieu !* (bis)". In 1894, the "scélérates laws, recently voted, oblige *Le Père Peinard* to interrupt its publication. The main anarchist militants were arrested and tried before the Seine assizes, the trial of the Thirty, but acquitted. Having taken refuge in England where he continued his militant activities, he began a critique of terrorism. The era of individual attacks is over, the era of minorities, acting within the masses, begins.

As far as Pouget is concerned, it seems that, during his exile in London, the trade-unionist movement largely influenced him, as shown by the London series of *Père Peinard.*

Thus Pouget traces the way to follow to those companions who complain that the anarchist propaganda becomes difficult. "*Let a friend try, let him join his Syndicale, let him not rush the movement, let him, instead of wanting to swallow his ideas straight away to the comrades, go about it gently and take as his tactic, every time an ambitious person comes to chatter municipal elections, legislative elections or other duke crap in four words: 'the Syndicale's aim is to make war on the patriots and not to deal with politics.' Smart enough not to give in to the lies of the aspiring cloggers, who will not fail to slobber on his account, he will see himself keenly listened to.*"

Pouget then criticizes the groups of affinity to which too many anarchists have complied and he continues: *"the problem is this: I am an anarcho, I want to sow my ideas, what is the ground where they will germinate the best? I already have the factory, the bistro..., I would like something better: a corner where I find proletarians realizing a little of* the *exploitation that we undergo and digging their heads to remedy it. Does this corner exist? Yes, for God's sake! and it is unique: it is the corporate group!"*

Pouget goes on to show that the government is always on the side of the bosses, that the *"workers"* laws are only applied to the extent that the workers force the employers to do so and that, consequently, they are absolutely useless: *"the monkeys will only take account of them if the good people have the nerve to force them to do so. Consequently, the law is useless, nerve is enough."*

So what should the Union's work be?

> *"Firstly, it must constantly watch out for the boss, prevent wage cuts and other crap that he is chewing on. If the proles weren't always on the lookout, the monkeys would have quickly reduced them to eating bricks with the sauce of rocks.*
>
> *Deuxiémo, in addition to the daily grind, which is the current meal, has another task, really nice: to prepare the ground for the Social.*
>
> *We suffer the boss, because there is no other way to do it. We know that it is from our work that he gets fat. If, for the moment, we are content to hold him in respect, we hope, one of these four mornings, to be up to the task of kicking him out. That's what we at the Union have to explain to the newcomers who come here to protect themselves against exploitation.*
>
> *The factory belongs to all of us: every brick of the walls is cemented with our sweat; every cog in the machines is greased with our blood.*
>
> *What a great day, the day we can take back our property - make the great Expropriation. Once that's done, we'll line up to work as brothers. And, if the ex-boss doesn't curse, we'll make room for him in the factory: he'll work on equal terms, kif-kif the camaro."*

Back in Paris, he continued his work in *La Sociale,* which exalts the General Strike as a tool of the Revolution. *La Sociale* was followed by a new series of *Père Peinard,* which ceased publication in 1900.

Pouget then became editor-in-chief of the weekly of the very young CGT, a revolutionary syndicalist very close to the anarchists, *La Voix du Peuple.*

He then devoted himself entirely to the syndicalist cause, which for him was identified with that of anarchy. He was one of the architects, with Pelloutier and Yvetot, of the union of the latter with the Federation of Labor Bureaus.

Pouget's attitude during the Dreyfus Affair deserves to be mentioned. From 1894 to 1897, this text from No. 72 of *La Sociale* sums up the initial indifference of the anarchists towards the captain: "*The Dreyfus kike is a gallant, a patriot to the tip of his toes, who, as a paper pusher at the Ministry of War, was pimping the dirty secrets that are preciously kept in this dirty box. He sold them to Germany. His dirty trade was prospering, when, two years ago, the pot-aux-roses was discovered...*" Still in 1898 he wrote in No. 65 of *Père Peinard:* "*Neither Dreyfusians, nor esterhazians*" he wrote, and he stigmatized in these terms the men who already, had taken sides: "*The old exploiter Scheurer-Kestner, a senatorial calf's head, the scoundrel Yves Guyot, the hideous Reinach, three malefactors who helped to create the scurrilous laws, parade in the Dreyfusian cart, and Clemenceau faces them with, as a tail-bearer, a bunch of guys we would like to see elsewhere. The Esterhazian cart is also a mess, the old anti-government man Rochefort takes his tips from the Ministry of War, follows in the footsteps of all the ink-sucking secretaries, and is in good company with Drumont, ex-collaborator of the policeman Marchal de Bussy.*"

The year 1899 saw a large number of anarchists, following Sébastien and *Le Libertaire,* enter the very heart of the Dreyfusian struggle. Pouget participated in the *Journal du peuple,* which was founded to take part in this struggle, which saw the President pardon Alfred Dreyfus in September 1899.

In parallel to his union activity, Pouget continued to write in *La Guerre Sociale.* Then he founded the daily newspaper *La Révolte* which had only

53 issues. He did not recover from this failure and his action remained confined to the trade union field.

During the war he signed, like many revolutionary leaders, a few articles in *Guerre Sociale* which became *La Victoire* and *L'Humanité.*

The revolutionary idea is dead, Pouget will survive it until 1931 when he dies in Lozère (Seine-et-Oise).

Pierre-Joseph PROUDHON (1809-1865)
Man against Leviathan or the legitimist of freedom

On June 30, 1840, a book was published in Paris in which, in the last chapter, one could read this kind of dialogue:

> *"Which form of government will we prefer? - Hey, can you ask?" probably answers one of my younger readers, "You're a Republican. - Republican, yes, but this word does not specify anything. Res Publica is the public thing, and whoever wants the public thing, under whatever form of government, can call himself a republican. Kings too are republicans. - Well, are you a democrat? - No, I am not. - Would you be a monarch? - No, I am not. - Constitutional? - God forbid! - So you are an aristocrat? - Not at all. - You want a mixed government? - Even less. - What are you then? - I am an anarchist."*

Proudhon was of the people, not of the proletariat, or of the plebs, but of the people. He was born in a peasant and artisanal environment which he will always remember with emotion. He belonged to this environment that fiercely defended communal liberties. It is within the framework of this kind of obotchina, as the community was called in the Russian populist tradition, that he draws the essential materials of his thought. His father was in turn a lumberjack, a winegrower, a cooper and a brewer. His mother was a cook and a maid for heavy work. "*I am noble,*" he wrote, because "*my ancestors, father and mother, were all free laborers, exempt from drudgery and death duties since time immemorial.*"

"I was born in Besançon on January 15, 1809 to Claude-François Proudhon, cooper, brewer, native of Chasnas near Pontarlier, department of Doubs, and Catherine Simon, of Cordiron, parish of Burgille-les-Marnay, same department..."

He is the eldest of the family and this family, if not being, is modest. We have recalled the peasant-community morality[28] which animated the Proudhon family. This morality of exchanges in kind which extended to the notion of fair price, antithesis to the immoral law of industrial profit, led the father Proudhon, when he opened an inn, to sell his beer made in family, at a price taking into account only this manufacture and the expenses in supplies. This practice led him to bankruptcy in a world where morality was no more than a mere pleasure of speech.

The first twelve years of Pierre-Joseph can only be described by himself.

> *"Until the age of twelve my life was spent almost entirely in the fields, sometimes doing small rustic jobs, sometimes tending cows. I was a cowherd for five years. I don't know of an existence that is both more contemplative and more realistic, more opposed to that absurd spiritualism which is the basis of Christian education and life, than that of the man of the fields... What a pleasure it was in the past to roll around in the tall grass, which I would have liked to graze, like my cows, to run barefoot on the smooth paths along the hedges, to sink my legs into the deep, fresh earth while re-shodding the green corn!*
>
> *More than once, on hot June mornings, I have left my clothes on and taken a dew bath on the lawn. What do you say about this dirty existence, Monsignor? It makes poor Christians, I assure you. I could hardly tell me from the non-me. I was everything I could touch with my hand, reach with my eyes, and that was good for me: not me was everything that could harm or resist me... All day long, I filled myself with blackberries, raipberries, meadow salsify, green peas, poppy seeds, roasted corncobs, berries of all kinds, sloes, blessons, alises, wild cherries, wild rosehips, lambusks, wild fruits. I gorged myself with a mass of raw vegetables that could make a middle-class boy*

28. That one finds in many places where the resistants to the leviathan monster have frozen the social relations to resist the heraclitean flow of the goods (Aragon and the Pyrenean world for example).

die and that had no other effect on my stomach than to give me a tremendous appetite in the evening... Mother Nature does not hurt those who belong to her.

Alas, I could not make any more of these superb pickings. Under the pretext of preventing damage, the administration has destroyed all the fruit trees in the forests. A hermit would no longer find his life in our civilized woods. The poor people are forbidden to pick up even acorns and faines; forbidden to cut the grass of the paths for their goats. Go, poor people, go to Africa and Oregon! Veteres migrate coloni!

How many showers I have wiped off! How many times, soaked to the bone, I dried my clothes on my body in the breeze or in the sun! How many baths I took at all hours, in the summer in the river, in the winter in the springs! I climbed trees, I went into caves; I caught frogs on the run, crayfish in their holes, at the risk of meeting an ugly salamander; then I did, without dismay, roast my hunt on the coals. There are from man to beast, to everything that exists, secret sympathies and hatreds of which civilization takes away the feeling. I loved my cows, but with an unequal affection. I had preferences for a hen, a tree, a rock. I had been told that the lizard is a friend of man, and I sincerely believed it...

Certainly, in this life of spontaneity, I did not think much about the origin of the inequality of fortunes, nor about the mysteries of faith. There was no famine, no envy. At my father's house, we ate corn porridge called "gaudes" in the morning, potatoes at noon, and bacon soup in the evening, all week long.

Thus was my education as a child of the people... It is this contrast of the real life suggested by nature and the false education given by religion, which gave birth in me the philosophical doubt, and warned me against the opinions of the sects and the institutions of the society".

Then his mother wanted her son to study. And the young Pierre-Joseph, a peasant at heart as we have just read, found himself a day student at the college of Besançon thanks to the support of the parish priest. In this exile of the soul and the body, he undergoes a thousand humiliations which are as many firecrackers which will later ignite the pyre of the anarchy. "*I underwent a hundred punishments for having forgotten my books: it is that I did not have any*". He had no shoes and had to leave his clogs at the entrance to the classroom so as not to disturb the class with their noise. During the vacations, he works in the fields or goes to get the hoops that his father needs in his business. It is in these experiences, which will order all his future attitudes, that he draws this disgust of the civilization (Rousseau is not far) conceived like a world of hypocrisies where the life is "*without color nor savour, the passions without energy, without frankness, the narrowed imagination, the affected or flat style*". The nostalgia of the natural life is thus reinforced with for corollary the rejection of the social world.

Not of idea, not yet, but of instinct, of feelings, and of experiences, he is already an anarchist.

So he dragged himself, in his own words, to rhetoric, his last year of college. Then he entered a printing shop as a journeyman. As a proofreader, he was called upon to read dozens of books at random and without method. There lies the source of his self-taught training. As a companion in the Tour de France, he travels around the country and discovers the industrial world then in gestation, an experience that no theorist of socialism or anarchy will ever possess. What made him leave his condition, without ever denying it, was the meeting with Gustave Fallot whose proofs he corrected for a book. They became friends and Proudhon followed him in his passion for linguistics. Although he was reluctant to accept ambition as a downgrade, he answered Fallot's call to come to Paris. An unfortunate attempt and return to Besançon. But this time it is a question of setting up his own business in order to "*make for his work, the leisure he needs to work and write his ideas*" of which he says that he has enough to "*feed two or three Chateaubriands*".

Fallot died in 1836 without having seen his prophecy come true: *"Here is my prediction, you will be, Proudhon, in spite of yourself, inevitably, by the fact of your destiny, a writer, an author; you will be a philosopher; you will be one of the lights of the century..."*

So he writes to cure himself of an illness whose nature is unknown, of overwork and of his sorrow. And this gives him back his health; however, this first work, *The Essay on General Grammar,* is read by no one but a few friends. And the printing house collapses and has to close.

So when he learns that the triennial pension offered by the Academy of Besançon is going to be put up for competition, he tries his luck. His memoir ends with a peroration that sounds like a challenge and a refusal to succeed. Notwithstanding this explicit threat, he was granted the Suard pension which, if it did not free him from all material concerns, allowed him to devote himself to writing. We are in 1839 when his first writing on a subject proposed by the Academy comes out: *De l'Utilité de la Célébration du Dimanche.* He himself felt and wrote to a friend that by this publication he was crossing the Rubicon. Then he leaves for Paris, this city which he hates, but where reputations are made and great polemics are conducted. For he has a project, matured in the revolt inspired by the tradition that we know and the daily poverty in which he struggles.

This project is a book that must "*kill inequality and property in a duel to the death; either I am blind or it will never recover from the blow that will soon be dealt to it*". This book, which was to settle its account with the old world, came out in 1840 and was entitled: *What is Property?* And he answers this question in a way that the bourgeoisie, and the proletarians who aspire to be part of it, or their leaders who dream of succeeding it, will never forgive him. He wrote that "*property is theft*". This word will weigh on his whole life and on his literary posterity.

Yet few have tried to understand the powerful thought that was manifested in this text. What was Proudhon saying? That property has neither its justification nor its origin in the law, which is only a revisable convention, nor in the right of occupation, which is the same for all, nor in work, since he who does not work or no longer works, remains the owner. It only proceeds from an initial appropriation secondarily legitimized by a right that can only be that of the most powerful. The supposedly universal recognition does not legitimize in any way what will always be a fact and not a right, whose primary origin is therefore a theft.

Beyond this society segmented by the individual and collective property, Proudhon foresees the community, golden age of the ancients, the primordial rise of the sociability, spontaneous movement by which it manifests itself, and its disadvantages. "*The systematic community, reflected negation of the property, is conceived under the influence of the prejudice of property which is found at the bottom of all the communist societies*".

The correctness of the reasoning, Marx will understand it and will say it a little later, is not enough to shake the bourgeois order, another force is needed.

> *"The community is oppression and servitude. Man wants to submit to the law of duty, to serve his country, to oblige his friends, but he wants to work at what he likes, when he likes, as much as he likes; he wants to dispose of his hours, to obey only necessity, to choose his friendships, his recreations, his discipline, to render service by reason, not by order; to sacrifice himself out of selfishness, not out of a servile obligation.*
> *The community is essentially contrary to the free exercise of our faculties, to our noblest inclinations, to our most intimate feelings. It violates the autonomy of conscience and equality."*

One then glimpses Proudhon's system, neither community nor property. But he does not venture beyond declarations of principle.

The five hundred copies published are dedicated to the academy of Bisontine which is indignant and summons him. Paradoxically, the representatives of the Church and the State supported his brief, and the Academy kept his pension. Similarly, the minister renounced to order prosecution on the advice of the economist Adolphe Blanqui, brother of *L'Enfermé*.

But here he is again with a *Second Memoir* in which he persists: "*I preach emancipation to the proletarians... I push for revolution by all the means in my power... my life is a perpetual apostolate*". Again Blanqui intervenes. And again Proudhon reoffends and this time cannot escape prosecution.

Brought before the assizes, as it was at the time, he is the revolutionary monster against whom all are united. But at the bar it is, in his own words, "*instead of a republican with a red vest, a goat's beard, a sepulchral voice, it is a small blond man with a clear complexion, a simple and good-natured face, a quiet demeanor*" who mystifies the court with a speech that is abstruse in its economic developments and so explicit in its satire of the possessing classes, that he is acquitted to the cheers and laughter of the public. It is his first triumph.

He will now, while criticizing the chimeras of others, produce some in his turn. It is in 1845 that the idea was born that will develop his thesis on the free credit in which he sees *The Solution of the Social Problem,* title of the work which will appear in 1848 and in which he exposes his doctrine.

And to clear the ideological ground, Proudhon publishes *The System of Economic Contradictions* (or Philosophy of Misery) in which he affirms that *"the real problem to be solved is not in reality the political problem, it is the economic problem."* For, he demonstrates, the economist has absorbed the political, and the social order, substance and form, is the product of transactions and exchanges. Universal suffrage appears then for what it is: a lure and an encouragement to submission. As for the laws which proceed from it, Proudhon is without ambiguity declares: *"I do not recognize any".*

Clear-sighted expositions and lucid syntheses that will abort in a solution that gets lost in the torrent of illuminism of the time: the mutualized credit of the workers as a lever for the rout of the capitalist institutions. In short, by creating a Bank of the People, he wanted to organize credit, and therefore initiative, by freeing men from the *"kingdom of gold"* because gold is *"the despot of circulation, the tyrant of commerce, the head of mercantile feudalism, the pivot of privilege, the material symbol of property."* He therefore wants to create equality between products by organizing the permutability of values without the intermediary of money, just as he wants to organize the government of society by all citizens without the intermediary of royalty, a presidency or a directoire.

At the same time as he was writing, Proudhon worked for the Gauthier brothers, his bosses. He is the clerk of his bosses of a water transport company, located in Lyon, who have entrusted him with the management of their legal affairs. Not only did he excel in this job, but this life of travel allowed him to meet many economists and political refugees, including Marx and Bakunin.

And then he dreams of taking a wife and also of fatherhood. Who has paid attention to this sentence from the *System of Economic Contradictions: "the family, a mystical institution, the most astonishing of all..."* And these from the *1859 Notebook* which, at a later date, reveal his feelings: *"Fatherhood is for me like a doubling of existence, a kind of immortality... Suffice it to say that I set so much store by fatherhood, that I am profoundly a family man and patriarchal, that for several years, my first and only love gone, I had the idea of becoming a father, in return for a pecuniary compensation, through the mediation of a poor young girl whom I would have seduced, if I may use this odious word, for that. And I would have done it, if I had not thought that, the child made, I would have ended up by spirit of justice, by marrying the mother, what it was better to do before than after".*

But he doesn't want a lowly blue. The long-awaited meeting occurred in Paris in 1847. It was in the street that he met a young embroiderer of twenty-five years, Euphrasie Piégard, with whom he was immediately in love. And according to the customs of the time, the family of the beloved agreed to his courtship[29]. It will last two years.

These years will be the most tumultuous of the pamphleteer's life. In order to give more audience to his thought than his little-read books offered him, he founded a newspaper. This weekly is called *Le Peuple.* It will have only one number so few subscribers.

To this bitter failure are added two bitter disappointments. The *Journal des Economistes, to* which his friend Auguste Blanqui contributes, delivers a very qualified opinion on his book *Système de Contradictions,* written by a certain Molinari*: "His book... is a heap of visible darkness".* In addition, there is a pamphlet from Belgium signed, in the French style, by a certain Charles Marx, whose title is an inversion of Proudhon's subtitle: *Misère de la Philosophie.* It reads *"M. Proudhon has the misfortune to be singularly unknown in Europe. In France, he has the right to be a bad philosopher, because he passes for being one of the strongest French economists. We, as Germans and as economists, wanted to protest against this double error."* And he hits hard. Proudhon, for him, is a restless little bourgeois who understands nothing of the modern world. The latter, who did not have the means, did not respond except in his *Notebook* where one can read these words that have remained famous: *"Marx is the tapeworm of socialism".*

His editorial failures broke his arms and legs. His employers planning to borrow to develop their business, Proudhon separates from them,

29. The following anecdote deserves to be told: the Piégeard family is of royalist legitimist tradition. The father is a Chouan registered in the secret militia of the king. He and his future son-in-law had a great mutual esteem. When he was embarrassed to write a petition to the king, it was Proudhon who took up his pen to write it for him. A newspaper will print it and will denounce the real author. The republicans will make a great scandal of it and, once again, Proudhon will find them ridiculous.

unable to bring himself to work for bankers. No longer hopeful and no longer in a position, he can only ask his betrothed to commit herself to waiting for him.

Moreover, his father died and his mother died, and sadness gripped Proudhon. It is the revolution of 1848 that will pull him out of his despair. After the shooting that left twenty workers on the pavement, Paris was covered with more than five hundred barricades. Proudhon, who took to the streets, was charged by Flocon, the director of *La Réforme,* with the printing of an important proclamation... to the riot. He attends the triumph of Lamartine whom he hates, on February 25. The author of *The History of the Girondins* imposes the tricolor flag against the red flag as emblem of the Republic. Proudhon is not fooled by the escamotage of the revolution, once more to the profit of the bourgeoisie.

Suddenly the darkness of solitude in which he believes himself forever locked up is torn apart. Workers in arms come to ask him to publish his *Solution of the Social Problem* and to collaborate in a newspaper, *The People's Representative.*

In the first days of April the work is proposed to an opinion which remains deaf. The solution which prevails and which signs, by doing so, the defeat of the revolution, is the universal suffrage.

For Proudhon, as we know, putting the future of a people to the vote is a folly. He has always thought so and he repeats it. He even writes it in an article of April 20, entitled "*Mystification of the Universal Suffrage*".

In May, he also protested against the warmongering that wanted to drag France into a war to support the Polish insurrection. He wrote: "*We rush to the conquests, and we forget the rest. The rest is the social question, the organization of work...*"

Proudhon was then a pamphleteer, a friend of noise and moreover little known, if not shunned by the press, including the political reviews of Louis Blanc, Pierre Leroux, and Victor Considérant *(La Revue du Progrès, La Revue indépendante* and *La Démocratie pacifique).*

Also, entering in his turn in the system of the contradictions, when his candidature to the Constituent Assembly is presented in 1848, he does not ask to be crossed out. He was elected and entered the Assembly "*with the timidity of a child and the ardor of a neophyte*". And very quickly he became famous as a "scarecrow". But, immersed in this artificial life he ceases to be sensitive to the events and does not see coming the insurrectionary days of June. When they broke out, wearing his tricolor scarf, he was everywhere there was danger. However, it was too late to repair *the "irreparable fault"* to which he had been led by his election and his life in the Assembly. He cut himself off from the people.

So he returns to the charge and the pamphleteer finds his breath on a ground where the bourgeoisie is particularly sensitive: money. The Bank of France had obtained a moratorium on the payment of its debt, so Proudhon demanded a moratorium on mortgage loans, on farms, on annuity services, in short, a moratorium on the whole usurious economy. And moreover he wants the remission of a third for all rents. This famous program is published in *Le Représentant du Peuple* under the title *Le 15 juillet.*

General de Cavaignac banned the newspaper immediately. Since he was deprived of the means to spread his ideas, he tabled a project taking them up. During the parliamentary debate that followed, it was quickly understood that this text was a declaration of social war. And if Proudhon is delighted with the good trick played to the bourgeois, his text is diffused with the expenses of the National Printing Office, he realizes very quickly that he has in front of him all the apparatus of the bourgeoisie and its most ferocious representative, Adolphe Thiers.

And it is the outpouring. Proudhon becomes *"the man of terror"*, delivered to the vindictiveness of the opinion and to the opprobrium of the republicans and state socialists.[30]

And this hatred increases tenfold when in November 1848 he is one of the thirty representatives who vote against the Constitution. He simply justifies his vote: *"I voted against the Constitution because it is a Constitution"*.

Then comes the presidential election which sees the victory of Louis-Napoleon Bonaparte. In his pamphlet on the presidency, our revolutionary has some strange words. *"They say of you that you are only a moron, an adventurer, a madman. You've been a police officer and a comedian, you have all the makings, except for the ferocity, which is no longer of our*

30. Although a poor speaker - "Proudhon writes well but speaks badly" said Victor Hugo -, his speech is frightening when he storms: "when I say we, I identify with the proletariat, and when I say you, I identify with the bourgeois class".

age, of Nero and Caligula. Come to put to the reason these bourgeois. Come to take their last child and their last shield! Come to avenge socialism, communism, cabetism, Fourierism! Come, the apostates of all the kingdoms are there waiting for you...", but strange only for the fools and the narrow-minded who are often the same. Proudhon does not consent to the threatening dictatorship, he scourges with his invective and his contempt the cowardice of a people of courtiers.

However, he did not forget his great work and on January 31, 1849 the statutes of the Banque du Peuple were deposited before a notary. The experiment will be short-lived.

Two virulent articles in *Le Peuple*[31], directed against the prince-president, earned him a three-year prison sentence. He left for Belgium before being arrested. But for months, as his correspondence testifies, his desire to marry had been nagging at him and he returned to France clandestinely. One day when he went out to get some fresh air, he was recognized and locked up again in Sainte-Pélagie. He stayed there for three years.

At the time, as harsh as prisons were, their regime nevertheless retained something of a human liberality. "*I am at Sainte-Pélagie about as well as one can be in prison. I occupy a square room of about five meters in size, with two windows and a view of the Pitié and the Jardin des Plantes. I was not so well housed at rue Mazarine, even when I was a representative. I eat the prison bread, which is good; I take the morning broth, which is twice fatty and five times lean during the week; I buy extra food at the restaurant. The administration provides us with wine at twelve cents a liter, which is higher than the wine merchants' price of 1.50 a bottle. I receive my visitors at home. I obtained the permission to receive brochures and newspapers; I had all my books brought in: all that I possess is finally like me, under lock and key. What I wish, in spite of the boredom of captivity and the physical and moral discomfort that follows, is to stay*

31. After a few ups and downs, this journal acquired a certain renown and on its best days had a circulation of 40,000 copies. Among its editors were some famous personalities: Doctor Crétin, one of the inventors of homeopathy, the chemist Louis Ménard, inventor of the Collodion, Charles Beslay, future director of the Bank of France under the Commune, the musician Chauvet, inventor of another way of writing music, and Ramon de la Cerna, a Spanish writer, who had deserted a Spain where there was no longer any place for Don Quixote.

at least eighteen months; I would be afraid that a too rapid success of the revolution would compromise the peace of the world." In addition, he can receive visits from his future wife, have lunch with her, and even go out two or three days a month. It is from this "*recognition of his wife*" that two of his three daughters were born. For he was allowed to marry during his imprisonment and his wife moved into a room, rented and furnished by him, opposite the "*room of the princes of Sainte-Pélagie*". Above the marital bed, Euphrasie placed a crucifix, for which Proudhon would be reproached for a long time.

But prison does not slow down Proudhon's activity. By various means he continued to collaborate with *Le Peuple* and then, when it disappeared under the censorship, with *La Voix du Peuple* which he had just founded. This led to his transfer to the Conciergerie, to incommunicado detention and then to his relegation to the citadel of Doullens, where he remained for a month.

It is also in prison that he will write his two most remarkable books: *Confessions of a Revolutionary* published in 1849 and which are the best on the revolution of 1848, and finally his *General Idea of the Revolution in the nineteenth century* from which Bakunin will draw so much, followed by *The Social Revolution demonstrated by the coup d'état* which will be published at his release in July 1852.

It is necessary to underline in the verbal torrent that represents tens of thousands of words and ideas... this rare pearl, at a time which gets drunk with the vapors of modernity and is doped with progress (technical, sanitary):

> *"Divine Plato, these gods you dream of do not exist, there is nothing in the world greater and more beautiful than man. There is nothing in the world greater and more beautiful than man. But the man coming out of the hands of nature is miserable and ugly; he becomes sublime and beautiful only through gymnastics, politics, philosophy, music, and above all, something you hardly seem to suspect, asceticism.*
> *The decadence will not be eternal; degenerate men will have learned two things, which will one day make them greater and better than their fathers. The first is that before God all men are equal; consequently, that by nature and providence there are no slaves; the second is that the duty and honor of all is to work.*

What neither gymnastics, nor politics, nor music, nor philosophy, have been able to do together, Work will accomplish. As in the ancient ages the initiation to beauty came through the gods, so in remote posterity beauty will reveal itself again through the worker, the true ascetic, and it is to the innumerable forms of industry that it will demand its changing, ever new, and ever true expression. Then, at last, the Logos will be manifested, and the human workers, more beautiful and free than the Greeks ever were, without nobles and slaves, without magistrates and priests, will all together form, on the cultivated earth, only one family of heroes, scholars and artists."

It is clear to those who, holding their breath, immerse themselves in this verbal deluge, to which Proudhon does not attribute any value, that this attests to his profound vision *"to the barbaric belief that equates human progress with the progress of mechanical inventions"*. Halévy and the work of which he speaks is none other than the free creative activity aimed at satisfying real needs, and not the productive act aimed at satisfying alienated needs.

On June 14, the Gallic Don Quixote left Sainte-Pélagie having served the entirety of a sentence for which the administration had not given him a one-day discount. After wandering around with his newfound friends and drinking a lot of cannons in the guinguettes, he drags Euphrasie and her two daughters to Burgille-sur-Ognon, the village of his childhood. They make the rounds of relatives and friends.

During the following years, Proudhon seems to retire. He was refused permission to publish *La Revue du Peuple* and if he published a few works of circumstance or commissions, it was very little.[32]

In truth, he has passed forty years and no longer believes in the revolutionary deceptions of pre-1948. Almost single-handedly he understood that the new world, which according to Marx was supposed to have produced a revolutionary class, was much less threatened by it than the fiery proclamations of the revolutionary cloud-makers had led one to believe.

Two works that are too often ignored mark this period of his life: *De la Justice dans la Révolution et dans l'Église* and nouveaux *Principes de*

32. A well-known scenario. Marx was wrong, when history repeats itself it is each time more tragically derisory.

la Philosophie Pratique. They are manifestos of positive anarchy trying to reconcile Stirnerian individualism and community aspiration. Of the first one, only the anticlerical vehemence has been retained. But he was never atheist, only anti-theist, refusing any transcendence but maintaining the notion of mystery. "*One has never finished fighting against God*". For him, against the Hegelian and illuminist idea of synthesis, the dualistic notion prevails: thesis and antithesis clash eternally, "*the antinomy is not resolved*", and history has no end. Between man and society, man is himself, the fight is endless.

This book is seized for insulting public and religious morality and its author is sentenced to three years in prison. He therefore crossed the Belgian border and settled in Ixelles. Sensitized to the questions of international politics, he writes *La Guerre et la Paix, a* book attacked by pacifists of all stripes, even though it was they, against Proudhon, who called for war in a strange munichoise anticipation.

At that time, the fate of Italy, Hungary and Poland moved public opinion. Proudhon replied: "*I would like it just as much if they talked to me about re-establishing the Saxony of Witikind, the kingdom of Austrasia or that of the Visigoths. Poland especially was mistreated.*"

Then it was Italy's turn. The madman of national independence, Mazzini, fulminated a manifesto against King Victor Emmanuel, whom he reproached for not taking Rome and Venice to achieve Italian unity, and he appealed to democratic Europe. Then on July 13, 1862, Proudhon answers him in an article which makes scandal and where he affirms that "*the Italian unity had for obliged consequence the consumption of the French unity and that the ancient patrimony of Charlemagne was owed (to Napoleon III) as indemnity of what he had just made at the request of Europe, for Italy*". The Belgian press was furious and reproached him for calling for the annexation of this country by France. And he had to leave his country of asylum to return to France where Napoleon III had remitted his sentence. It is done in December.

It was in France that he waged his last battle. His articles, once again, earned him general hostility, and he replied in a book *entitled The Federative Principle,* in which he developed *"this approximation of anarchy"* which, in his eyes, was the Federation. In this he went against history. Feeling that the era of Empires was coming, five or six, he said, and in order to avoid "*this purgatory of a thousand years*" for humanity, well before Orwell, he called on people to oppose the federal idea to the unitary idea and to a world super-state with all the powers.

And for that he wants to remake, to refound the party of the revolution, and to propose precise actions. The elections of 1863 offer him the opportunity. Against the Empire and against the centralist democrats and the reds he calls for abstention. This will be his ultimate contribution. He will write to Chaudey *"in two words; from the point of view of principles we cannot vote under any pretext..."* And he develops this anarchist policy: to abstain is to refuse any essential reality to the power, to the governmental apparatus that pretends to be the emanation of the universal suffrage.

All this culminates in the prodigious formalization that is *The Political Capacity of the Working Classes, the* last work in which he takes up all his ideas and affirms, against Marxism and all the authoritarian variants, that the association can be constituted *"without engulfing the worker in the community ocean" nor making him "a serf of the State".*

A few months later, on January 19, 1865, the man who wrote *"man no longer wants to be organized, to be mechanized... freedom is the eternal contradiction that stands in the way of any thought and any force that would tend to dominate him"* died.

Gabriel RANDON (1867-1933)

"Jehan Rictus, the poet of the streets and cobblestones, the singer of misery"

Who has read *Les soliloques du pauvre*, the poem that was at the center of a successful show at the *Cheval Bleu* (Montmartre)... and especially who remembers it?

Son of a nobleman and a commoner, he was born on September 23, 1867 in Boulogne-sur-Mer, spending the first years of his life between France and England, where his father came from. But his parents separated when he was eight years old and he ended up in Paris with his mother in poverty.

The studious and gifted schoolboy is forced to leave school at the age of thirteen (he finds himself alone, poor with his mother, a mean woman who leads him a hard life) and to work at a thousand small jobs (errand boy, sweeper, laborer, runner at a publisher's and then at a hosier's, etc.). This miserable childhood is the subject of his novel *Fil de fer*.

At the age of eighteen he was on the streets of Paris, wandering from shelter to shelter and learning the language of the street. However, he frequented Montmartre and the anarchists, found a job as a paper-pusher at the Hôtel de Ville and began, encouraged by Albert Samain, to publish poems. He knows a period of wandering, quits his job, founds, without success, evenings of poetic diction, etc.

But the literary circle La Butte, which he frequented, gradually ensured a certain success for his poems, published in Parnassian and symbolist reviews. This fame and his collaboration to various reviews allow him to reach a certain ease, so much so that his poems *Les soliloques du pauvre*

(The poor man's soliloquies) are declaimed at the *Quat-z-arts* cabaret then at the *Chat Noir* (1896).

He then adopted the pseudonym of Jehan Rictus, who signed the publication of his collection *Les Soliloques du Pauvre* at the *Mercure de France.*

While writing for various magazines and newspapers, *Le Matin, Le Soir...*, he tried to produce, without much success, shows and concerts. He is praised by Jules Lemaitre, Taillande... and Léon Bloy who wrap him in a Nessus tunic that he will never leave... but ensures him a lasting success... from which he will live without renewing his verve nor digging new furrows.

He then published a pamphleteering essay, a literary bluff *The Edmond Rostand case,* a pantomime *The Woman of the World* and other small collections.

Then, gradually, the spokesman of the misery and the popular soul turns to, we are in 1914, the nationalism, becoming an ardent Camelot of the king in 1930.

He will die at the age of sixty-six, totally retracted, having shunned himself and absolutely forgotten or disowned by his former public.

However, let's remember what he was able to write before he became doddery and a stranger to himself.

THE SOLILOQUIES OF THE POOR

The Revenant
Extracts

Sometimes I think, when I'm driving to
doubled... to the left and without knowing my
poor thing in need of hope, and I see
I'm not allowed to sit or snooze
on the sidewalk or the tarmac of "my" house
Homeland; I say to myself: all the same, if there
r'viendrait!
Who? Well what! You know who,
eul'l'trimardeur galiléen, l'rouquin au coeur
bigger than this!

Of what? Well, it's him who's all larder
rolled in beautiful swaddling clothes because
his double daron was so tell'ment purotin
that he had to lay him on the manure, like this
the hard way, the cool way, to prove that the
of its crib sailed in the dung of
cow...

Extracts

If he would come! If he would come,
The blue man who walked on the sea
And what was the faith in stroll...
The guy who was swallowed by the women
(To the point that it was scandalous)
...
The Man with the beautiful eyes, the Man with the
beautiful dreams,
The carpenter is always on strike,
The artiss, the leader, the anarcho,
The burglars' interlude
(It would be a paradox
The gas that was worn on his back
Eune aut'croix qu'la Légion d'honneur!)

Mathurin RÉGNIER (1573-1613)

Herald of the license

His life is even more poorly known than his work, as the documents that attest to it are fragmentary and random. He was born in Chartres on December 21, 1573 to a father who was a notable in that city and a mother born Desportes, sister of the poet of the same name.

His father owned a game of paume on the Place de la Halle called *Le Tripot Régnier*. Mathurin was later accused of being congenitally debauched. This is pure slander because his father rented the establishment and exercised the worthy profession of alderman. Although he was destined for the ecclesiastical state and the succession of his uncle, which led to his being tonsured at the age of seven, the young boy's conduct during his youth was not very edifying, and he would even have composed satires calling into question the friends of his own family, which earned him some paternal corrections. At the age of twenty, he entered the service of the Cardinal de Joyeuse as a page, accompanying him on his mission to the Holy See during six trips. There he discovered the burlesque Italians and assiduously frequented the tripots. Left by his protector, he returned to France where he led a miserable life for ten years until the day when the death of his uncle Desportes (1606) left him a pension of 2,000 pounds that Henri IV allocated to him, and a canonry in the church of Notre-Dame de Chartres, of which he was the holder.

While continuing his life of bamboozler he writes. In 1596 having sung in his verses Gabrielle d'Estrées, the king's mistress, he became one of the official poets of the Court. This accomplished Latinist is also a lover of Montaigne, of Rabelais to whom he is close by the inspiration and the style, and of the authors of the Pléiade through whom he defends, making himself the herald of all the liberties, the absolute freedom of the inspiration. It is about them that he quarrels with Malherbe who was his friend, to whom he reproaches to be incapable of imagination. At the beginning of the 17th century, in 1608, he published his first ten satires which were very successful. The first edition is entitled *Premières Œuvres,* the second one published one year later, *Satyres.*

Having gathered around him a sort of literary cenacle whose humanism was the cement, he divided his time between Paris, where he was commissioned to write various works, and his abbey of Royaumont. He was never officially made a canon, as he did not complete the six-month residency in Chartres that this status required.

He was also ill, probably suffering from gravel like Montaigne, and ended up consulting a renowned surgeon in Orleans. But the operation failed and he died in October 1613 in an anonymous hotel room.

His satires are action portraits. He accumulates the details aiming at unmasking those which he depicts... with a sober ferocity. This one underlines the ridicule proceeding from the smugness of the narrow-mindedness. And the targets are reached.

Before tasting his satires, let's resurrect his epitaph:

"I lived without any thought
Letting myself go gently
To the right natural rent,
And if I am surprised why
Death dared to think of me
Who never thought of her".

Nicolas Edmé RESTIF de la BRETONNE (1734-1806)
The scorned Balzac

Nicolas-Edmé Restif, who will later add to his name de la Bretonne, was born in 1734 in Sacy in the Yonne where his father owned a small property. The eldest child of a second marriage and the eighth of fourteen children, he was born into a simple and hard-working family. As a result, he took on a country dress that he wore for many years.

However his fetishism of the feet, that of the young girls, and the shoes, was worth to him to enter by the small door, the door of the bottom, in the universe of the seduction. It will be the object of an intense attraction near the very young women, so much so that at the age of fifteen, rushing in the writing, he wrote an erotic poem dedicated to his twelve first mistresses. This precipitation in the universe of debauchery and sexual consumption was worth to him to be directed by his father towards an apprenticeship at a printer of Auxerre... of which he seduced without waiting the wife who did not cease to live his literary world under the name of *Mrs. Parangon.*

Leaving then Auxerre to carry out his companionship to the royal printing office (in Paris), he will be cried by all the grisettes of the city. His life will continue on the same pattern with the comedians, the nymphs of cabaret counters, the four-season merchants, the little and big ladies, blond as well as brown or redheaded, but whose feet charmed him. Continuing his quest for good fortune, he nevertheless married Agnès Lebègue in 1760, appeasing their continuous wars of delicate armistices with multiple conquests.

However, misery lurks, he is thirty-three years old and the printer's worker sometimes without work despite his unceasing quest for work as well as love(s).

This period precipitates him into the literary world and his first work *La Famille vertueuse* is not successful. But he continued with *Lucile* who brought him the sum of three louis... with which he lived for four months. This licentious work, as will be the following ones, such as *La Confidence nécessaire, Le pied de Fanchette,* is worth to him an increasing vogue.

From then on, he decided to be, in addition to a novelist, the *"legislator of a new morality"*. He publishes *the Pornographe* denounced as absolutely contrary to good morals. However, Mr. de Sartine, lieutenant general of police, alerted, allows, on his own initiative, the edition (as well as the emperor Joseph II in Vienna).

His success led him to persist in the path of *"societal reform"* by writing *Le Mimographe ou le théâtre réformé par une femme,* then to cease his vain effort to return to the literary essence through *Le Ménage parisien, a* violent satire of the people of letters and their milieu. From this contempt for this world that he judges artificial and contrived, is born *Le Paysan perverti,* a merciless satire of the society of marquises and duchesses, of the promised frills, of the brandished glories. This book which puts in scene a peasant entering in training with a painter, (besides magnificently illustrated), is the major work of this marvellous polemicist.

I prescribe, without revealing more its contents, the reading of this work of which Mercier said this: *"the absolute silence of the literati on this novel full of life and expression, and of which so few of us are capable of having conceived the plan and formed the execution, has well right to astonish us, and engages us to point out the injustice or the insensitivity of the majority of the people of letters who admire only small cold and conventional beauties, and who do not know how to recognize or to acknowledge the most striking and the most vigorous features of a strong and picturesque imagination. Would that the reign of imagination would be totally extinguished among us, and that one would no longer know how to sink into these vast, moral and endearing compositions which characterize the works of the Abbé Prévost and of his happy rival, M. Rétif de la Bretonne".*

This work precipitates Restif in the heart of contemporary literature and fortune. In less than ten years, he amasses more than 6,000 francs, becomes famous and courted by the booksellers. He remains for all that the worthy peasant, abstaining from occupying a place among the writers of the time, being the object of criticism and disdain, but also of the friendship of some, of which Crébillon, the son, to quote only him.

Restif also remains the most intrepid runner of adventures that can be imagined and that nothing scares. From this ceaseless quest for beauty comes *Les Contemporaines ou Aventures des plus jolies femmes de l'âge actuel,* these sixty-five volumes recounting his excursions (often nocturnal) and his persistent spying (which some have imagined to be related to police "*missions*") through Paris.

The vogue of his writings has gradually ceased to be only a library (and bibliophile) memory today.

For all that, this peasant, son of a peasant incarnate, fiellishly described as the Voltaire of the chambermaids or the Rousseau of the Halles, had a life adorned with titled or notorious company: the Duchess of Luynes, the Abbé Sieyès, the Duke of Mailly, the Countess of Argenson as well as Beaumarchais, Joseph Chénier, Mirabeau, Grégoire?[33]

The French Revolution did not suspend his existence, he continued his nocturnal wanderings, protecting women assaulted and rejected by their men, the drunkards, wandering in the most sinister districts under the benevolent eye of the maréchaussée. He will evoke this troubled period in the last volume of the *Nuits de Paris* in a noticeably bitter tone.

However, this period was fatal to his image and his fortune and a decline began in 1794. He is alone, isolated, and is fed by his daughter Marion[34], herself a widow and mother of three children. His work *Monsieur Nicolas, which* has had very modest success, is the story of this existential disintegration. The few écus he had left fueled the publication of his last work *Posthumes ou lettres du Tombeau,* a description of the last days of a poor old man. The seizure of this work, in the new era of freedom (to be silent?) brings him the coup de grace.

He stops seeing the world but persists in frequenting cabarets, and provocations in the street(s) against the public order, which is worth him some arrests.

33. He is received but also receives... with dignity.

34. He had with his wife Agnes Lebègue two daughters, Agnes the elder and the younger Marion who, after her widowhood in 1778, never left her father to whom she returned.

The passing of time did not offer him the peace of age, but an accumulation of infirmities which precipitated him into the refuge of his house of the Bûcherie where he expired on February 3, 1806 at the age of seventy-two.

When he was buried in the Montparnasse cemetery, his funeral was attended by nearly 2,000 people and a delegation from the Institute.

In short, his death resurrected the author and the scorned man.

Small final illustration in front of the author's tomb:

> *"A fat man, an energetic man, a superstitious monster, can only say that it is an outrage to reason, to morals, and to sound philosophy to say that education is independent of any sentiment, of any religious principle. Base morality, you atrabilious fools, on reciprocity; it is the only reasonable basis, and God is the author of reason! It is blasphemy to say that our reason deceives us! All religions were an error, convenient to the first teachers of societies, harmful to the deceived.*
> *One cannot conceive of the hatred that some sophists have shown against religion. Vile and deceitful man who speaks thus, look at the evil that priests have done and are doing... Look at the Vendée, at Belgium, and get out of your astonishment!*
> *As for the worship of the supreme being, it is praiseworthy. But it is still an absurdity to say that it has been left at the disposal of man, who could deprive the supreme being of it! No, no, the physical homage which the whole nation pays, and which does not depend on man, is the only one necessary.*
> *Moral homage is necessary to man if it is not necessary to God. It is to agree with me that it is useless."*

Auguste-Jules RICHEPIN (1849-1926)
The tribune of the beggars

Auguste-Jules Richepin - Jean Richepin is his pen name - was born on February 14, 1849 in Medea, where his father, a doctor in the army, was stationed. His tanned complexion made some people say that he had Arab blood in his veins, others that he was descended from the bohemians - those who had settled in the 16th century in the north-east of Picardy, in the Thiérache.

In truth, his roots were deeply rooted in deepest France: his ancestors, farmers, ploughmen, sheep breeders, are to be found in the department of Aisne, since 1778.

His father was the first to rise in the social hierarchy. His father's travels allowed young Auguste to travel, not only to Algeria, but also to France. The child is at ease everywhere. When his father left for the Crimea, the mother and her son, aged six, settled in Paris, in Belleville to be precise. It is perhaps from this period that his sympathy for the poor of the capital dates. His ability to learn is great; he acquires during his travels a rich vocabulary, both in the official language and in the dialects heard here and there.

A student at the Lycée Charlemagne in Paris - top of the class - he passed his baccalaureate at the age of sixteen. His father wanted his son to be a doctor, but he wanted to be a writer. In 1867, he was admitted to the École normale supérieure. It is in the order of things, he is a brilliant subject. At the end of his life, he will write :

"I passed my degree, the first in my section, I confess. My second year was cut short by a four-month leave of absence, supposedly because of illness. Then the war came and I was never cube.
From my sixteen years at EN, I kept some very good memories, two and three dear and solid friendships, the benefit of lively philosophical and literary discussions in a society of alert, sharp, curious minds, a copious supply of substantial readings and above all the training for long work sessions."

He is a voracious reader, all styles and genres interest him. Gifted with an extraordinary memory and an innate gift for languages, he amazed his teachers. It is, during his stay at the EN that he begins to write, in verse. Some poems of this time will appear in *La Chanson des Gueux*. By the time he left the EN, his tastes and personality were already firmly established.

"A passionate humanist, deeply sensitive to the beauty of words and rhythm, he dreamed of an art rejuvenated by the verve of the people, an art both familiar and refined that would be that of a great poet and a village minstrel. Thus at twenty years old, Jean Richepin was already himself" (Émile Mâle).

Like many other writers, Richepin entered literature through the door of journalism.

He was a journalist at *L'Est*, a newspaper in Besançon, when war was declared with Prussia. He knew "*the cold, the rainy skies, without officers, without food, without hope*". When the armistice was signed, he returned to Paris and found the capital in the hands of the Commune. He had sympathy for the ideals of the Communards, but their excessive violence shocked him. One of his biographers will say that "*from the roof of the house he occupied in rue Vaugirard, in the manner of Nero before Rome burned, Jean Richepin throwing a Spanish cape on his shoulders, in a great state of excitement, he will declare the poem of Victor Hugo 'The Fire of Rome,' while the flames consumed the Tuileries and the City Hall."*

Did this theatrical attitude, this display of insouciance, correspond to the reality of his most intimate convictions, or was it only provocation?

He then went through a bohemian period, during which he frequented the Latin Quarter, gave private lessons and even became for three months a professor of literature at the preparatory school of Saint-Cyr, near Paris, whose students were particularly insolent, rowdy and rude. Shortly after his admission to this school, he was elected to the French Academy.

An American newspaper reports the first contact of the future Immortal with the students of Saint-Cyr:

> *"The next morning Richepin sat at his desk and waited for the students. They came running in, whistling, stamping their feet. A deep, low voice stopped them dead in their tracks and they heard, surprised: 'Young people, I ask you to know that I am not here for my pleasure. I am here to earn a living. Is there anyone among you who wants to stop me? If there is, let's go out into the yard and explain ourselves, but with the understanding that you and I are about the same age, it is with our fists that we will explain ourselves.' And just as he finished his sentence, he banged the desk so hard that the papers flew out. The students behaved like lambs afterwards."*

Thereafter, Richepin wrote articles for more or less obscure publications that few people read; he was paid little, but what did he care, his name was published.

He then wrote in *Le Mot d'ordre, Le Corsaire, La Vérité,* and in literary journals, *La Renaissance littéraire et artistique* and *La Revue Moderne.* The twenty years following the war were marked by a proliferation of literary coteries, whose members displayed extravagant behavior during noisy demonstrations. The Parnassian movement extinguished, the literary scene became a battlefield on which rival groups fought to win the war of words. Richepin adheres to the movement with all the vigor of his superb youth. His picturesque personality, his courage, his good humor, make him known, admired and loved by the writers of the Left Bank. He adopted eccentric, sometimes aggressive clothing that served these young writers as "publicity support".

"One could not reproach him for having endowed himself with the relief that gave a young writer very eager not to be ignored, a large gray felt hat, a Tyrolean hat brightened by two red tassels, a velvet jacket and Hungarian hussar pants: what is this large hat, murmured the already conquered crowd?

And there was always someone to answer: "It's Jean Richepin, a young poet with a future. They say a lot of good things about the works he will write". (Ernest Raynaud, *La Bohême sous le Second Empire).*

Around 1868, he frequented the salon of Nina de Villard in Montmartre, the most chic place in Paris. Famous poets rubbed shoulders there: Leconte de Lisle, Bainville, Hérédia, Coppée, Anatole France; painters: Manet, Degas; musicians: Berlioz, Wagner; pamphleteers: Jules Vallès, Camille Pelletan, Henri Rochefort.

This heterogeneous group had a common enthusiasm for new ideas, a hatred for academic art, and a deep disdain for bourgeois materialism. There was such an atmosphere of easy mockery, irony, and fantasy in this salon that it could be considered as the precursor of the *Chat Noir.* The plays written in collaboration were performed; the women cut and sewed the fancy costumes, the men set up the stage, painted the scenery. Richepin reigned supreme over this group of amateurs. Many people crowded into this place where they laughed, shouted, sang, danced, ate and drank a lot. All these young people had a lot of fun and wrote, among others, *Le Moine bleu,* a buffoonery, a parody of Hernani, Marion Delorme, Tristan and Yseut.

After the 1870 debacle, the young French intellectuals, the Bohemians of the Left Bank, among whom Jean Richepin was the master of thought, proclaimed their defiance of laws, conventions, in a word, of the established order. It is however a bohemia *"less ragged than the old one, more intellectual than pecuniary".*

Adolphe Brisson, evoking the Richepin of the inter-age period, wrote: *"he took the bohemian life seriously and sincerely believed that a lyric poet cannot, without falling apart, adhere to a regular existence and that he is obliged by human respect, to mix with the Court of Miracles.*

He was a being as uncomplicated as possible; one should not look in his work for disturbing underbelly, nor for enigmatic beyond".

His dress code attracts attention. All the young writers know each other, meet in the cafés near the Pantheon or the Odeon. Richepin seduces them with his physique, his smile, his kindness, his theatrical gesture. In the Latin Quarter he met Paul Bourget, Adrien Juvigny, Maurice Bouchor and Raoul Ponchon, the closest of them all, who wore zinc rings in a spiral pattern on his fingers. Richepin immortalized the astonishing figure *"À Raoul Ponchon"* in *La Chanson des Gueux* :

"You smell of wine, O exquisite unleavened dough...".

In 1873, he meets Mounet-Sully who will become the great French tragedian. He scratched him, *"at last a young man has entered classical tragedy like a young bull in the store of a potter"*. Mounet-Sully invites him, he is seduced: *"I saw entering my house a very handsome boy with long black hair, a newborn beard, a strangely sympathetic physiognomy"*. Very quickly, the two young men become friends. Mounet-Sully will interpret thereafter, at the Comédie-Française, plays by Richepin, *Par le Glaive, La Martyre* and an adaptation of *Macbeth.*

It was also in 1873 that Richepin and the caricaturist André Gill wrote together a short verse piece, *L'Étoile.* It is thanks to André Gill that *La Chanson des Gueux was* created in 1876. Here is how: at the end of a good meal, well watered, Gill recited *Le Vieux Lapin* in front of Georges Decaux, editor of *La Lune Rousse* and *L'Éclipse,* two periodicals in which Gill drew regularly. Decaux was moved to tears and wanted to know the author.

And Richepin wrote, *"Gill took advantage of the emotion in which he had thrown Decaux to give him the right blow of the book to be published, by presenting me to him as the author of these verses which had brought tears to his eyes, of the author in need of a publisher.*

We got together and that's how, thanks to a good lunch, La Chanson des Gueux, *already so many years old, was born in June 1876."*

This work was considered an outrage to morality, to good manners, a threat to the social order, and an affront to French literature.

The Charivari addressed an open letter to Richepin:

> *"The volume that you have just published under the title of* La Chanson des Gueux, *is an unhealthy, guilty and deeply useless work. If it has, by chance, the pretension to make an act of social protest, it does it very clumsily because it makes perfectly odious those whose portraits it illuminates. She exhibits their vices too complacently for us to care about their misery. If she has literary ambitions, these ambitions are disappointed, because in this jumble of deliberate coarseness, premeditated brutality, and cynicism, there is nothing that smacks of lived and sincere inspiration. The young people, formerly, had another ideal that the words of the prison, the lupanar or the mastroquet".*

The Charivari posing as a champion of virtue, this may surprise you!

Louis Veuillot, the *"Catholic pamphleteer"*, wrote: *"the author wanted and perhaps believed that he was not doing politics, but several verses of his Song contain the very sonorous notes of the "new" layers. In the place of Mr. Gambetta we would take care of these peasantries which could become more effective Marseillaises than the old one... ".*

Richepin was condemned in the name of the Moral Order: *"the condemnation of Richepin for the outrages to morality contained in certain pieces of* La Chanson des Gueux *marks one of the stages of our national life under the 3rd Republic, that of the 'Moral Order'".*

Arthur Christian, a young lawyer, defended him, *"the Song of the Beggars is not the work of a professional of bohemia; neither it is appropriate to consider it as a thesis; it is only a game... These characters sketched by the poet, are not, certainly, of an edifying morality, but they are true, real, alive. Does one heal a wound by diverting the germ?...*

Among the 75 poems that make up the Chanson des Gueux, *there are only six in which one can find passages of this nature. If the same security had been applied previously to the literary works which thus would have reached us intact of those which today make our admiration?"*

The court pronounced a sentence of one month's imprisonment, a fine of 500 francs and the loss of his civil rights. Decaux the publisher and Debous the printer were fined 500 francs. Richepin protested against the sentence in an article published in *La Tribune*, a socialist newspaper, in August 1876: *"What was struck from my book was indeed the freedom to write and the freedom to think.*

In spite of the Revolution, in spite of the modern spirit, we still have neither the freedom of the pen, nor the freedom of speech... I painted the little ones, the barefooted, the starving. I tried to show the mud in which society forces them to live; I stirred up this mud with a cynical but pitiful hand. I wanted to bring down a ray of sunshine, and they found it unhealthy, immoral, monstrous...

In a word, I wanted to make the Beggars sing, and the honest people have just brutally shut my mouth with the eternal war cry of the happy 'the beggars have no right to speak. Silence to the poor!'"

Later, in the preface to the second edition of *La Chanson des Gueux,* he wrote: *"I protest with all my might against this absurdity, Justice controlling Literature. Art is one thing, and Morality is another, and these two things have really nothing to do together... I believe that it is essential for the poet to be of his time, to be interested in the life which fights, suffers, cries or sings around him, and I estimate that one can produce a really human work only on the condition of being fundamentally human".*

Fortunately for him, the regime of the Sainte-Pélagie prison where he entered on September 10, 1876 was not too harsh.

His imprisonment reinforces his fame; he is considered a martyr of the freedom of thought. He recovers his civil rights; the young authors admire him more. A few years before the publication of the Chanson des Gueux, in 1874, the three friends, Richepin, Bouchor and Paul Bourget, founded their own literary movement, Les Vivants, in opposition to the Parnassiens or Impassibles. Their ideal, always the same: to change the conditions of society. The group did not become very important: Ponchon, Maurice Rollinat, Gabriel Vicaire and Charles Cros were the only new recruits.

In their *Histoire de la poésie française depuis 1850*, Paul Fort and Louis Mandin draw a parallel between this new poetic trend and the naturalist novel:

> *"The upheavals of 1870-71, the fall of personal power, the advent of the republican regime, by bringing to the forefront of the news public affairs, the power of the people and the agitations of the crowd, were like a signal to which soon responded the blossoming of a more popular literature, full of the sounds of the street and which, sometimes, liked to frolic even in the stream. In prose, it is the naturalist novel... In poetry, it is the joyful companions, Richepin, Ponchon, Bouchor".*

The aspirations of the group Les Vivants were legitimate, but they did not become a school. They were satisfied to translate with humor scenes of the everyday life of the petty bourgeois, people of modest origin, the poor. The group of the Vivants did not form a restricted circle and Verlaine and Rimbaud joined them. Richepin is attracted by Rimbaud: *"a clumsy peasant's look, big hands and feet, thatched hair, but angelic eyes, unforgettable eyes. Good poet and better than good, but what a bad sleeper!"*[35]. Rimbaud's more than extravagant behavior - he often exceeds the limits - drives some away. Verlaine and Richepin continued to be close to him, spending most of the time in the cafés of Boul'Mich

35. Richepin, *Germain Nouveau and Rimbaud* - memories and unpublished papers - *La Revue de France*, January 1927 page 125.

drinking absinthe. Richepin was different from Rimbaud: he was affable, not *"addicted"* to absinthe. In spite of Rimbaud's bad manners, of his immorality, he never condemned him and recognized in him a genius. Germain Nouveau was also a disciple of Richepin, he was of the same temperament as Rimbaud: a party animal but an admirable rhymer.

For Verlaine, it was different. After the publication in 1884 of *Blasphèmes*, a collection of atheist poems, Verlaine wrote a pamphlet full of contempt and malicious insinuations for Richepin. But Richepin forgave Verlaine, as evidenced by the very friendly letters they exchanged at the end of the latter's life.

After Verlaine's death, Richepin wrote a very moving tribute: *His Funeral*, in which he evoked *"the delicate color of the winter sky on this day of sadness, the old Church of Saint-Étienne-du-Mont, and the composition of the afflicted crowd that came to accompany him," "no one who came by simple duty of politeness or by desire to be present without more! Not a single indifferent person! All friends and sincere admirers".*

He was angry with the Parisians for having abandoned Verlaine, the descendant of François Villon, for having let him die in great poverty. *"He was glad to know that somewhere in the Latin Quarter there was an incorrigible refractory to bourgeois life... a kind of modern hoodlum, having taken up the tradition of the 'bad boys' of the Middle Ages and continuing those of the poets dedicated to the hospital. He was delighted in Paris to have a similar 'number' in his gallery of curious beasts."*

Richepin gave lectures on Verlaine in several European countries (a death mask of the poet was one of his most cherished possessions).

After 1876, it is very difficult to establish a chronology of Richepin's overflowing activities, especially since the legend has taken hold of him: he travels through France with a group of gypsies, he unloads ships in Bordeaux, he embarks in Nantes on a merchant navy vessel... What is certain is that he did indeed have an experience as an apprentice fisherman on *the Hirondelle* off Dieppe.

The impressions he received from the wind, the waves and the sky, appear in *La Mer* and *Le Flibustier*. Speaking of the sea, Richepin will write *"I have known its 'sweet' and its 'bitter'; I have sailed in nutshells, throwing the net or taking the watch, I have plunged into it, I have abandoned myself to the rocking of the waves... I don't love the sea, I love it! And I have sung it with the fervor of a poet celebrating his ideal mistress and*

I am sometimes referred to by this name, the poet of the sea, of which none could make me prouder."

Back in Paris, Richepin frequented the literary circles of the Left Bank, including *the Club des Hydropathes,* founded by Emile Goudeau.

In October 1878, about fifty people gathered at the Café de la Rive Gauche heard Paul Mounet, Goudeau and Rollinat read their works. Soon the group had to move to the Café de l'Avenir, at the corner of the Boulevard Saint-Michel and the quay. Famous people, Guy de Maupassant, Jean Moréas, François Coppé, Charles Cros, Sarah Bernard meet there. A newspaper, *L'Hydropathe, was* even published; it gave the minutes of the meetings and published the writings of its members. It was during one of these evenings that the baritone Georges Fragerolle performed several poems by Richepin that he had set to music: *Le Noël des Gueux, les Vieux Papillons, Le Bain à Quat'sous.*

The *Hydropaths* were moderate drinkers, preferring poetry and music to the fumes of alcohol: *"From nine o'clock to midnight, the poets followed the singers; it was not mutual admiration, no, it was simply a cure of art, spirit and gaiety for each of the participants. When leaving the sessions, one felt better, thanks to Beauty, who, for three hours, had reigned as sovereign mistress".* (Jules Lévy, *Les Hydropathes*)

The Hydropathes remained active until 1881. Then it was, under the impulse of Rodolphe Salis, *Le Chat Noir,* Boulevard Rochechouart in Montmartre, which became their headquarters: *"the Latin Quarter became then like a small desert. Richepin had left it to live in Montmartre. Bouchor made only rare appearances there..."*

In 1879, Richepin married Eugénie Constant in Manosque, a talented pianist and student of Emmanuel Chabrier. She was the opposite of her husband. Three children were born from this union.

It is from this moment that Richepin ceases his wanderings, although he does not lead a cloistered life. All the great ones are his friends: Barbey d'Aurevilly, François Coppé, Jules Renard, Edmond Rostand. When Richepin was qualified by some of his detractors as *a "circus rider",* as a *"Genghis Khan of the fairground circus"*, it was Coppé who defended him: *"Get drunk on harsh and popular wine, but frank and pure, and you will love, as I do, this true poet in whom art has not killed nature, in whom letters have not stifled naivety, descending in a straight and legitimate line from Villon and Saint-Amand."*

When he converted to Catholicism, Richepin lost some of his friends. He also had enemies among the men of letters: Émile Zola, Jules Vallès and Léon Bloy.

Zola refuses to recognize in him the poet of the little people. He certainly admires his slang, from which he will probably draw inspiration to write *L'Assomoir* published one year after *La Chanson des Gueux*, but he considers that Richepin lacks sincerity: *"one feels that the scoundrel details in Richepin's work are not lived, that he has put them there to make an effect. The painters have an expression which expresses clearly the thing: it is made of chic, it is a fantasy which plays the nature but which was not copied on it... Thus Mr. Richepin who poses as a realist, seems to me to be even more romantic"*[36].

The relationship between Zola and Richepin was not at its best. In a review by Huysmans *À vau l'eau*, Richepin dares to predict that *"Naturalism, as a system, will pass as did the first Romanticism, both equally to hell, whether in holy water for the one, or as the other in water of brimstone."*

However, with his usual loyalty, Richepin declares that Zola is a great novelist in spite of his pseudo-scientific theories and proposes him for the cross of the Legion of Honor: *"He's a bad head all right! A grumpy person who pushes all his colleagues with his fists and* his *feet, so be it! An acerbic and unjust critic, that's understood! But he is a hard worker. And even those who don't like the man like me, take the hat off to the writer, for his valour, his stubbornness in the work, for the pieces of mastery that there are in his pile of clay"*.

When *Germinal* appears, Richepin writes to Zola to express his enthusiasm. Zola is very touched: *"I am very touched, very proud, all the more proud that there was sometimes some bitterness between us. All that is far away, and there is always room for esteem and admiration between workers. Thank you for your bravado in extending your hand to me, which I shake very affectionately."*

The quarrel between Jules Vallès and Richepin arose from a satirical drawing, *Le convoi du pauvre (The Poor Man's Convoy)*, by Gill, in which Vallès was depicted as a mangy dog with a saucepan attached to his tail, following the poor man's hearse. At the same time, Gill wrote an open letter to the *Figaro* in which he disavowed the activities of the Communards. On

36. (Zola, *Literary Documents*, page 148).

his return from exile in 1880, Vallès learned that Gill was ill, that his brain had gone haywire, and he took advantage of this illness to accuse him in three articles published in *Le Réveil*. Richepin did not admit: *"I used to love Vallès very much, but today it's over, I am content to admire him, but without understanding him and I don't love him anymore".*

Léon Bloy was not tender with Richepin either, calling him *"a man with guts"*, a *"bourgeois stallion"*, an *"ideal and definitive ham"*. *The Song of the Beggars* is for him a work of violent effort.

Whatever the case and whatever the opinions of some and others, Richepin is definitely a man in the spotlight. He can't take a step, say a word, without the gazettes being immediately buzzing. He shares his fortune with Madame Sarah Bernard. Like her, his life, his adventures, his physiognomy, are known to all. He is a restless, boisterous, restless personality, a talent discussed by some, praised excessively by others, but denied by no one.

The year 1897, with *Le Chemineau,* marks the peak of Richepin's success.

In 1901, Richepin divorced to marry Mrs. Louis Gamme from whom he had two sons that he legitimized. Until the end of his life - he died in 1926 - he knew glory, fame, even if, sometimes, the new generation was not very tender with him. Thus Benjamin Crémieux wrote in 1926, in *Les Nouvelles Littéraires* :

> *"He is not so much a great writer as a powerful, typical and living figure. His memory, in the absence of all his work, deserves to be perpetuated. There would be a beautiful life of Jean Richepin to be written, where one would see him entirely, from his childhood in the garrison of Médéa to the afternoon when he received Joffre at the Academy, and the unity of this existence would be provided by his worship of poetry and by this gift, donquichottesque but admirable, to democratize poetry, without betraying it... With him dies a beautiful ideal".*

The poems which made condemn Jean Richepin :

Son of girl, Ballad of happy life, Idyll of poor, Thug, Brother it is necessary to live, Sonnet argotique.

Antoine de RIVAROL (1753-1801)
The impertinent highness of the salons

Voltaire, whose wickedness could not be disputed, said of him: "*He is the Frenchman par excellence*". This beautiful praise did not convince a forgetful posterity. Of Rivarol there remains the title of a weekly newspaper, a unanimous recognition of a literary court with unknown rulings, from Sainte-Beuve to Jünger and a note in the various encyclopedias.

Antoine Roch was born on June 26, 1753 in Bagnols-sur-Cèze in Languedoc. His father owned the inn of the Croix Blanche at the Porte des Peyrieres, which still exists. He was also a "silk miller" and "controller of the rights gathered in the department of Alais". In short, he was a notable and above all a man of great quality, a scholar, with a perfect knowledge of ancient history but also of Latin and Greek. In addition to his official functions, this man taught young people in Bagnol... and practiced versification. The child had everything to succeed in life: an honorable family, caring parents, a cultured father and sufficient means to push himself through life. Of course, he will have to share with the fifteen children that his father Jean-Baptiste will have after him with Catherine Avon, but only five will reach adulthood.

If her family is of middle-class life, she is of aristocratic ancestry. And even of very old ancestry since we find mention of it in the Italian Parmesan where it received in 1050, from the Emperor Conrad II, the fief of Rivarolo. The multiple movements of its ancestors will lead this branch of the family to France. If some have doubted and laughed at it, such as Sophie Arnould who exclaims, when she learns that Rivarol is adorned with a noble title: "*It's a count for a laugh that we are being made here*", the facts are stubborn: the former is not a usurper.

It is from his father, of whom he was the favorite, that Antoine received his first rudiments. Then he went to the Joséphistes college in Bagnols and finally, at the age of eighteen, to the Sulpicians' seminary in Bourg-Saint-Andéol. It is with the small collar and the title of abbot that he leaves the Sainte-Garde seminary of Avignon to appear, according to the formula, in the world.

In 1777, he arrived in Paris where he would later say "*Providence is greater than anywhere else*" and settled in the Hotel d'Espagne.

In less time than it takes to wear out a suit, his refined elegance, his acid and penetrating mind, the extraordinary seduction of his conversation... and his charm open the salons to him. It is true that he also had the chance to be helped in this hard conquest by one of the most brilliant minds of this fertile century, d'Alembert, whom he met, according to the story, in the Luxembourg garden.

Very quickly he becomes a figure of this universe of salons, where the world and the demi-monde cross in a rustle of vanities and a agitation of ideas which testify of the fever of agony of a society. It is the time of light and piquant opuscules of which the first is the *Letter on the poem of the gardens* of the abbot Delille.

This courtier of the aristocracy sees himself crazy for having neglected the people of the vegetables. And this gives: "*Delille will pass, the turnips will remain*". This is followed by a parody of the *Songe d'Athalie*, a letter to Monsieur le Président... and articles in *Le Mercure* created by Panckoucke. This from 1778 to 1783: a meager record, but Rivarol is above all an improviser who does not like "*the writings*". He also composed a character of nonchalant dandy (as Barbey d'Aurevilly will describe him) managing to sustain a sparkling conversation without any previous effort. In truth, there is a lot of coquetry and facade there. He works at night, in his bed, and notes ideas, good words and formulas which will be so many materials skilfully arranged, and where the improvisation will be reduced to the superfluous. In short, an enormous preparatory work as his friends and collaborators Chênedollé and Dampmartin will attest.

We are in 1784, Rivarol has produced little but he is famous[37]. He is thirty years old, and therefore old enough to establish himself. His wife,

37. His apprenticeship years are over and he is considered the arbiter of elegance.

Miss Matther-Flint is English. "*God preserve you from the Love of an Englishwoman*", he will write later; she is older than him, rather pretty and pedantic. She was older than him, rather pretty and pedantic. Moreover, she had no money and a rapacity that the poor boy would have to pay for: by marriage contract all the couple's property belonged to her. They have a son, but very quickly a certain incompatibility of moods begins to emerge.

This strong character is also a possessive and narcissistic wife: "*I was his wife par excellence,*" she writes, "*the one who took the place of everything*". In fact, she dismisses the merrymakers and the companions of ribaldry and the scenes multiply.

One year later he left and their divorce will be pronounced on XII Brumaire, year III. He was a bad husband, because he had a bad wife.

In 1784 he published *Le Discours sur l'Universalité de la langue française* which was awarded a prize by the Berlin Academy. The success of this work earned him the title of member of the Academy and a pension from Louis XVI. In this work which consecrates the superiority of this language:

> "*It is a question,*" he says, "of *showing to what extent the position of France, its political constitution, the influence of its climate, the genius of its writers, the character of its inhabitants and the opinion it has been able to give to the rest of the world, to what extent, I say, so many diverse causes have been able to combine and unite to make this language such a prodigious fortune.*"

He affirms that language is part of a whole and cannot be dissociated from economy, culture, literature, politics...

> "*Between the language and the speaker,*" he explains, "*there is an intimate agreement that can only be achieved in the mother tongue. The great national languages tend towards the universal. It is to underline the spiritual origin of the language. Rousseau had anticipated it in his Essay on the origin of languages.*"

He then compares the different languages of Europe, their disadvantages and virtues, but he also develops, with an astonishing modernity, an analysis of the genesis of a language which makes him one of the very first linguists.

The superiority of French, of which he affirms that "*what is not clear is not French*", leads him to proclaim: "*The time seems to have come,*" he adds, "*to say the French world as once the Roman world*".

This speech is followed by a translation of Dante's *Inferno,* the first in that language. This one is qualified for some as "*beautiful infidel*"; however, Rivarol's bias is to translate sensations and for that he resorts to a poetic prose.

In 1788 he publishes *Le Petit Almanach des Grands Hommes,* a Pantheon of nothingness, for the year, and puts to the sword of ridicule the cutists who pretend to conquer fame and engages in a work of merciless literary police that discourages the swindlers of talent. *The Letters to Necker* follow in which he denounces the deism of this one in the name of the ignored reason. He also accused in this last one who, "*being in charge of a water mill looks where the wind comes from*", in short an opportunist, what the future will confirm. He is not yet strictly speaking a royalist. Like everyone else, he was influenced by a few extraordinary people and was influenced by his environment and his century. His political thought and his conception of the society are inspired by the ideas of Montesquieu. He will never cease to be faithful to him and will write at the end of his life, addressing himself to Chênedollé: "*Here is my man. He is the only one I can read today*". But he accepts all the ideas that he then analyzes and adopts or fights them: "*One does not fire guns at ideas*". His contempt is not for the ideas he does not share or for those who profess them, but for those, especially leaders of society or clerics, who do not have any and talk about them. Foolishness, and wickedness its double, are his two favorite targets and characterize those in whom he sees enemies, but also, the infidelity to their convictions, their friends and their family. In short, to the foolish and the wicked, we must add the opportunists and the cowards.

At the dawn of the Revolution, he published *Le Petit dictionnaire des grands hommes et de la Révolution* dedicated to Madame de Staël as it was a list of her worshippers. In this almanac, written like a dictionary, he portrays without kindness all those who play a role in the revolutionary process. His strokes are directed against those whom he considers as "*worms of the social body [of] intriguers thirsty for power and money who use the lights of the old people to overthrow everything*". He wages what must be called an intellectual war against those whose project is to destroy civilization.

He was not a member of any club because he was too concerned about his freedom. But he accepts, at the request of the abbot Sabatier de Castres, to write the famous *Journal politique national* from July 1789 to October 1790 where Burke will draw the main arguments of the counter-revolutionary thought. The journalist Rivarol paints pictures of events in the manner of a painter. From these pictures he nourishes a political theory. His papers are sober, documented, rich in ideas as well as facts, without superfluous comments and idle digressions, punchy and above all of a total freedom of speech. He is then rather open to changes and critical towards the Court and its theory of greedy and vain courtiers. But he does not want violence. So when on September 11, 1789 the Assembly suspends the right of veto of the king, he understands that it is finished with the monarchy and writes:

> *"The wrongs of the Capital, or rather its crimes, are too well known: it has already provided subjects of tragedy to posterity and terrible arguments to the enemies of freedom. Woe to those who stir up the depths of a nation! There are no centuries of light for the rabble".*

His pen is unleashed. Louis XVI "*is now only the grand officer of the National Assembly. The title of king is preserved to him like an ancient decoration... France is now a democracy armed with a crown*".

And he senses that France is moving towards dictatorship:

"*Your real crime, National Assembly, is to have slandered the revolution, by making it bear poisoned fruit... yes, we will owe you the despotism of one...*"

Counter-revolutionary he will be from now on, but not conservative. Of the division of the society in distinct orders he thinks that it is about a "*Gothic use born of barbaric centuries*", of the privileges and feudal rights that "*the nobles take their memories for rights and are not more than the masks of their ancestors*". What he refuses is physical violence and the destruction of the civilizational heritage. He does not want either a pure democracy with Sieyès because "*when the people are king, the rabble is queen*".

He is an elitist, but this elitism is not that of wealth and he denounces a revolution made by the people but "for the 6,000 capitalists", hence his aversion to the power of money.

Politics must take into account natural situations and inequalities, intellectual (spirit, talent, intelligence...) or social (leadership skills, vigor at work, willingness to promote oneself...) are a fact. "*On the contrary, it has made them very unequal; one is born strong and the other weak; one is healthy and the other infirm, not all are equally skilful and vigilant. The masterpiece of an ordered society is to make equal by laws those whom nature has made so unequal by means.*"

He joins from then on, to lead this ultimate fight of denunciation of a terror in gestation, the team of Peltier to the Acts of the Apostles (apostles of the freedom and the royal democracy). He finds there some characters of which Champcenetz, of which it is necessary to say two words. René Ferdinand Quentin de Richebourg de Champcenetz, Knight of Malta, was born in 1759. He was a remarkable swordsman, a wonderful journalist, a merry man and even a libertine. He was a faithful friend and an unparalleled collaborator. They were called *Guyenne* and *Gascogne*. As a polemist writer, Champcenetz was nicknamed Gobemouches sans souci. Collaborator of the *Acts of the Apostles* he refused to emigrate and was arrested. To Fouquier-Tinville who announced his condemnation to the scaffold he asked: *"Can I be replaced in this case as in the army? - No! Why? - Because I would like you to be my replacement"*. He will be guillotined laughing on July 25, 1794.

The other companions are Peltier, Suleau and Mirabeau-tonneau, the younger of Mirabeau-tonnerre. It is not only a question of laughter and their newspaper is a newspaper of combat.

However, the spirit is never absent, as this text shows:

> *"Article 1: Starting July 14 of this year, days will be equal to nights for the entire surface of the earth, with the day beginning at five o'clock.*
> *Article II: At the time when the day ends, the moon will begin to shine and it will be in its fullness until the sunrise.*
> *Article III: There will reign constantly from one end of the globe to the other a moderate and always equal temperature.*
> *Article IV: Lightning and hail will never fall except on forests. Humanity will be forever preserved from floods and the earth, in*

all its extent, will receive only salutary dews which will make it bear fruit to the advantage of all its inhabitants without distinction.
Article V: This decree shall be sent to all municipalities and made public in both hemispheres, etc."

A funny way of denouncing the egalitarian nonsense that has not ceased to flourish since.

It is on June 10, 1792 that Rivarol, having nothing to do in France but to die there, according to the word of Mr. de Lescure, leaves France. This was a useful precaution, since shortly after his exile, the discovery of the papers in the iron cabinet decided the Convention, in December 1793, to arrest him.

He leaves in good company since Mariette accompanies him. We know almost nothing about her and first of all her name. She was an embroiderer, occasionally traded in her charms and had no mind. Their union will last eight years.

Here is the poem dedicated to him that describes the nature of their relationship.

"You, whose innocence rests
On the kindest pivots,
For whom every book is a closed letter,
Who, far from distinguishing verse from prose,
Do not inquire if the goods or words
Have the ink or paper for cause,
If there are other laurels or other poppies
Only those that a gardener waters,
And who only suspect feathers to the birds,
In the difficulties that the study opposes me
Or a few bits of thread to sew my words together,
Ah! Keep all those nice zeros for me
Of which your head is composed.
If anyone instructs you
All my happiness will be destroyed,
There's not much you can do about it.
Always taste to me like a good fruit,
And spirit like a rose".

Rivarol first took refuge in Brussels where he took part, with reserve, in the activities of the emigrant circles. When *the manifesto of the Duke of Brunswick* was published, which threatened the French nation insolently and made traitors out of the emigrants who associated themselves with it, he retorted by publishing his letter to the French nobility in which he ridiculed the author and his writing.

The advance of the republican troops forces Rivarol to take refuge in London *"where he dislikes extremely"*[38]. It is thus in Hamburg that he settled in 1795 where he found his sister the baroness of Angel, companion of the general Dumouriez. He met the bookseller Fouché-Borel, who edited the royalist newspaper *Le Spectateur du Nord*, and commissioned him to write a book that he had been dreaming of writing for a long time: *Le Nouveau Dictionnaire de la Langue française.*

He will write only *Le Discours préliminaire in* spite of the cease and desist of the publisher and the advances of money (1,000 francs per month) which allow him to live. To escape from the latter, Rivarol took refuge in Hamm, hosted by the Jewish banker David Cappadoce-Pereira, where he created a kind of literary workshop.

The future Louis XVIII entrusted him with a mission in Berlin, which failed because of the hostility of the Prussian king's entourage. But he consoles himself for his failure with a pretty Russian princess who shows him great tenderness.

In 1797, *Le Discours préliminaire (The Preliminary Discourse), a* true treatise on the philosophy of language, was finally published and met with great success. This work is the preamble of what could have been, sixty years ahead of Larousse, the first encyclopedic dictionary of the French language.

The project is explained at length in *the prospectus* which preceded it by eighteen months and which weaves the fabric of the work to come. The *Discourse* is a dissertation on language, accompanied by a general study on what we would call today the cognitive apparatus of man. He adds 80 pages called of recapitulation which comprise complements on his theories concerning *"the intellectual and moral man"*.

38. Despite the warm welcome of Prime Minister Pitt, and Burk who called him "the Tacitus of the Revolution".

Forced to leave Hamburg because of the threats of the Directory, he arrived in Berlin in 1800. There he fell ill in 1801, probably with pneumonia, and died on April 11.

He is buried in the Dorotheenstadt cemetery, but the exact location of his grave has been forgotten. Thus passed away the one who had "*adorned and armed reason with the weapons of the spirit*", according to his biographers' beautiful words. On his grave was the epitaph he had wished for:

"Laziness took him away from us before he died."

He leaves a work to be rediscovered, full of depth and lucidity, of witty and sarcastic remarks... and of common sense.

"A poor man asks you for money out of pity for himself, a thief asks you for money out of pity for himself, and it is by mixing the two ways that governments, alternately beggars and thieves, always have the people's money."

Henri ROCHEFORT (1831-1913)
Or the chivalrous insolence

Let us remember the verses of Hugo with whom Rochefort maintained such close relations:

"Rochefort, the proud archer, the bold sagittarius
Whose arrow is on the side of the fallen Empire"

For such is Rochefort's destiny in the face of history; it was the blows of his *Lanterne* combined with those of Hugo's *Châtiments* that precipitated the fall of the Second Empire. Who does not remember this epigram of the first number of this famous *Lantern*: "*There are in France 36 million subjects without counting the subjects of discontent*".

Nothing however predestined Rochefort to become the prince of pamphleteers, except perhaps the profession of his father, a journalist and vaudevillist well known under the name of Armand de Rochefort.

Armand's real name is Claude-Louis-Marie de Rochefort-Luçay. He is a former marquis and of the oldest and highest nobility. His ancestor Guillaume was Chancellor of France under Louis XI and Charles VIII, and Guy, the brother of the former, was in turn Chamberlain to Charles the Bold, First President of the Parliament of Dijon and Chancellor under Charles VIII. His grandfather had been lieutenant of the marshals of France under Louis XV and his father, a lieutenant-colonel, had emigrated and served in the Condé army. Before fleeing Paris, he had sold all his property, castles and forests to avoid confiscation. But he was paid in assignats which precipitated his ruin. The young Claude, in order to help his mother, became at the age of fifteen an employee of a bookstore, then secretary for three years to the governor of the Bourbon Island. When he returned to Paris, he fell in love with a young girl, Nicole Morel, whom he met in literary circles, and married her. She became Henri's mother.

Collaborator of the royalist newspaper *Le Drapeau Blanc* and then of *La Quotidienne*, the marquis frequented all the legitimist celebrities but was more concerned with his vaudevilles than with political quarrels.

When his fourth child, Henri, was born on January 31, 1831, the first boy to be preceded by three girls, the father wrote *"It's too late to come"*. This did not prevent him from loving tenderly this boy whom his three sisters, his mother and the old maid Louise revered as a young God. He was a child of poor health, excessively nervous and shy, but gifted with a brilliant intelligence and a prodigious memory.

His rebellious temperament dates from childhood. He could not stand constraint and was resistant to authority. In 1848, during the revolutionary days, he ran away from school and joined the ranks of the insurgents. He was also sometimes seen at the meetings of the Central Republican Society, the club founded by Blanqui.

With his baccalaureate in his pocket, he started working as a ghostwriter for a historical novel and collaborated with the *Dictionnaire de la Conversation* where he met Jules Vallès. Above all, he obtained a job at the Hôtel de Ville where his immediate boss was Drumont père, who took him under his protection. This was the beginning of his pamphleteering career. He wrote the verses on the Badinguette that everyone hummed. This song entitled *Madame César* celebrates with rosserie the marriage of Napoleon III and Eugénie de Montijo.

He then collaborates with the *Mousquetaire*, founded and directed by Alexandre Dumas père, and becomes drama critic of the Presse théâtrale. Then he joined the satirical newspaper *Le Charivari* where he met the cartoonists Cham and Daumier. But the regime to which the press was subjected did not allow him any freedom except that of approaching politics in a direct, light and gently boulevardière way. In short, he scratched, not stabbed.

While participating in the *Charivari*, he wrote the *Courrier de Paris* for Aurélien Scholl's *Le Nain Jaune*, among whose pens were the Goncourts, F. Sarcey, Barbey d'Aurevilly, etc. At the same time he devoted himself to the theater, writing and performing 19 plays. Articles and vaudevilles having brought him fame, it is ratified by his entry into the *Figaro* of Hippolyte de Villemessant, a great periodical entrepreneur. This *Figaro,* which had a fairly large circulation (40,000 copies), was the newspaper of the opposition to the Empire and welcomed all those who would play a role during the Commune or the Third Republic.

In *Les Aventures de ma vie* Rochefort tells of the creation of *La Lanterne.* Having felt a certain jealousy of the success of *Propos* de Labienus de Rogeard, remembering Alphonse Karr's periodical *Les Guêpes,* encouraged by Paul Véron, sponsored by Villemessant who presented him with titles among which he retained *La Lanterne,* Rochefort allowed himself to be tempted by an adventure that he felt conformed to his personality.

The first issue appeared on May 30, 1868.

- *How much do you print*? asks the printer Rochefort who wonders about the success of the company.

- *To fifteen thousand,* answers this one.

Rochefort is dismayed, convinced that the stock will be at least 10,000. There will be multiple printings and finally 120,000 copies will be sold. And the success is not denied for the following issues. This success is due to the vigor of the line, to the quality of the style, alert, frenzied, to the freedom of tone, to the audacity of the subject. No reservations or half-words, the attack is frontal, nominative. It sparkles with intelligence and courage.

Here is what he answered when he was accused of being an enemy of Bonaparte and the Empire.

"I have been accused," he writes, *"of being a declared enemy of the present state of affairs and a supporter of the old parties. This insinuation was all the more unfounded because (I do not have to hide it here) I am deeply Bonapartist. One will allow me however well to choose my hero in the dynasty. Among the legitimists, some prefer Louis XVIII others Louis XVI others finally place all their sympathies on the head of Charles X. As a Bonapartist, I prefer Napoleon II; it is my right.*

I will even add that he represents, for me, the ideal of the sovereign. Nobody will deny that he occupied the throne, since his successor is called Napoleon III. What a reign! Not one contribution; not one useless war, with the decimals that follow; not one of these distant expeditions, in which one spends 600 million to go and claim 15 francs; not one devouring civil lists; not one minister cumulating each one five or six functions at 100,000 francs each; that is the monarch as I understand him. Oh yes, Napoleon II, I love you and admire you without reserve! Who will now dare to claim that I am not a sincere Bonapartist?"

Then the trials rained down which, in the thirteenth number, earned him a sentence of thirteen months in prison and ten thousand francs, not to be confused with those already pronounced.

This last sentence is pronounced by default, because Rochefort took the train from Brussels where Victor Hugo welcomes him. The publication of *La Lanterne* will be continued until the 74th issue. Banned in France, it penetrates there by all kinds of tricks, including in the busts of the man who is enthroned in the Tuileries.

The success of *La Lanterne* gave rise to a lot of competition... which did not harm it: Victor Noir's *Le Pilori*, J.B. Clément's *Le Casse-tête*, G. Maroteau and E. Vermersch make a pale figure and disappear as soon as they appear.

For Rochefort's success was dazzling and everything contributed to it: prosecutions and convictions, exile, duels. His influence was enormous. In 1880, Rochefort reissued the 74 issues that had been published, preceded by a preface in which he declared:

> *"The Empire was never a government. The odious siesta that drunkards took for twenty years on the second floor of the Tuileries Palace was never a reign.*
> *No you will not enter the history, scoundrel! said Victor Hugo. All that will remain of all these moral and political obscenities is a kind of stench impregnated to our clothes, a kind of chemical precipitate, as if it were a verminate of infamy or a crapulate of despotism.*
> *Under these conditions, I asked myself if it was patriotic to put before the eyes of the nation the daily march of the unmentionable disease that has eaten away at us for so long. What makes me decide to do this is that it is intolerable to let the world think that thirty-eight million human beings could live twenty years with a pillowcase over their eyes. When one reads later on this adventure of the great road, which has been called until now the Empire, and when the less nervous will write: 'How! Did the French put up with this harlequinade for more than twenty-four hours? How! Men who are reputed to be serious have allowed this pencil merchant to*

attach crosses of honor to their chests? What! it happened one day that this Lagingeole, having pretended to put himself at the head of the army, which he pretended to lead to the deliverance of Italy, the people of Paris unhitched the horses of his carriage? When, after many snows fallen on the hills, the grandfather will be able to say to his grandchildren pale with surprise: Look well at this old man who drags himself today on his stalks; well! He was once among those who were jocular enough to subscribe to the loan decreed by Bonaparte". When the next generation refuses to believe its ears, it seems to me consoling that the historian can answer: *"It's true! But read* Les Châtiments, *read* Napoleon-le-Petit, *read* L'Histoire du Deux-Décembre, *read even* La Lanterne, *and you will recognize that through the dirty paws of Piétri and the jails of Pinard, public indignation escaped and went far away to recruit soldiers for the real France. There were the dead, the desperate, the flattened; but there were also the vigilant who watched for the hour and whose every blow of pickaxe, pen or revolver, widened the hole from which the Republic was going to come out."*

In 1869 Rochefort enters the Legislative Body after a first failure and with the support of the most radical fraction of the electorate. He forms a small group of extreme left with Raspail.

It was at this time that Rochefort launched a new newspaper with Victor Noir, Gustave Flourens, Paschal Grousset, Benoît Malon and the communists Millière and Dereme, members of the International, as collaborators. The first issue of *La Marseillaise* appeared on December 19, 1869, and Rochefort wrote in his inaugural article: "*Since it is now well established that the people have their own opinions, it is only fair that they also have their own newspaper.*" It is openly a newspaper, in agreement with the Blanquists and the Internationals, defending the socialist claims.

It is welcomed with enthusiasm by the popular masses, and with spite and fury by the governmental circles. Thus Pierre-Napoleon Bonaparte, son of Lucien and one of the most dubious representatives of the family, will mount a provocation that leads to the assassination of the young Victor Noir.

The next day, Rochefort, in deep despair, wrote:

"I had the weakness to believe that a Bonaparte could be something other than an assassin!
I dared to imagine that a fair duel was possible in this family where murder and ambush are tradition and custom.
Our collaborator Paschal Grousset shared my mistake and today we mourn our poor and dear friend Victor Noir, murdered by the bandit Pierre-Napoléon Bonaparte.
For eighteen years now, France has been in the bloody hands of these cutthroats, who, not content with machine-gunning Republicans in the streets, lure them into filthy traps to slit their throats at home.
French people, don't you think that's enough?"

But it was *La Marseillaise* that was seized and Rochefort that was pursued. Also, nearly two hundred thousand people beat the Parisian pavement during the civil funeral of the journalist, led by Rochefort and Delesclare and all the militants of the International and the Blanquist sections. Some people waited and hoped that Rochefort would give the signal for a riot, but he did not, and the crowd dispersed without major incident.

Rochefort will be imprisoned in Sainte-Pélagie from where he will get out only during the troubles that precede the establishment of the insurrectional Commune. Pierre Bonaparte will be acquitted and *La Marseillaise will be* suspended, it will have lived seven months.

Two months after the declaration of war to Prussia, on September 2, Napoleon III capitulated at Sedan. Rochefort was extracted from his prison by force and participated for a few weeks in the provisional government before withdrawing. He then published *Le Mot d'Ordre* and was elected deputy of the Seine. He resigned from the assembly that was sitting in Bordeaux and refused to defend the country to the fullest and left to rest in Arcachon. It was his illness and his absence from Paris that prevented him from being elected as a member of the Commune. Nevertheless, he will support in his newspaper the government of the Hôtel de Ville until the last minute. He was arrested in Meaux and handed over to General de Galliffet.

Tried by the Council of War, he was sentenced to deportation for life in a fortified compound. Like thousands of other Communards, he was sent to the hell of the Caledonian prison from which he escaped after three months, on March 20, 1874, with five comrades, first to Australia and then to New York. From there he moved to London where he reissued *La Lanterne* but its distribution was difficult. So he moved to Geneva and it is from there that *La Nouvelle Lanterne* will radiate for two years.

In 1876, a radical-socialist daily newspaper *Les Droits de l'Homme* is founded in Paris and calls for his collaboration. Rochefort signed his articles first X then X...y. It was in this first issue that he coined the term opportunity. "*Voters are warned: 'en temps opportun' is a term of parliamentary slang which means: Never!*" In another article he points out a "*new disease*" in parliamentary circles:

> *"Our excellent republicans attack the ministers so as not to appear too satisfied with the morbid state in which the Republic is languishing; but they use against them speckled foils that barely skin them, or pass through their bodies rubber daggers that fold back on themselves like in the old theater of the Funambulists.*
> *Doctors have named 'hospital rot' a kind of typhus that suddenly invades wards crowded with wounded and transforms the slightest scratch into a mortal wound. The patient, without any apparent cause, suddenly loses his strength and expires just when he was thought to be saved. I take the liberty of pointing out to political doctors an analogous disease resulting from the cohabitation of deputies in a restricted space and which could be called 'assembly rot'."*

Crushed by the trials, the newspaper disappears and is succeeded by a new daily *Lanterne* where Rochefort vilifies Thiers, Mac Mahon and the Moral Order. And at the same time he writes novels of which Zola will speak very highly.

Amnesty, the great demand of the time, was finally voted on July 11, 1880 and Rochefort's return to Paris was triumphant. A few days later he published the first issue of *L'Intransigeant*, which was to be the newspaper of the advanced radical-socialists, the intransigents and the revolutionary socialists.

In October 1885, Rochefort was again elected deputy of the Seine and again he resigned in February 1886, not being able to bear the parliamentary stifling.

Then it was to be the Boulangiste adventure in which he allowed himself to be drawn. Unaware of the general's dealings with the Orleanist and Bonapartist right, temporarily forgetting his disdain for the saber-runners, Rochefort saw only his hatred for the blandness and spinelessness of this opportunist regime. But with Boulangisme definitively defeated and the republic assured of its future, Rochefort returned to the essential, the social question. Socialism was then a growing force both in its anarchist and Marxist forms around Jules Guesde and Paul Lafargue. On May 1st, 1891, there was a major mobilization of the working class and a savage reaction by the State, whose troops in Fourmies shot at a harmless crowd and killed fifteen demonstrators, injuring thirty-five. And Rochefort denounced the *"bandit Constans"* (Minister of the Interior) who was greedy for fresh meat.

In 1892 he took the side of the Carmaux miners and the following year, during the general strike of the workers of the North and Pas-de-Calais, he dealt with the judicial repression that was being inflicted on them:

> *"Alexandre Dumas, in* The Three Musketeers, *portrayed the executioner of Bethune: the judges of Bethune are certainly much more abominable. There is, in fact, no execution by the sword that can rival, in ferocity, the sentences inflicted on these wretches, not only on the arrested minors, but on the witnesses, guilty of coming to testify in their favor. This is the first blow to that bitch called French justice. The wretches of the court of Bethune have struck from the code, the right to defense."*

On October 29, Rochefort returns to the charge against these Robert Macaire toques and petticoats, against these Laubardemont of small city:

> *"It is the regime of arbitrariness and good pleasure. Just like prostitutes with lovers at heart and maintainers who provide them with the material, the judges of Bethune and elsewhere allow everything to the director of the mines who represents the crusher, and they do not have enough gehenna for the miners who represent the crushed."*

Rochefort was then very close to the socialist group La Petite République and its leader Jean Jaurès. He supported the candidacy of

Gérault-Richard from England where he had taken refuge once again to escape repression. The victory of the latter sounded the death knell of the Casimir-Perier ministry and his successor Alexandre Ribert had an amnesty voted.

The return of the great outlaw, according to the title of a song of circumstance, saw thousands of people cheering Rochefort on the way and 10,000 people giving him a standing ovation in Paris, chanting: *"Long live Rochefort, Long live the Social, Long live the Commune, Long live the honest people."*

During the Dreyfus Affair, his supporters had, for a moment, expected Rochefort's support. But it was with his usual vehemence that he joined the anti-Dreyfus ranks. And every morning, along with the members of the "Reinach-Jewish ball" government, the man of the revision was denounced as a spy and foreign agent. The reasons for this commitment are mysterious and probably multiple: rivalry with the newspaper *L'Aurore* directed by his former collaborator Ernest Vaughan, and above all this patriotic feeling so present in this blanquist current voluntarily cocardier and revanchard. Rochefort will be faithful to his nationalist position until his death.

On October 10, 1907 he published his 9948th article in *L'Intransigeant.* It will be the last one. The next day the management passes to the hands of Léon Bailby who bought the shares in underhand.

No longer a major combat newspaper, Rochefort would henceforth give free editorials to *La Patrie* until his death, despite the discomfort that this absolute atheist felt in this clerical and conservative environment.

He died on July 1st 1913 in Aix les Bains where he had gone to rest. With him disappears one of the last representatives of French socialism and one of the greatest polemicists.

"My philosophy is that I don't like to be bothered, neither the people I love nor my country."

The greatest libertarian polemicist has not had a successor worthy of this program or of his talent.

Colette REMY, known as SÉVERINE (1855-1929)
Our Lady of the Tear, grandmother of the Revolution

"I am not and will never be part of any group or organization. I love my independence too much to commit it to anything and anyone." The one who wrote this also said: *"I have too much horror of theories and theorists, of doctrines and doctrinaires, of school catechisms and sectarian grammars..."*

And her life will be in the image of these declarations, independent and tumultuous, contradictory and passionate. Collaborator and friend of Jules Vallès at the *Cri du Peuple,* founder of the boulangiste newspaper *La Cocarde,* journalist at Drumont's *La Libre Parole,* she was not anti-Semitic, a passionate feminist at a time when it was necessary to be one, she defended Captain Dreyfus in *La Fronde,* a women's newspaper defending the cause of women during the affair of the same name. Pacifist in the midst of the war madness of the Great War, she was inflamed by the Russia of the Soviets and joined the Communist Party after the Congress of Tours. She will be excluded in 1923 at the request of Moscow the doddering.

Who is this woman whose place is not in a panel of housewives under fifty years of age any more than in a museum of literature? Her name was Caroline Rémy and she was born on April 27, 1855 in the heart of elegant and worldly Paris, just a stone's throw from the Boulevard, deserted by the spirit of revolt of the Second Empire. It is therefore a "*proper*" family of the petty bourgeoisie that welcomes this child and gives her the good education necessary for the peaceful and sanitized life to which her milieu predestines her.

Her parents, followers before their time of E. Badinter's a-historical thesis on the love of children, adored their daughter and kept her under wraps, but were stingy with all the manifestations of tenderness that nourished the sensitivity of children. Hence, no doubt, this stormy need for external signs of affection that will govern her temperament.

For Caroline will always overflow the mold in which she is to be cast. She is not a small thing, and quicksilver flows in her veins. Bulimically curious, she learns to read, on her own, in six months and in the newspapers, to understand what is said in the evening at the table. The staid education she received at the boarding school in Neuilly and then at the Bessières Institution in Paris revolted her and she resigned herself to it, apparently, only while waiting for something better.

This is how she accepts the marriage arranged by her parents, because at the age when every young girl of her milieu (and of her time) dreams of a more or less charming and silver prince, she dreams of theater. "*To be the spokesperson of the great poets, to make the public soul vibrate, to feel the verses fly from her lips like birds, their flight towards freedom, their shivering of joy*." But her father Onésime exclaimed one day when she was talking about it: "*I would rather see her dead*". And as she did not want to be a teacher, she accepted Henry Montrobert, a Lyonnais, employed at the Parisian gas company, as her husband. She was sixteen and a half, he was thirty.

Twenty years later in *Le Gil Blas,* and in a series of articles entitled "*L'Eternel masculin. Diary of a woman*" she will tell her wedding night, legal rape, during which the exquisite suitor becomes again the eternal male predator. "*This, eh, what, this is it? ... this infamous action, this bruising, this defilement, this crushing of the weakness by the force, of the will under the violence, this torture, this profanation of all the physical being while the brain judges and that the heart fails, it is the marriage...*"

Two years later, and despite the birth of a little boy, who will be raised by his father, Caroline asks for the separation of body and property and returns to the family home, bruised but infinitely revolted.

But she had to earn a living and after odd jobs, piano lessons and embroidery, she became a governess for Mrs. Guebhard, a rich widow of Swiss origin. She married her son, a scientist. He loved her all his life, despite her wanderings, her flamboyant loves... and a 35-year separation. So much so that he will come to join her and die beside her, in the evening of his life, in Pierrefonds (Oise).

But for the moment, with Adrien and his mother, in the secret of their affair, she finds peace and from this union is born, in Belgium where she went to give birth, a second child.

It is in this city, refuge at the time of the French opponents to the imperial extinction and to the sordid Third republic incipient, that her life will rock. During an evening at the home of Dr. Semerie, a republican who directed the ambulances of the Paris Commune, she met another Frenchman: Jules Vallès. He was returning from a distant exile and was awaiting the amnesty that would turn the page on the last great, and true, workers' revolution. She saw him again, by chance, a few days after that evening; they sat down to a lemonade and talked for a long time. Or rather he speaks and she listens to him *"deeply disturbed, dazzled by too much light".* And she is deeply seduced by the character, because Vallès, more than a man, is a personification of revolt. It is another world, another universe, that reveals itself to her.

While she resumed her quiet life in Paris, it is Vallès who takes up with her about a Commune outlaw who needs help.

After a suicide attempt that expresses her ultimate revolt against this milieu that wants to keep her away from the world that attracts her, from this life that she feels is hers, Caroline, now free to dispose of her time as she pleases, officially becomes Vallès' secretary. The and not the secretary, because from the outset a militant camaraderie was established between them, an intellectual and political companionship that would decide her intellectual and journalistic training.

Then came the year 1881; one evening in July, the law on the press, still in force today, had just been voted, which finally liberalized the publication of newspapers. Vallès was enthusiastic because it was the complete freedom of printing and publishing that was proclaimed.

If everything was now possible, in principle, money was needed, less than in the past since the bond had been abolished, but money nonetheless. These funds were provided by Adrien Guebhard, Caroline's husband, the Doctor, as Vallès respectfully called him. 100,000 francs and the new *Cri du Peuple* resurrected the one from the Commune: *"a dead newspaper, a newspaper that had its name hung in shame and fell with a bang on the battlefield."*

Le Cri du Peuple will be a militant newspaper "*social, human, pearled with tears or spangled with dreams, open to all, free tribune*", but also a newspaper of information which will present "*a review as complete as possible of all the political, literary and artistic events*". In short, a real popular newspaper capable of competing with the big newspapers of the time.

But very quickly, Vallès, overwhelmed by illness, had to step back and rely on his secretary. Caroline will be the faithful executor of the "*boss*" and, more and more, she embodies in the eyes of the latter, the new generation. She signed her first article under the name of Séverine, disparaging the good poet François Coppée. Very soon her *Notes d'une parisienne* will receive the definitive signature of Séverine. The journalist was born, of whom the Goncourts, always full of accusations, would say: "*Vallès is a unique individual. We will never do it again. He took a mistress who had a bit of literature, and he made her erupt weekly, with thoughts of her own, all his fellow writers who made more noise than he did. It was Daudet, Zola and me.*"

She, unperturbed, continued her business but never for a moment stopped paying attention to Vallès, whom she had installed with her in a neighboring apartment in the same building. And she always kept an eye on *Le Cri*, Vallès' beloved child.

But in 1885 the old lion died, and a war of succession began between Séverine and those whom Vallès called "*the good men of Nuremberg*", dogmatists of a shoddy Marxism or a republicanism of incense. If it wins, it is also by introducing an unexpected ally. For it was not a militant of this or that school but a journalist from *L'Écho de Paris whom we* met at Vallès' funeral. This Georges de Labruyère was a handsome man, and a young one at that: he was thirty years old.

Acquainted with modern journalism, already called "*American style*", that is to say, adept at fieldwork, reports and interviouves, he will contribute to the evolution of the *Cree*, as the new boss wishes, to conquer new readers and ensure its survival. Also, in addition to investigations, press drawings and entertaining articles such as the song of the day (by Jules Jouy) were developed. It was the time of sensational articles such as this report by Séverine herself, on the murderous fire at the Opéra-comique, whose tone anticipated that of *La Cause du Peuple* during the fire at the dance hall in Saint-Laurent-du-Pont; those responsible were designated: *"the management of the theater which had condemned an exit, locked the fire escape for fear of free-riders, which had been criminal through stupidity."*

Having become a famous woman, she did not abdicate her personality or her ideas. Thus her anti-parliamentarianism - she calls the deputies the deputaille - leads her to greet the election to the presidency of the Republic of Sadi Carnot in these terms: *"This election has only one good side, it is to prove the perfect inanity of the Presidency".*

But she went further and got herself hired as a worker in a refinery. She wanted to experience, in order to bear witness to it, the sufferings of the workers riveted to their line(s) for twelve hours a day. And then it is still necessary to relieve the miseries, all the miseries. So she opens subscriptions, putting into action solidarity, or is it charity?

She welcomes in her home the disinherited, the poor struck by injustice and all the misery of the world. And this exasperates the doctrinaires who are annoyed by this exacerbated sensitivity, they say sensibility, and its emotional procession of tearful alum. Also one will take advantage of two rather sordid affairs, where his private life is spread out, in particular his affair with Labruyère, to push him aside.

But she did not leave without resisting. Thus, during the Duval affair, which tore apart the editorial staff of *Le Cri*, she first took the advantage. Duval is a partisan anarchist, and practitioner of individual recovery. More simply, he is a thief who claims the insurrectionary character of his acts. This individual recovery also shares the anarchist milieu; some see it, such as Sébastien Faure and the Recluses, as a revolutionary act: *"private property is theft, if a restitutor touches it, I have no problem with it."* Others, such as Jean Grave, saw in the restitutors *"vulgar enjoyers".*

The doctrinaire socialists who are beginning to pick up their first electoral stamps and are settling, while waiting to wallow, in the republican and prebendary system, are absolutely hostile. Following their mentor Jules Guesde, they proclaim that the ballot paper will henceforth be the source of all wisdom.

Séverine denies any validity to the theory of individual recovery but tries to understand its human foundations: *"This theory worries me, seems to me likely to keep the hesitant away from us, to intimidate the simple, to frighten the fearful. But in my trouble, I feel that there is there the most painful social problem which ever stirred the world... and my thought remains undecided, my judgment remains uncertain."*

And to evoke an article of Vallès: "*I do not see the shadow of a danger in this explosion of suffering while the danger would be mortal if one believed oneself authorized, in the name of the discipline of the parties, to condemn the undisciplined of the tribune*". And a few days later, she goes further in an article that casts the brightest light on what today would be called the positioning problem of the formalized labor movement; she writes in this article entitled "*The Responsible*": "*We spend our lives telling the humble that they are being robbed, exploited, slowly murdered; that they are machine fodder, that their daughters will be pleasure fodder, that their sons will be cannon fodder. We stir up anger, we inflame the minds, we set the souls on fire; we turn these outcasts into rebels in the name of supreme justice and sovereign equity.*"

Therefore, by what right, and in virtue of what, to stigmatize "*the impatient, the exalted, those who have the imperious hunger or the greedy hatred... all those who cannot be satisfied to give credit to the Society for a few years of distress and sacrifice*".

For the partisan socialists there is a declaration of war because she refuses and rejects a doctrine with which they have signed an emphyteutic lease. Then Séverine is accused of anarchism and threatened with an ostracism that would remove her from the *Cries*. She reacts quickly and proclaims once again that the Cri remains a free forum open to all revolutionary currents, and she takes over the journal from Guesde and the others.

This freedom of thought, which she claims, leads her, it is the reverse side of her doctrinal indifference, to compromising curiosities, in the eyes of some.

Thus she flirted with Boulangisme, as well as many men of the left, even of the extreme left. Her companion Labruyère, she now lives with him, left the editorial staff of *Le Cri* to found *La Cocarde* which weakens her position in the editorial team and accredits the idea of her own conversion. She reacts: "Le Cri du Peuple *is, and will remain socialist*" and she analyzes saying their fact to the "*makers of Caesars*". These are the leaders of today who are chewing up her work and are going to lead her by the hand. They make the cover of the bed where "*the savior*" will sleep.

But the crisis is too strong and her resistance gives way: she resigns. From then on she wrote in all sorts of newspapers and all sorts of things, taking, as she nicely put it, the paths of "*the truant school of the Revolution*". She wrote six thousand articles and chronicles for a hundred newspapers until her death in 1929.

With her, an emblematic figure of the revolutionary movement and of the workers' movement will pass away. Whatever the case, Séverine embodied spontaneity and freedom of thought, off the beaten track of theories that had become formal oppositions, before becoming virtual, to the new triumphant capitalist society. She belonged to the era of refusal.

Laurent TAILHADE (1854-1919)
An imprecator among the lackeys

Laurent Tailhade is the man of a harsh century: the 19th century. He was born in Tarbes in 1854. After solid classical studies at the Lycée de Pau, he began studying law at the Faculty of Toulouse where his destiny awaited him. Distinguished in a poetic competition of "jeux floraux", he decides to make writing his profession. Believing that the profession of plumitif is in no way honorable and does not constitute a state, the family decides to marry him to a young woman suitably endowed.

To distract himself from a bourgeois life that bored him, Tailhade began to compose the pieces that made up the poetic collection *Jardin des Rêves* (1880). Fortunately, the death of his wife freed him early and he moved as soon as possible to Paris, where he met writers and painters of the Parnassian school: Mallarmé, Samain, Verlaine and Moréas... While squandering his wife's fortune in bamboozling, he was noticed by other talents than that of a party man. Indeed, he enjoys an astonishing classical culture built up since his childhood.

If the anarchist bomb of Vaillant, which exploded in 1893 in the Chamber of Deputies, and the other attacks of the partisans of direct action and individual recovery, terrified the bourgeois, he praised these acts with this scathing word: "*What does it matter about the victims if the gesture is beautiful?*" He was forty years old at the time and this remark, which caused a scandal, propelled him out of the restricted circle in which he had been languishing. Especially since a year later, in 1894, he was in turn the victim of the bomb that Emile Henry threw at the Café Terminus. He came out of it disfigured and lost an eye, but he entered the anarchist fight and became one of the most beautiful jewels of its press. He will, from then on, lead a fight without respite and without nuance against the stooges of the writing board who prospered then, and still today, in the press. He collaborates with Sébastien Faure's *Libertaire* in which he publishes a resounding article. It was indeed the time of the Franco-Russian alliance (1901), an alliance of a *"democracy"* and an *"autocracy"*. It was an unforgettable time when Tsar Nicholas II was received in Paris with the Tsarina and celebrated by all the plumitifs, led by Edmond Rostand who wrote an ode to the Empress.

In this flurry of republican praise for the Moscow tyrant, where one can see that the selective indignation of self-proclaimed intellectuals is not new, Tailhade's article, *Le Triomphe de la Domesticité,* brutally and sumptuously, causes a scandal. Justice, in the eternal service of the masters of the moment, is moved and Tailhade gets a year's vacation in the prison of La Santé. As soon as he was released, Tailhade was present at all the avant-garde meetings and events. He deploys his eloquence supported by a trumpeting voice and a wide gesture. He knows brilliant triumphs there.

Thereupon, Abbé Charbonnel founded *L'Action, a* fiercely anti-clerical daily. Tailhade is part of the team. He will then bring the contradiction in the churches during the services. When the newspaper disappeared, he took part in the adventure of *L'Internationale, a* superbly illustrated weekly, lively and combative as hell. Then, after a long period of silence, it was *Je dis tout, a* fearsome and dreaded paper in which he attacked the *"cagots of the Lodge"*, the Freemasons, of whom he said: *"the Masonic clergy is as stupid as the others, with the aggravating circumstance that the Commies pride themselves on being free spirits".*

But illness begins to eat away at him, and it will keep him as far away from the front lines of combat as disillusionment. In the meantime, in this *Je dis tout,* he attacks two of the most formidable writers of the time: Gustave Téry and Urbain Gohier, of the newspaper *L'Œuvre.* The result is two duels with pistols and embraces with Gohier, whose courage seduces Tailhade. It is in another duel, against Maurice Barrès, about the Dreyfus affair (Tailhade is an ardent Dreyfusard), that he will remain crippled in the right hand. At the end of his life, his health still weakening, he stepped back from the fight, but never gave up. After the

Great War, a convinced pacifist, he collaborated with *La Vérité* and the *Journal du Peuple.*

But the disease overwhelms him and he is hospitalized at the Maison Dubois. However, when Méric asks him to participate in the new review *Le Merle Blanc,* he replies: "*That's fine. We are going to titillate some of these gentlemen of literature and politics*". Death did not leave him time and took with him a whole era of furious polemics and virile fights.

Jules VALLÈS (1832-1885)
Freedom without shores

How to portray an icon, the perfect representative of a generation of revolutionaries whose life cannot escape hagiography?

Talking about his childhood is a difficult exercise because he did it so well in the first volume of his autobiographical trilogy under the character of Jacques Vingtras, *L'Enfant.* But his youth, adolescence and young adulthood, as well as his literary and political career, are just as wonderfully evoked in the next two volumes, *Le Bachelier* and *L'Insurgé.*

So, disregarding the embarrassment that a monument can inspire, we will dare to paint a broad picture of this refractory. This is indeed how Vallès wanted to be, a bristling character blurred by an unhappy childhood (or lived as such), or dismantled by an excessive sensitivity.

Thus *L'Enfant* is dedicated "to all those who died of boredom at school or were made to cry in the family, who, during their childhood were tyrannized by their teachers or scolded by their parents.

This child, a victim of abuse, as we would say today, and who would end up at the DDASS rather than on the barricades, is this progress? was born under the exact name of Louis Jules Vallez in Puy-en-Velay (Haute-Loire) on June 11, 1832. His parents were small, very small bourgeois, from the peasant world. His father, a schoolteacher and then a tutor in a college, was a hard worker, a small winner, his eyes fixed on the blue line of social success. At his side, his mother, a defrocked nun, half-crazy, greedy and rapacious, remembers her son. If these memories are not exact, it is the legend of Vallès-Vallez-Vingtras poured with big emotional broths in this trilogy, monument of the autobiographical literature, at the same time bitter and tearful.

But if he moans about his childhood and makes his memories cry, Vallès is proud of his peasant ancestry and of his Auvergne region, which makes him the "country of" Vercingétorix. And then this mistreated child is a good student, even very brilliant, that we find studying in Paris at seventeen years preparing the École Nationale Supérieure. At that time, his father, so timid that he let himself be beaten by the older brother of a student he had slapped, who feared for his tiny job, considered him crazy and had him committed. This painful experience, reminiscent of Mirabeau's, left its mark on the young man's rebellious and fearless soul.

The revolutionary days of 1848, the purest expression of the revolutionary impulse of the young working class, are still present in people's minds and the air is red. Vallès is instinctively on the side of this violence that beats within him, nourished by all the humiliations and resentments of his childhood and by this unreserved lucidity. So he rubs shoulders with this multitude of circles, cenacles, casts his energy into the militant mold and participates in a plot to kidnap the prince-president Bonaparte.

First stay in the prisons of the Third in Mazas which is not very long.

But here he is initiated into the revolutionary bohemia. Yes, initiated, because it is indeed an informal brotherhood with codified rites, with singular customs, an intelligentsia as we would say today, before the noisy media success. He lived from small writing jobs, freelance work, and temporary jobs: repeater, clerk... his pen was used wherever he was temporarily welcomed from the *Figaro* to *L'Événement.* And he wrote so well that after having gathered his articles in a book entitled *Les Réfractaires* (1866), he created his own newspaper, *La Rue* (1867).

In these two titles, *Les Réfractaires* and *La Rue,* one can read all of Vallès: admiration for those who have freedom at any price and refuse the aseptic and mercantile universe proposed by the bourgeoisie, and faith in a future that is played out in the street, on the barricades of revolt and in the passion of insurrections. In truth, he had little choice, for an attempt to work at Girardin's house ended in his being put on the index. Here is the portrait that Vallès draws of this great boss, one of the initiators of the modern press:

> *"I find him,"* he says, *"in a blue jacket, with a rose in his lapel; he comes to me with his hand outstretched and a smile on his face.*

- Bulldog, we're going to unleash you! You'll be doing the column on Sunday... And let's hear you bark, shall we?
His lips curl up and he meows while crossing his claws.
- I gave a shout out and it didn't take long! Girardin was ordered to shoot his dog. He did not make one or two moves and sent his manager to tie the stone to my neck and throw me into the river.
- He could have waited, though..."

But *La Rue* did not last because non-conformism was not in fashion in the last years of the Empire. And then Vallès dipped his pen in vitriol and spared nothing and no one, not even the State, Hugo, Baudelaire, etc. Then came the fines, the harassments and the prison (Sainte-Pélagie).

Two years later he founded *Le Peuple* and ran for office. He is the "*candidate of the misery*" who calls to the revolt against the "*soldiers, the gabelous, the priests, the* rats-of-cave, *the magistrates...*". "*Obey your memories of the defeated*" he shouts to his voters. It appears that 780 have memory against 30,000 who vote for the opportunist republican Jules Simon.

The war and the defeat find him in prison and free him. During the siege he was naturally a supporter of the war in excess, patriotic and republican as one would say fresh and joyful. Then the capitulard government suppresses his newspaper. But after the proclamation of the Commune on March 18, 1871, he regains the freedom to write. This freedom, just like Rochefort, he will defend it for all and will protest against the suppression of reactionary newspapers. If he was enraged, this did not prevent him from analyzing the events and refusing to take action (which was very rare). These analyses sometimes lead him close, very close, to compromise. Thus when he writes in *Le Cri du Peuple,* after having denounced "*the lazy bourgeoisie... which does not produce, which froths, which gathers...*", "*But there is a working bourgeoisie, honest and valiant... it is by its courage, and even by its anguish, the sister of the proletariat*". The patriotic sans-culottism and this attachment to the craft industry that one finds in Blanqui and the quaranthuitards are the source of this confusion and this blindness.

His courage is exemplary and he leaves his post only at the last hour. His post was not in a paneled room but behind a barricade in Belleville.

Here is the story as found in *L'insurgé* (volume II of the Jacques Vingtras trilogy):

> *"We are at the giant barricade at the bottom of Belleville Street, almost in front of the Favié Hall.*
> *[...] I have fought more against the Federated than against Versailles until now. Now that there is only this suburb free and that there are no traitors or suspects left to judge, the task is easier. It is only a question of holding out for honor and of going to stand by the flag, like the officers near the main mast when the ship sinks.*
> *Here I am.*
> *We respond with rifle and cannon to the terrible fire directed against us.*
> *At the windows of* La Veilleuse *and all the houses on the corner, our people have put straw mats, whose bellies smoke under the hole of the projectiles.*
> *From time to time a head makes Guignol on a balustrade.*
> *'Touché'!*
> *We have a room served by silent, valiant gunners. One of them is not more than twenty years old, his hair the color of wheat, his eyes the color of cornflower. He blushes like a little girl when he is complimented on the accuracy of his shooting.*
> *One hears cries towards the street Rebeval.*
> *- Would they have come from behind, while their messenger diverted attention? Vingtras, go and see!*
> *- What's up?*
> *- There is that here is a private individual who is in the middle of us and who refuses his share of work.*
> *- Yes, I refuse... I am against the war!*
> *And the good man, forty years old, with an apostle's beard and a calm appearance, comes up to me and says:*
> *- Yes, I am for peace against war! Neither for them nor for you...*
> *I dare you to force me to fight...*
> *But this reasoning is not to the liking of the federates.*
> *- You think we wouldn't like to do what you do better! You think it's a joke to exchange prunes! Come on, take this snuffbox and sneeze... or I'll make you sniff myself... and shut up!*

- I am for peace against war.
- What an animal name! Do you want the snuffbox or the tobacco? He snorted at the tobacco and followed the other, dragging his gun like a crutch.
[...] Suddenly, the crusaders are disengaged, the dike collapses. The blond gunner let out a scream. A bullet hit him in the forehead and made like a black eye between his two blue eyes.
- Lost! Run for it!"

If the Commune executed seventy-two people, the Versailles of M. Thiers had at least fifteen thousand victims. Vallès was not one of them, but they thought they had captured him, and a poor bastard was arrested and shot in his place. He, disguised as a doctor, took refuge in the Pitié hospital. After months of clandestine wandering, sentenced to death in absentia, he took refuge in London where he taught French, Latin and literature, then in Brussels where he languished in a shabby furnished room in the Gare du Nord which he nicknamed *Le Punaise-Hôtel.*

It is precisely there that he meets the one who will become Séverine. But for the moment, he waits. He waits for the amnesty for which for ten years voices have been raised, including that of Hugo who, although hostile to the Commune *"a good thing but badly done"*, pleads for civil peace and the return of the statutes of limitations. He was heard on July 10, 1880.

He returned to Paris on the 13th in the company of B. Malon, welcomed by a large crowd of pandores and faithful friends, André Gill, Hector Malot, etc. His first gesture as a Parisian was to attend the review of the troops the next day, where he was moved to his great surprise by the sight of the three colors: *"I thought I would be horrified to see this tricolor flag in the name of which we were shot. Well no, it is necessary to have lived in exile!..."*.

Vallès never stopped writing. In the numerous French colony in London, small and ephemeral newspapers of immigrants multiplied, where all points of view were fiercely disputed. Moreover, some friends who had remained in France, Hector Malot and Aurélien Scholl, opened the columns of *L'Evénement* and *Voltaire* to him. And then he wrote *Jacques Vingtras, the History of a Child, which* was first published as a serial in *Le Siècle* and then as a volume by Charpentier. The sequel

Les Mémoires d'un révolté was published in *La Révolution française* and then in volume after his return from exile. But after this one he had difficulty to readjust. And here he is, hanging out in cafés and brasseries, living the life of literary bohemia and making friends or renewing acquaintances with Barbey d'Aurevilly, Bourget, Maupassant.

He took his time and wrote very little, a few articles in *La Vie Moderne* and *Le Citoyen de Paris* and a historical serial, *Les Blouses,* for Clemenceau's *La Justice.* But he organized collectivist dinners with political friends or literary days that brought together journalists from all sides and men of letters. People eat a lot and solid food and drink a lot.

And then Vallès wanted to "*remain an outsider, even in the camp of the revolted*". He was also reluctant to join any of the many different groups of the nascent socialist movement. He therefore wanted a newspaper that belonged to him. So while he worked on the third volume of the trilogy of the *Adventures of Jacques Vingtras* and on *La Rue* à Londres, which he dedicated to Séverine, he prepared the rebirth of *Le Cri du Peuple.* He wants a newspaper that escapes the "*rhetoric*", the "*biblicism of the sentences that drowns the idea in the shadow or wets it in the fog*".

He wants a journalism of reports with "*the fact, the fact, the fact, the life and not of silly, inflated, criminal literature*".

And then came the new *Cri du Peuple* offered to him by Séverine, whose husband, the Doctor as Vallès respectfully called him, advanced 100,000 francs: "*I am resurrecting a dead [...] newspaper, which had its name hung in shame and which fell with a bang on the battlefield.*"

This newspaper will be a militant newspaper, "*the great organ that [the people] need in their daily struggle against the economic and political exploiters.*" A newspaper of revolutionary action, certainly, but also a newspaper of socialist unity. "*Social, human, beaded with tears or spangled with dreams, open to all, a free forum, that is what* Le Cri du Peuple *wants to be.*" Vallès, who had always marched "*with the people, but always as close to them as a free soldier, without a regimental number on [his] kepi,*" refused on this occasion to join any of the schools - "sects", one might say - that were being torn apart in the name of socialism. If they are willing, the new *Cri du Peuple* will be their "*meeting place*": the newspaper will campaign "*so that we bury all the hatreds from group to group, and so that from this reconciliation a generous organization will be reborn, into whose frameworks will enter all those who want us to cut off the arms of Capital, as in the past we cut off the wrists of parricides. (...) At* Le Cri du Peuple, *we are revolutionary socialists; we are neither anarchists, nor blanquists, nor possibilists, nor guesdists."*

In the editorial staff there are confirmed journalists: Meunier, Duc Quercy, Caze, Pain but also Jules Guesde, the future deputy of Roubaix and pope of a sepulchral Marxism embodied by the Workers' Party founded with Paul Lafargue (Marx's son-in-law). The first issue came out on October 28, 1883 and the boss wrote the following in his first editorial[39]:

> *"Certainly we will go to war with the comrades against the official power whose mask must be torn off and whose face must be blown off. But above all we will campaign against the invisible mask and the mysterious fatality that gnaws at the entrails of a race and devours the hearts of the resigned and humble. We will go to the isolated and discreet pains as well as to the public and irritated pains, to the miseries that have never moved a pavement, as well as to those that tear the mourning shawl from the shoulders of the widow of a striker to make of it, one morning of famine, a black flag. And here people of all opinions will find their place, in their rank of distress and sorrow, in proportion to their sufferings. It is the federation of all those who are, because of the capitalist organization, exploited and crippled, thrown into misfortune or into evil. The Revolution must have a more open hand and a wider heart than in the days when it conspired in cellars and was forced to sharpen its daggers in the dark. She has entered into the fullness of life, she has walked into the sunshine! She no longer has to sort out her protégés, she has to pick up all the wounded on the paths she has sprinkled with her blood."*

Le Cri du Peuple is above all a militant newspaper, determined, without complex. It denounces the trifling and palinody of politicians, the repression and the agiotage, the concussion and the spinelessness. It is also a popular newspaper that deals with current events from the point of view of the unreserved: these are the sections Miscellaneous facts and

39. "Do not speak to me," wrote Vallès, "about the cloudy and humanitarian conceptions of Marx".

Courts, then there is a social section evoking the "*questions of society*" and literary or historical feuilletons. The reception is favourable and 20 to 25,000 readers come every day.

But Vallès is ill. It is the price of a dog's life that has worn him out, aged him prematurely, whitened his beard and hair, stooped his spine, reduced his breath. And on top of that, there is this diabetes that only the diet fights but that emanates so quickly. So Séverine, his secretary but also his nurse, brings him back to her house, rue Soufflot, close to the Doctor, her husband. And she accompanied him during the summer of 1884 to Mont-Dore so that he could regain some of his strength. There they met Zola and his wife, who were concerned about Vallès' condition and spread the news to the journalistic and literary world of Paris.

Vallès was too weak to go to the newspaper, but he continued his activity with the help of Séverine, a faithful liaison with the editorial staff. She was in charge of a thousand commissions and instructions, one of which was to prevent the newspaper from becoming the parish bulletin of the "*constipated of the Social*".

But his health declined day by day and he died on February 14, 1885.

It was to the cries of "*Long live the Commune, Long live the Social Revolution, Long live Anarchy!*" that several thousand people (nearly 15,000 according to the police) accompanied Vallès to Père-Lachaise in a forest of red and black flags. Séverine said, "*The revolution had just lost a soldier, literature a master.*" On his tombstone it is written *"What they call talent is only made of convictions".*

HENRI

Clément VAUTEL (1876-1954)

The great reactionary or the giant of reaction: my priest among the journalists

Those who still know him say the worst about him and suspect him of the worst things. Yet he was one of the most popular journalists of the interwar period, collaborating alternately or simultaneously with *La Liberté, Le Charivari, Gil Blas, Cyrano, Le Matin, Le Rire,* etc. He was also the author of the series *Mon curé chez (les pauvres, les riches...)* which met with exceptional success, each title approaching or exceeding 500,000 copies. Theater and cinema will amplify the echo of his work but will not deepen its furrow nor will valorize its image. Who was he?

Born in Belgium, in Tournai in 1876 and naturalized French, of his real name Clément-Henri Vaulet, he died at 78 years in Paris on December 23, 1954. Initially a wallpaper designer, and, it seems, a remarkable one at that, he began his career as a journalist as a caricaturist at the *Charivari...* at the time of the Dreyfus Affair, which M. Winock considers to be the birth of the intellectual[40].

He was anti-Dreyfus *"by temperament, by instinct"* even though he thought Dreyfus was innocent. He wrote in 1941 in *Ses Souvenirs* that this affair was *"a revolution made by a passionate and audacious minority",* which reality will testify through the growing power of journalists, who very quickly became the instruments of various and sometimes

40. What Orwell and then the situationists would develop, emphasizing the artificiality of points of view that only aim to maintain illusions and submission to false realities. M.Le Goff evoked for his part the 12th century as having given birth to the intellectuals (and in particular to the Goliards such F. Villon), but it was, at the time, about professors registered in a corporatist dimension and not about the plumitifs ancestors of our mediocrats.

antagonistic forces of the system. The writings of Bourget, France (who would end up a hundred percent Bolshevik), Gide (who would follow the same path), Bloy, Bernanos, Daudet, Barrès, Séverine, Rochefort, Drumont and Tailhade... and the list could only get longer, as a testimony and the meaning of the Dreyfus Affair can be read in this way, of mistrust, incomprehension, hostility, the qualifiers are declined according to the intensity of hostility to modernity... vis-à-vis the developing capitalist society of which the Jews (the Jew) would be the agents and the beneficiaries.

This anti-Semitism is also the fruit of refusals, let us think of Huysmans and Bloy in particular, of the degradation of morals and of the de-civilization phenomenon that is beginning.

It was in 1921 that the Tharaud brothers wrote *Quand Israël est ici* and in 1922 that Lacretelle published *Silberman "métèque... raclure de ghetto".* Thus, Vautel's anti-Semitism is part of a collective ideology that has not yet been stigmatized.

Likewise his antifeminism; he is hostile to the female vote and considers that universal suffrage constitutes moreover *"a plague"* sufficient among men. And thus considers that it would be vain to extend this one to the women, what takes part of an anti-parliamentarism congruent with the conservative vision that he displays. The jealousy of which he was the object, as well as his participation, during the Occupation, in the press supporting Vichy and the Marshal, earned him in 1945 five years of sidelining or closet.

The novelist and the journalist Clément Vautel combined all the scorns, and André Dahl will publish an anti-Vautel writing of pamphleteer appearance in which, with a superb disdain, he says: *"It is known that the critic never reports on the works of Clément Vautel. It would seem that he does not fit into the literature".* Even those who would be predisposed to praise, such as Jacques Laurent, do so with caution. Only Marcel Aymé, with proven courage, will say: *"The extraordinary importance that had in the life of the French, this series of novels in apparently anodyne, all the series of* Mon curé chez*".*

In any case, Clément Vautel and his friend and literary accomplice Georges de la Fouchardière[41] have the honor (political and literary) of

41. Georges de la Fouchardière, former left-wing anarchist, looking carefully to the right.

having promoted right-wing anarchism and both deserve to be recognized (re-recognized).

Finally, in *Ses Souvenirs,* he claims to be a journalist, underlines the frequency of *"snobs"* among writers and does not hesitate to recognize that oblivion already strikes, more systematically, the plumitifs than the people of the spectacle (Michel Simon, Fernandel... whose artistic genius he praises).

The political and social context which is ours led us to privilege among the works of Vautel *Le Fou de l'Élysée,* and each reader will make the interpretation that he wishes. It is advisable, evoking this writer so forgotten, to recall as previously quoted that he was collaborator of multiple famous newspapers because he wants to be above all journalist and not writer because it is *"an easier job and in which the snobs do not miss".*

He can therefore be honored as one of the first right-wing anarchists and his memory flattered by the disdain of the pisces of historical bien-pensance. He simply prides himself on embodying common sense, work that is not servitude, and bourgeois values (understood in the manner of Georges Sorel); he is also the uncompromising defender of a vigorous literary and artistic conservatism: the true and the real against the false and the snobbish.

Alfred Sauvy will write of Vautel *"He was full of spirit, this man".*

He died in 1954 in Paris (16th district) and was forgotten for his historical notoriety... and especially because of his ill-thinking and the commitments it generated. A few excerpts from *Le Fou de l'Élysée* in which Clément Vautel sheds light on the antics of statesmen and in which all the democratic baudruches take to the stage, from the president to the ministers, deputies, mayors and other harlequins of the political show business:

> *"Parodying the helpful peacekeeper who leads an old lady from one sidewalk to the other, he took the head of state by the arm and led him across the avenue:*
> *- One sees well, he says to him, that you are not pedestrian any more but by chance... Always in the carriages of Marianne! But what are you doing, at this hour, in the street? A quarter of an hour ago, if I had thought of you - it happens to me - I would have said to myself:*

'This sacred Alexis does not trot like me, so early in the morning, on the pavement of Paname! He sleeps in, in a historic bunk, with a member of the Comédie-Française. After all, it is allowed to him, he is single, and it is easy for him, since he only has to throw his handkerchief to the sultana he has chosen...' Say, would you have slept over? [...]

- I always thought the Republican court was missing a jester.

- Do you think so? I've been told that buffoons abound.

- Yes, but these ones don't do the trick. They are boring with their marotte, each of them has his own and has nothing in common with that of triboulet. They are not, alas, madmen, they are fools.

- To know what is more dangerous for a people, the foolishness or the madness of those who govern it?

- One does not prevent the other. Well, considering what differentiates the Louvre from the Élysée, the president of the Republic from the king of France, the old regime from the new one, it seems to me that you can play, as a jester, a useful role. Perhaps the kings didn't listen enough to their fools and that's why they did foolish things, not to mention stupid things... It is up to you to create your character, to pose it, and even to impose it. I think it will carry in one way or another.

- What will the courtiers say?

- The greatest lords should not intimidate you. By the way, it seems to me that you were hardly intimidated by the president of the Senate?

- But the press, the public?

- Do you see yourself putting your feet in all the dishes, throwing paving stones in all the frog ponds, trampling in the begonias, expressing, by joking, the desires, the complaints, the angers, the disgusts of the good people of France? What a success my old Ludo !

- However, the French do not have the right, on the whole, to say they are unhappy. - One can be unhappy, and even happy without knowing it, while one has the very clear feeling of being content or discontented. Your subjects, O Alexis, are discontented.

- It is a tradition with them.

- This tradition has rarely been followed, it seems to me, with such ensemble.

- What are we complaining about?

- We don't even complain anymore... The national curmudgeon is on the way out. There will soon be only one left, and it may be me in the museum. People are disgusted, and disgust is usually expressed by a silence that can also be eloquent.
- Yet citizens still vote, at least the majority of them, and isn't that proof that they still believe in the republic?
- Do you think that all parishioners who go to mass are believers? The same is true of voters who go to the polling station.
- Is it the regime that disgusts them so?
- It's more like his staff... You know; the French love, hate, despise individuals much more than systems, institutions, regimes. In France, there has never been a revolution against royalty or the Empire, but against a king or an emperor... Not even against bad ministers, bad advisers, bad servants of the State or the Prince. If one day there is one more revolution, it will not be against the Republic, but against those who plunder and dishonor it... Only it is possible, it is even probable that Marianne will pay the price, like Louis XVI. Better her than you, my poor old man!"

And a few lines to finish illustrating the portrait of Vautel, from the excellent series *Mon curé chez...* In this case *My priest at the rich people :*

"The afternoon was devoted to a visit to the Basilica of the Sacred Heart: the parish priest of Sableuse found it beautiful and it is, indeed. In the imposing nave, a pilgrimage was taking place, singing hymns. Then a preacher went up to the pulpit and to the peasants who listened to him, he addressed a homily bristling with Latin quotations, stuffed with purely theological arguments, entangled with redundant and nebulous sentences. A heavy boredom fell from the high Byzantine dome; all this pious eloquence put the tired pilgrims to sleep.
And the priest of Sableuse thought: If all the apostles had spoken like that, it is certain that they would not have converted the people and that our holy religion, instead of spreading in the world, would have remained in the cabbages".

Louis VEUILLOT (1813-1883)
The pamphleteer in the sun

It is on October 11, 1813 that this son of a modest cooper was born in Boynes in the Loiret. Educated at the mutual school, he had to leave school at the age of thirteen. This experience of misery will never cease to haunt him. For it is an important matter to be born poor, one learns the concern for daily bread and the fear of unemployment and, sometimes, the necessity of silence and submission.

At first he was a courier for a solicitor, then a civil servant, secretary to Bugeaud in Algeria and attached to the cabinet of Guizot. As a teenager he began to write some literary texts and one day, infected forever by the virus of journalism, he first collaborated to several provincial newspapers before becoming editor of the *Mémorial de la Dordogne,* a governmental sheet.

During these years he questioned his religious and political convictions. When he left the direction of his newspaper, he made a trip to Rome which was to be decisive. There he met God and became unwaveringly attached to the cause of the Church. He then became a contributor to *L'Univers,* whose motto was "Catholique avant tout", and a few years later, its editor-in-chief. He succeeded his *"little"* brother Eugène. We are in 1843.

He can then realize his wish, to settle with his sisters in a large apartment in the rue Babylone. Did he think about marriage? To those who ask him, he answers: *"I have married my sisters".* And indeed, only Rome preoccupies him because it alone promises eternal life. So he subordinates his entire existence to it. And then he wants to make of this *Universe* a newspaper of combat. Nevertheless, at the age of thirty-two, he married a young girl of twenty-one and had six children in seven years, six girls. Of his wife he will say: "*Much naivety, enough spirit, no literature at all... It is well what I wished, only I would have wanted a person a little fatter*".

Then the bane of his life came to ruin this happiness: four of his daughters and his wife died within three years. God has tested him!

He leads a bourgeois lifestyle but does not forget his plebeian roots. To his daughter, who married a colonel, he wrote: "*Don't forget, Madame the almost colonel, that one of your grandfathers was a cabaret owner and the other a pastry cook. As for your father, he was a small clerk of a solicitor. There is nothing more small thing*".

His first fight, in 1844, was to defend Abbé Combalot, a priest who denounced from the pulpit the authority of the University (i.e. the State) over education. Then he lends his support to the Count of Montalembert who created an Electoral Committee for religious freedom. He approves the coup d'état of Bonaparte but he opposes the Italian policy of the French government which lends its assistance to the Italian unification and reduces the states of the Pope and the temporal power of this one. The newspaper is prohibited in 1860. It published provocative works such as *Le Parfum de Rome. L'Univers* reappeared in 1867 and fervently supported the dogma of papal infallibility pronounced in 1870 by Pius IX during the First Vatican Council. Its freedom of tone and its intransigence gave the newspaper a large audience.

After the defeat of Sedan in which he sees a divine punishment inflicted on Napoleon III, he joins the legitimist party. The newspaper is again prohibited in 1870 because of its attacks against the Italian monarchy and Germany of Bismarck. He then passed on the direction of his newspaper to his brother Eugène and continued the publication of his literary works: *Les Odeurs de Paris, Rome pendant le Concile, Paris pendant les deux sièges.*

He continues there the same fight that he never stopped leading in *The Universe.* Against the Empire, against the conservative and self-righteous world insofar as this world refused to fight and submitted to the modernist demons, against the dry bourgeoisie and armored with money who destroy the Christian faith, against the socialist demagogy, against the press slave of the bankers, against the liberals and the democracy, the *"free thinkers"*, against, against, against.

This medieval Catholic had many enemies and he was a lifelong rebel because that was his temperament. Every day, without weariness or irritation, he took up his subject and delivered his article. But in addition, he wrote dozens of pamphlets and more than fifty books.

He never suffered from the dearth of ideas of which Sainte-Beuve spoke, and despite his devoutly sacristan side, *"a bit of a cockroach"* as Léon Daudet wrote, this pamphleteer deserves to be recognized as one of the most furious, bitter and pertinent polemicists of the prodigious 19th century.

Theophile de VIAU (1590-1626)
Poet of dishonor

He was born in 1590 in Clairac in Agenais in a Protestant family of small nobility and with whom he spent a gray childhood. He studied medicine in Bordeaux before becoming a poet for hire and following a troupe of itinerant actors.

In 1615, he enters the service of the Count of Cancale as a secretary. With him he participated in the Wars of Religion, the civil wars of the time, in the reformed camp. When peace returned, he led the brilliant life of a fashionable young man at the Court, after a few months of exile, but he returned to fight in the royal army and then converted to Catholicism in 1622. Author of numerous odes and stanzas, satires and epigrams, he published a first collection entitled *Œuvres poétiques* in 1621 and a second one in 1623 followed by the *Parnasse satyrique.* His spiritual libertinism is so candidly affirmed that two zealous defenders, Jesuits, of the morality in force are offended. He was arrested in front of the scandal caused by the success of his works and thrown into prison at the Châtelet. He stayed there for two years from 1623 to 1625 for the offences of atheism, sodomy and insubordination to the monarchy. He wrote there some of his most beautiful works, *The Letter of Theophilus to his brother, The House of Sylvia...* During his trial, and thanks to the intervention of his friends, he escaped the stake and was condemned to banishment.

He died of the consequences of his captivity in 1626 at the age of thirty-six.

By Way of Conclusion Dialogue with the dead

The triumph of death is oblivion. In literature, textbooks are full of obituaries. On these, on their existence and on the benignity of their judgments, depends the survival of authors and their works. Sometimes even these authors survive only as historical characters, second roles of a history that expels them by expelling their productions. The antiquarian booksellers are then the last intercessors with these dead on borrowed time.

I wanted to engage in a dialogue with those who have existed and must continue to live through our thoughts, our dreams, our emotions and our revolts.

The choices I have made are arbitrary and I claim them as such. The degree to which men and works are forgotten or misunderstood varies. However, they all have one thing in common, that of having played a role in the movement of ideas that inspires the lives of men and of being sympathetic to me in one way or another.

This means that I believe their lives to be interesting, and, why not say it, instinctive. But also that the reading of their works, even today, is of a nature to get this strange and formidable pleasure which makes us feel as fleshed out, denser, sometimes inhabited, and that we are going, in our turn, to play this role which, as modest as it is, adds meaning in the succession of the ages.

To realize this work I privileged, too much perhaps, the narrative to the detriment of the style, eager to say and to show by withdrawing behind the words. And for materials, I plundered without scruples those that a monogamous passion had attached to trace the life of such or such. The biographers, these craftsmen of literature, also have the right to escape silence and death.

Table of contents

Best sellers Max Milo Editions

Hitler's banker, Jean-François Bouchard

Confessions of a forger, Éric Piedoie Le Tiec

The Koran and the flesh, Ludovic-Mohamed Zahed

Governing by fake news, Jacques Baud

Governing by chaos, Collectif

A political history of food, Paul Ariès

Mad in U.S.A.: The ravages of the "American model", Michel Desmurget

Mondial soccer club geopolitics, Kévin Veyssière

Putin: Game master?, Jacques Braud

Treatise on the three impostors: Moses, Jesus, Muhammad, The Spirit of Spinoza

TV Lobotomy, Michel Desmurget

www.ingramcontent.com/pod-product-compliance
Lightning Source LLC
LaVergne TN
LVHW060836170826
845678LV00007B/1774

* 9 7 8 2 3 1 5 0 1 2 0 7 7 *